SUPER
GIANT
GRAB A PENCIL®
BRAIN
BOOSTERS

SUPER
GIANT
GRAB A PENCIL®
BRAIN
BOOSTERS

RICHARD MANCHESTER

BRISTOL
PARK
BOOKS

Please visit www.pennydellpuzzles.com for more great puzzles

First Bristol Park Books edition published in 2020

Bristol Park Books
252 W. 38th Street
NYC, NY 10018
www.bristolparkbooks.com

Bristol Park Books is a registered trademark of
Bristol Park Books, Inc.

Published by arrangement with Penny Press, Inc.

ISBN: 978-0-88486-747-0

Printed in the United States of America

BRAIN BOOSTERS PUZZLES

Enjoy hundreds of puzzles designed to give your brain a fun mental workout. The required skills associated with solving the puzzles are provided for you. They are listed as LANGUAGE, MATH, SPATIAL, LOGIC, VISUAL, and DECODING. The puzzles are broken down into 52 weeks' worth of solving, but you can complete as many as you please on any given day!

PUZZLES

BULL'S-EYE LETTER

LANGUAGE

Add the SAME single letter to each group of three letters, then rearrange the letters to form six everyday 4-letter words.

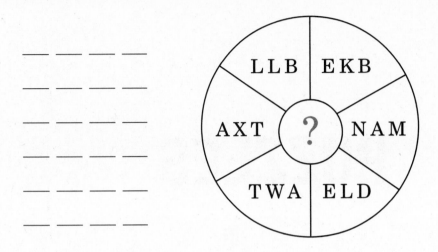

— — — —

— — — —

— — — —

— — — —

— — — —

— — — —

MAGIC NUMBER SQUARES

MATH

Fill in the empty boxes so these groups add up to the number below each diagram: 1. each row; 2. each column; 3. both diagonals; 4. the four center squares; 5. the four corner squares; 6. each quarter of the diagram. A number will be used only once per diagram.

1.

	21		
14			11
	9	8	22

58

2.

33			9
		19	
		21	35
			15

96

ANAGRAM MAZE

WEEK 1

The diagram contains 36 words, 17 of which are anagrams of other everyday words. Start at the top arrow and anagram LEAN. Move up, down, right, or left to the only adjacent word that can be anagrammed. Continue until you arrive at the bottom arrow. There is only one path through the maze.

1 LEAN	2 OXEN	3 WOOL	4 MUCH	5 SOUR	6 CLAM
7 RIDE	8 MAZE	9 HOOT	10 CANE	11 KNOW	12 HATE
13 NONE	14 TERN	15 BUST	16 LISP	17 BANK	18 NODE
19 TINY	20 GRIT	21 FANG	22 LILY	23 VEIL	24 INCH
25 MALT	26 MINK	27 LESS	28 BEAU	29 CLAY	30 FERN
31 MAKE	32 AFAR	33 HAVE	34 CELL	35 PEST	36 MEAT

ALL IN A ROW

Which row below contains the most groups of consecutive numbers adding up to 10? Look carefully, because some groups may overlap. We've underlined an example of a group in each row to start you off.

A. 5 6 3 2 <u>1 2 2 5</u> 7 4 1 2 6 1 8 4 3 5 2 9 4 7 1 1

B. 9 4 7 1 5 6 2 2 5 4 2 1 2 1 3 5 4 8 <u>7 3</u> 2 6 3 4

C. <u>5 5</u> 6 1 4 3 1 3 3 5 4 2 7 8 2 7 1 1 5 8 4 1 2 3

WAYWORDS

A 7-word thought can be found beginning with the word EVERY. Then, move to any adjacent box up, down, or diagonally for each following word. You won't use all the words.

EVERY	COUNTRY	SHOULD	SOON
PERSON	SORROW	BE	PERFECT
KNOWS	FORGOTTEN	WILL	AND
WHAT	MAYBE	ABLE	PASS

SENTENCE TEASER

Read the four statements A–D below, and assume that these statements are all true. Next, read statements 1–4 and, using the information received from statements A–D, try to determine if the final four statements are true or false.

A. All short-haired cats have long tails.

B. Long-haired dogs with long tails have green eyes.

C. Cats with long tails have blue eyes.

D. Dogs with green eyes have black fur.

• • •

1. No short-haired cat has black fur.

2. Long-haired dogs with green eyes have black fur.

3. Short-haired cats have blue eyes.

4. All cats with blue eyes have long tails.

ARROW MAZE

Starting at the S and following the arrow leading out of it, see if you can find your way to F. When you reach an arrow, you MUST follow its direction and continue in that direction until you come to the next arrow. When you reach a two-headed arrow, you can choose either direction. It's okay to cross your own path.

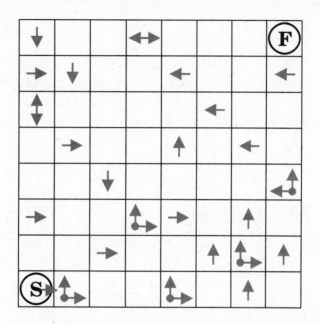

DECODING

SYMBOL-ISM

This is simply a Cryptogram that uses symbols instead of letters to spell out a truism. Each symbol stands for the same letter throughout. For this puzzle, we've already indicated that the ☆ = P.

DEDUCTION PROBLEM

LOGIC

Sammy owns three beautiful parrots, one of which is named Polly. All three can talk a blue streak, but not always the truth! Each parrot said one of the following three statements and only one of the three is true. Can you figure out which one is actually named Polly?

Parrot #1 said, "Parrot #2 is Polly."

Parrot #2 said, "I am Polly."

Parrot #3 said, "Parrot #1 is not Polly."

MIXED MENAGERIE

VISUAL

Find the row or column that contains five DIFFERENT birds.

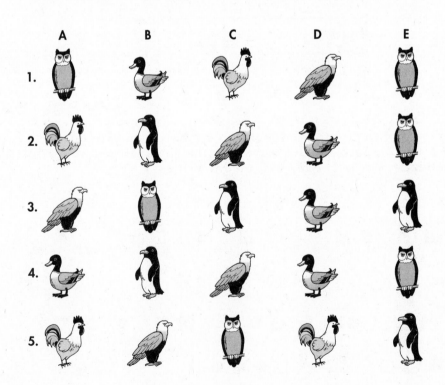

SUDOKU

Place a number into each box so each row across, column down, and small 9-box square within the larger square (there are 9 of these) contains 1 through 9.

				7		8		
	7	6	2					
		9	1			3	2	7
	1	8		5				9
			7	2	9			
3				6		7	5	
6	5	1				4	9	
						7	5	4
		7		9				

THE LINEUP

While scrutinizing the lineup of letters below, can you answer the five given questions correctly in five minutes or less?

DUVXWILTMSITHREATENEDPKDEFYCRYINGOZBITEJ

1. Which letter of the alphabet does not appear in the lineup?

2. What 10-letter word — with its letters in correct order and appearing together — can you find in the lineup?

3. Which letter of the alphabet appears exactly three times in the lineup?

4. What 6-letter word — with its letters in correct order and appearing together — can you find in the lineup?

5. Other than the answers to Questions 2 and 4, how many everyday words — with their letters in correct order and appearing together — of four or more letters can you find in the lineup?

TARGET SHOOT
LANGUAGE

Find the two letters which, when entered into the center circle of each target, will form three 6-letter words reading across.

1.

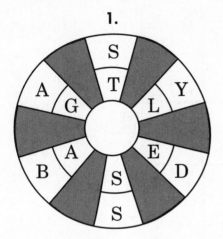

2.

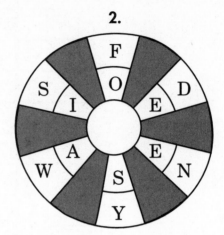

FUN WITH FACTS AND FIGURES
MATH

This puzzle tests you on a lot of little facts and figures. Solve the quiz in the order given since each answer is used in the next statement. There are no fractions used here.

1. Take the number of sides on a square and multiply it by the number of seasons in the year.

2. Next, add the number of doughnuts in a baker's dozen.

3. Now multiply by the value of the Roman numeral III.

4. Subtract the number of nickels in $1.45.

5. Add the number of people who perform a duet.

Our answer is the number of seconds in a minute. Is *yours*?

WHAT'S YOUR NUMBER?

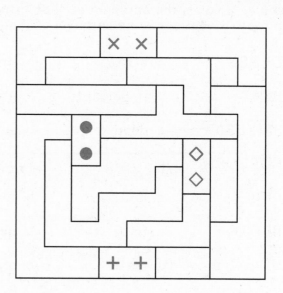

WEEK
2

Can you figure out the sequence of numbers in the diagram and what missing number goes into the space with the question mark?

6	7	13
8	4	12
14	11	?

VISUAL ◆ SPATIAL

IN THE ABSTRACT

Fill in each section with one of the four symbols so no sections containing the same symbol touch. Four sections are already complete.

15

U.S. N's

The list below consists of the names of 10 U.S. states, but we've removed all of their letters except for the N's. Can you write one letter on each dash to complete the names of the states?

1. N __ __ __ __   __ __ __ __ __ __ N __

2. __ __ N N __ __ __ __ __ N __ __

3. __ N __ __ __ N __

4. __ __ N N __ __ __ __ __ __ __

5. __ __ __ __ __   __ __ __ __ N __

6. __ __ N __ __ N __

7. __ __ __ __ __ N __ __ N

8. __ __ __ N __

9. N __ __ __ __ __

10. __ __ __ __ __ N

ANTONYMS QUIZ

An antonym is a word that is opposite in meaning to another word; for example, "cold" is the antonym of "hot." One of the words following each capitalized word is the antonym of that word.

1. DENSE   a. brittle   b. limber   c. sparse

2. PETTY   a. important   b. attractive   c. rich

3. SPECIFIC   a. deep   b. general   c. stagnant

4. EUPHORIC   a. frugal   b. mystical   c. unhappy

5. LIBERATE   a. mutate   b. confine   c. petrify

6. BLEAK   a. hazy   b. healthy   c. cheery

7. BRAWNY   a. weak   b. brave   c. smart

8. PLACID   a. formal   b. agile   c. stormy

CARD SENSE

Five playing cards were shuffled and put in a pile, one on top of another. Using the clues below, can you identify each card's position in the pile?

1. No two black cards are adjacent.

2. The three is somewhere above both clubs.

3. The heart is somewhere below the queen.

W COUNT

Here's an eye exam that's also a W exam! First, read the sentence below. Next, go back and read the sentence again, but this time count all of the W's. How many W's are there?

WHEN WOODROW WENTWORTH WENT

WESTWARD TO DOWNTOWN WARSAW

WITH HIS WILLOWY WIFE WANDA,

WOODROW WATCHED WAINWRIGHTS

WORK ON WAGONS WHILE WANDA WAS

BROWSING AT A NEWSSTAND.

ELIMINATION
LANGUAGE

Cross off the capitalized words below according to the instructions given. The remaining words, in order, will form a truism.

EVERY FORTUNE DAY PLUME SHOULD PINNACLE OFFER PREDICT BLEACH SOMETHING CARVE NEW ONION

Eliminate the word...

1. that has letters that appear the same upside down as right-side up.
2. that has a beverage in it reading backwards.
3. that is composed of letters from the first half of the alphabet.
4. that is a fruit when a letter is removed.
5. that, when the letters are rearranged, will spell out two numbers.
6. that is another word when two consecutive letters are switched.
7. that, when its third letter is removed, spells out a bird when the letters are rearranged.

WORD VISIBILITY
LANGUAGE

There are six 5-letter words below. The first letter of the answer is found in the first pair of letters, and it is either the top or the bottom letter. Continue across each pair.

For example, the word GIRL would be found thus: G A R L
                                                 L I T X

1. T H U G M
   S B I C H

2. P R O P A
   G A C W N

3. E W R E L
   N A S C Y

4. F C W U T
   S I O D E

5. T R C T O
   M I U B H

6. F R U P E
   G I A K O

LICENSE PLATES

Each box contains six letters of a past or present female TV talk-show host's name. The top three are a part of the first name and the bottom three are a part of the last name, in order.

1.
```
MAR
WAR
```

2.
```
PRA
FRE
```

3.
```
ROS
DON
```

4.
```
LEN
RES
```

5.
```
YRA
NKS
```

6.
```
ELL
RIP
```

ASSOCIATIONS

Below, you'll find eight groups of three words that can be associated in some way with each other (example: mantel, fireplace, logs). Cross out each group as you find it. The initial letters of the remaining words will spell out the answer to the riddle:

WHY WAS THE CAT THROWN OUT OF THE CARD GAME?

BREAD RAT EAT BOUND FLANNEL CAVE BRAVERY

MARIGOLD AVENUE URGE LILAC SENT COURAGE EVENT

SCREWDRIVER HAIR DAISY DIAMOND EACH EMERALD

WAIT ARGUE HAMMER JUMP SHARE LEAP ASK LINEN

CHEESE PECAN HEAVY CASHEW RUBY EDGE SQUIRREL

VALOR EFFORT BURLAP TAME MOUSE AMPLE ALMOND

HINT PLIERS

SKILLS TEST

LANGUAGE

Identify the following capital-state pairs by their initials. For example, "A, G" would be Atlanta, Georgia.

C, O _____

T, K _____

L, M _____

P, A _____

H, C _____

HEXAGON HUNT

VISUAL

In this diagram of six-sided figures, there are 10 "special" hexagons. These 10 are special because the six numbers around each one are all different from each other and the center. We've circled one of the 10. Can you find the other 9?

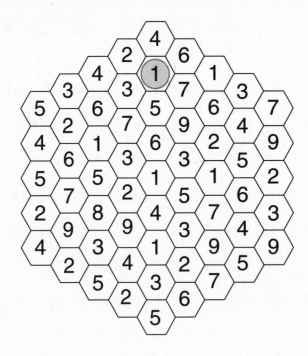

PATCH PUZZLE

WEEK 3

Place the correct vowel (a, e, i, o, or u) into each blank space in the diagram, and you will have a finished crossword with everyday English words reading across and down.

M	T	■	C	L		W	■	S	L		D
	R		R	L			C		D		
W	L	C	M	D			R		L		
■			S		■	D			P		R
R	N	T	S	■	L		N		■	■	■
	R	T	S	■	K		N	D	N		S	S
F			W		N	G	S	■		S	
T		D	P		L		S		S	T		Y
■		■	R		N	■		S			T	S
S	P	R		N	G		T		R	M	■
N			N	■	R			N	F		L	L
	L	S	■		G		S	■		T		Y
G		T	S		M		D	■		W

CODE WORD

Decipher a quote and the Code Word's ten letters, represented by the numbers 1 through 10. So, if the Code Word were "FORMULATES," 1 in the quote would be F, 2 would be O, etc.

$$\overline{1}\ \overline{2}\ \overline{3}\ \overline{4}\ \overline{5}\ \overline{6}\ \overline{7}\ \overline{8}\ \overline{9}\ \overline{10}$$

10 4 7 3 3   1 O 5 6 10   7 R 9   6 O 8   O F

4 2 1 H   V 7 3 2 9   6 O W 7 D 7 Y 10 ,   B 2 8

7   D 5 4 9   1 7 6   B 9   7   8 9 R R 5 F 5 1

10 1 R 9 W D R 5 V 9 R .

21

MARCHING ORDERS

MATH ◆ LOGIC

WEEK 3

Using a different two-step sequence of addition and subtraction, can you make your way from Start to Finish in each puzzle? We've started the first one for you using the sequence -2 and +5; continue this sequence to reach Finish. You will not cross your own path or pass through any square twice.

1.   FINISH ⬆

9	12	11	20	27	25
10	18	12	10	14	22
17	7	11	15	16	24
9	8	12	13	22	19
4	5	4	18	10	21
6	3	7	6	16	9

⬆ **START**

2.   FINISH ⬆

14	19	38	35	42	39
16	17	31	37	34	23
11	13	34	27	30	26
12	8	6	12	9	19
5	3	9	14	11	22
6	4	10	7	18	15

⬆ **START**

DOVETAILED WORDS

LANGUAGE

Two related words, with their letters in the correct order, are combined in each row of letters. Can you find both words? In a line like POBOOXDELER, or POboOxDeLEr, you can see the two words POODLE and BOXER.

1. U N A C U L N T E   _____ _____

2. P D E L I U C A C N K   _____ _____

3. S Q U R A S A D H I S H   _____ _____

4. C A P H E P R R Y L E   _____ _____

5. Y E G R L E L O W E N   _____ _____

22

SYMBOL-ISM

Directions for solving are on page 11.
For this puzzle, we've indicated that the ▲ = L.

LANGUAGE

PRESIDENTIAL VOWELS

The list below consists of the names of 10 U.S. Presidents, but we've removed all of their letters except for the A's, E's, I's, O's, U's, and Y's. Can you write one letter on each dash to complete the names of the Chief Executives?

1. A _ _ A _ A _   _ I _ _ O _ _

2. _ O _ A _ _   _ E A _ A _

3. _ E O _ _ E   _ A _ _ I _ _ _ O _

4. _ _ E O _ O _ E   _ O O _ E _ E _ _

5. U _ Y _ _ E _   _ _ A _ _

6. _ _ I _ _ _ _   E I _ E _ _ O _ E _

7. _ A _ _ I _   _ O O _ I _ _ E

8. _ O _ _   _ U I _ _ Y A _ A _ _

9. _ A _ E _   _ O _ _ O E

10. _ I _ _   _ _ I _ _ O _

23

COUNT THE TRIANGLES

VISUAL ◆ SPATIAL

Write down the three letters that describe each triangle (a three-sided figure). How many can you find?

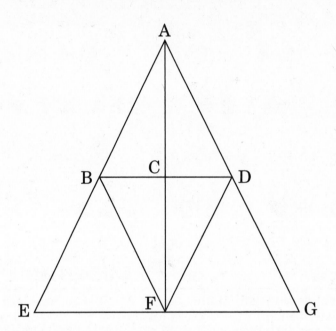

EASY PICKINGS

LANGUAGE

Cross out one letter in each pair below to spell out a lighthearted observation.

OI AF   TG LH EI DR AE ' YS   BN EO

AD WL TO EF RQ IN UA GT IP BV SE,

VT HE WE DR OE ' YS   NM OY

PF ER IO VB LI ZE YM.

TRI, TRI AGAIN

WEEK 3

Fit the nine triangles into the big one so six everyday words are spelled out reading across the arrows. Do not rotate the triangles.

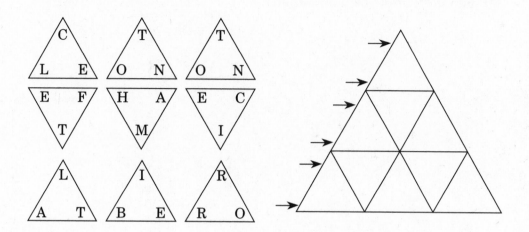

MAGNIFIND

Figure out which area of the drawing has been enlarged.

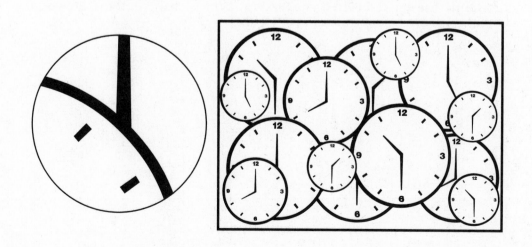

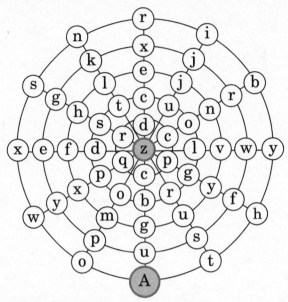

ALPHABET CIRCLE MAZE

VISUAL

WEEK 4

Start at A at the bottom, continue through the alphabet only once, and finish at the Z in the center. You will pass through other letters when going from one letter to the next, but move in only one direction, either around a circle or along a spoke. Don't enter or cross through the Z until you are finished.

SALT & PEPPER

VISUAL ◆ MATH

Examine the salt and pepper shakers below and then answer these questions: 1. Which row contains the most SALT shakers? 2. Which row contains the most PEPPER shakers? 3. Which row contains an equal number of SALT shakers and PEPPER shakers?

1. P P S S P P P P S S

2. S P P S S P S P S P

3. P P S P S P S S S S

4. P P P S S S S P P P

5. S P S P S P S P P P

6. S S S P P P S S S P

7. S S P P S S S S S S

26

ONLINE NETWORK

In each two-column group, take the letters in the left-hand column along the paths (indicated by the lines) and place them in their proper boxes in the right-hand column. When done, you'll find a thought in the two groups by reading the letters in the right-hand columns from top to bottom.

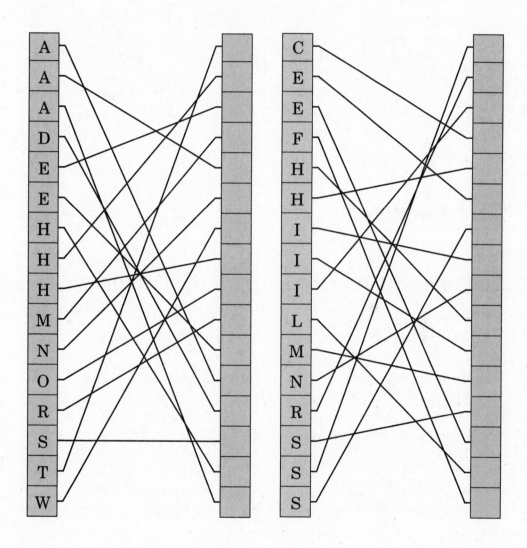

WAYWORDS   LANGUAGE

Directions for solving are on page 10. This time, you'll be looking for a 9-word thought beginning with FAR.

FUTURE	FINAL	LOVE	HEART
ISLANDS	FAR	THE	SEEM
FROM	SMART	BLESS	FROM
THE	EYES	IS	FAR

THE LINEUP   LANGUAGE

Directions for solving are on page 13.

QJAMSBWGIRAFFEEXITKHIEROGLYPHICSDUZESTV

1. Which letter of the alphabet does not appear in the lineup?

2. What 13-letter word — with its letters in correct order and appearing together — can you find in the lineup?

3. Which letter of the alphabet appears exactly three times in the lineup?

4. What 7-letter word — with its letters in correct order and appearing together — can you find in the lineup?

5. Other than the answers to Questions 2 and 4, how many everyday words — with their letters in correct order and appearing together — of four or more letters can you find in the lineup?

BLOCK PARTY

WEEK
4

Study the different views of the block, and draw what should appear on the face that has a question mark.

 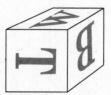 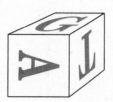 

VISUAL ◆ LANGUAGE

WORD CHARADE

Find each letter in the diagram according to the instructions, and write each letter on its dash to spell out an 6-letter word.

My first letter is directly above an R and to the immediate left of a U.

My second letter does not appear in any perimeter row or column.

My third letter is the only letter from the first half of the alphabet that appears in one of the columns three times.

My fourth letter appears in every odd row.

My fifth letter is the middle letter of a word that reads right to left in one row.

My sixth letter is the last letter of a word that reads bottom to top in one column.

R	D	W	N	H	A	X	B
K	C	U	J	B	G	L	S
P	N	P	H	T	P	U	Q
I	L	Q	O	W	R	T	G
J	T	S	E	R	C	N	O
X	F	A	W	L	M	I	C
M	B	N	F	O	U	A	K
S	R	T	U	H	E	F	P

— — — — — —

29

MAGIC NUMBER SQUARES

MATH

Directions for solving are on page 8.

1.

		16	
	37	31	
			43
	49	52	

130

2.

	56		
		32	38
41			
50		17	

146

DEDUCTION PROBLEM

LOGIC

Three high school boys, who are on the varsity baseball team, each is capable of playing all three outfield positions depending upon where the coach wants each. At practice the other day, the coach heard the three discussing the lineup for Saturday's away game.

Al said, "I'd like to play center field."

Bob said, "I want either left or right field."

Chuck said, "I don't want to be in left field."

The coach looked down at his clipboard and said to the three guys, "I'm sorry, boys, but only one of you is going to get what you want."

Can you determine what position each will play?

SUDOKU

WEEK 4

Directions for solving are on page 13.

			8		9	7	2	3
		2	6					4
1		9		2	7			
	9	5		8				7
		3	9		6	2		
6				4		5	3	
			5	6		1		8
8					3	4		
9	5	4	1		8			

LANGUAGE

BULL'S-EYE LETTER

Directions for solving are on page 8.

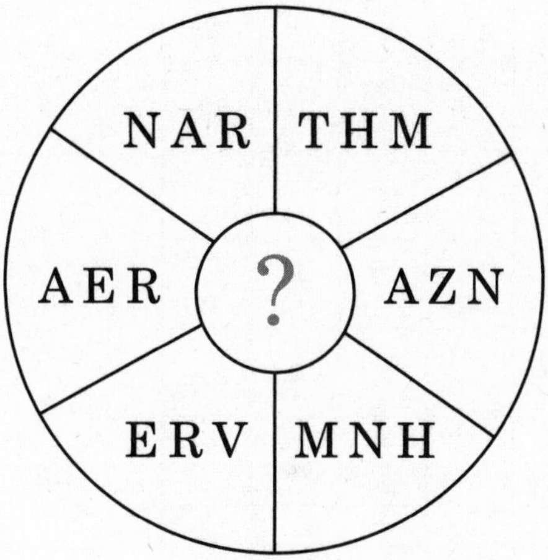

NAR   THM
AER   ?   AZN
ERV   MNH

_ _ _ _ _

_ _ _ _ _

_ _ _ _ _

_ _ _ _ _

_ _ _ _ _

SENTENCE TEASER

LOGIC

At the Bethesda Institute of Research, scientists experimented with carrots and broccoli in an attempt to discover if the vegetables had any effect on personal or psychological traits. After a battery of tests, what they discovered was:

A. People who eat carrots have good memories.

B. People who eat broccoli are generous.

C. People with good memories are generous.

D. People with good memories work hard.

In a follow-up study, based on results A-D, could these statements be proven valid?

1. Everyone who eats carrots works hard.

2. Everyone who eats broccoli works hard.

3. People who eat carrots are generous.

4. Everyone who eats broccoli must have a good memory.

ARROW MAZE

VISUAL

Directions for solving are on page 11.

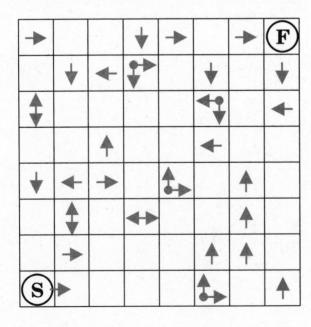

WORD HUNT

Find words by moving from one letter to any adjoining letter. In the first puzzle, you'll be searching for 3- and 4-letter fruits and vegetables (like FIG) and in the second puzzle, look for 5-letter fruits and vegetables. You may start a word with any letter in the diagram. In forming a word you may return to a letter as often as you wish, but do not stand on a letter using it twice in direct succession. We found 12 fruits and vegetables in the first diagram and 11 in the second.

1.

D	A	T	N	C
N	B	E	R	O
K	E	Y	A	K
G	I	M	L	E
F	L	U	P	E

Your list of words:

_____

2.

B	E	R	E	S	A
V	A	Y	R	C	S
N	G	U	O	I	P
A	R	O	H	N	R
M	P	C	E	O	U
E	A	P	L	M	B

Your list of words:

33

ALL IN A ROW

MATH

Directions for solving are on page 9. This time, look for the row with the most groups of consecutive numbers adding up to 15.

A. 4 9 4 1 2 8 6 3 1 6 5 2 1 8 9 3 2 1 6 5 8 2 6 2

B. 5 4 7 1 4 3 3 3 1 7 2 9 6 1 1 1 2 3 5 3 9 2 2 2

C. 7 8 6 2 8 5 4 6 2 2 3 2 9 1 6 7 4 4 1 1 6 4 4 2

FUN WITH FACTS AND FIGURES

MATH

Directions for solving are on page 14.

1. Take the number of months in a year and divide it by the number of sides on a triangle.

2. Next, add the number of kings in a standard deck of cards.

3. Now multiply by the number of letters in the name of the U.S. state that contains Columbus, Akron, and Cincinnati.

4. Subtract the number of letters in the alphabet.

5. Add the number of blind mice in the children's song title.

Our answer is the number of innings in a regular game of baseball. *Is yours?*

ANAGRAM MAZE

WEEK 5

Directions for solving are on page 9.
This time the first word you'll be anagramming is SNOW.

1 NOTE	2 SNOW	3 WOOL	4 QUIT	5 MALT	6 ZINC
7 HOST	8 WHOM	9 JUMP	10 THAW	11 PROD	12 PEAT
13 REEF	14 APES	15 OXEN	16 SAID	17 TELL	18 MARS
19 DANK	20 CUSP	21 SILO	22 BOLT	23 HALF	24 BUSH
25 LESS	26 LEVY	27 FORK	28 SPRY	29 TAME	30 NEWT
31 WALK	32 MAZE	33 ROOF	34 KIWI	35 SKIS	36 JADE

MARCHING ORDERS

Directions for solving are on page 22.

1. FINISH

19	21	23	27	26	32
20	17	24	20	30	33
16	9	13	21	25	29
5	6	8	10	17	18
1	2	7	12	16	14
3	5	9	13	11	15

START

2. FINISH

23	27	25	30	31	36
13	11	22	24	28	33
5	12	10	15	19	25
8	7	9	13	17	21
4	6	4	12	18	16
3	1	5	9	10	18

START

TIPS OF THE ICEBERG

MATH

This chart shows the gratuities each waiter earned on a recent breakfast shift at the Iceberg Diner. All you have to do is some careful addition and then answer the following questions:

1. Who made the most in total tips?
2. Who made the least?
3. Which two waiters made exactly the same amount?

EMPLOYEE	TIP 1	TIP 2	TIP 3	TIP 4	TIP 5
Al	$3.30	$3.20	$3.75	$3.05	$3.35
Brenda	$3.45	$4.30	$0.20	$3.00	$3.65
Charlie	$3.75	$3.20	$3.50	$3.30	$3.30
Dena	$3.30	$0.20	$0.75	$2.00	$3.30
Ed	$3.35	$0.20	$3.00	$3.00	$3.00
Flora	$3.30	$3.40	$3.00	$0.75	$3.30
Greta	$3.00	$3.35	$3.05	$3.00	$3.00
Hank	$3.35	$3.35	$3.35	$3.00	$3.00
Inez	$3.35	$3.00	$3.00	$3.00	$3.30
Jack	$3.35	$3.30	$3.10	$3.55	$3.35

CROSS PATHS

Start at the arrow. There are three circles in that box, so move three boxes, either across or up. Each time you land in a box, move the number of dots in that box in only one direction, up, down, or across. You may cross your own path, but do not retrace it.

LANGUAGE

POP!

The balloons in a dart game are arranged so their letters spell out the word "ABRIDGE." To win, you must pop six different balloons with six different darts, but after each pop the remaining letters must spell out a new word reading across from left to right; your word may differ from ours. Do not rearrange the balloons. Can you determine the order of the balloons to pop and the words formed?

A B R I D G E

CARD SENSE

LOGIC

Directions for solving are on page 17.

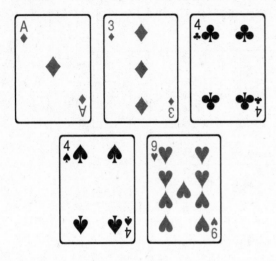

1. The diamonds are somewhere between the fours.

2. The nine is somewhere between the diamonds.

3. The heart is somewhere above the club and below the three.

IN THE MONEY

MATH

How quickly can you convert each bag of money into dollars and cents and determine which one contains the greatest amount?

1. 55 quarters
2. 320 nickels
3. 1,202 pennies
4. 135 dimes

TRIANGULAR SQUARE

WEEK 5

Place the nine numbered squares into the diagram so that the four numbers in each of the diagram's four large triangles equal the number outside of it. The patterns have to match and you may not rotate the squares.

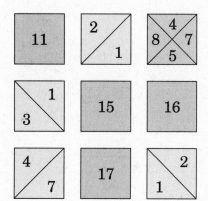

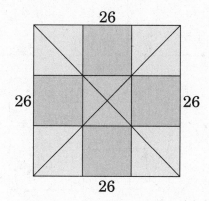

IN THE BALANCE

Scales 1, 2, and 3 are perfectly balanced. Determine how many triangles it takes to balance scale 4.

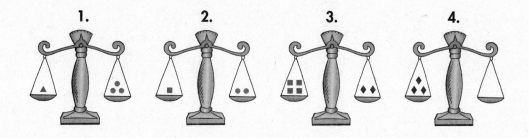

CARD SENSE

LOGIC

Directions for solving are on page 17.

1. The six is not the top card.

2. The two is somewhere below both clubs.

3. The heart is somewhere above the four.

4. The king is not adjacent to a red card.

POP!

LANGUAGE

Directions for solving are on page 37. This time, you'll be using the letters in the word "STREAMS."

CROSS PATHS

WEEK 6

Directions for solving are on page 37.

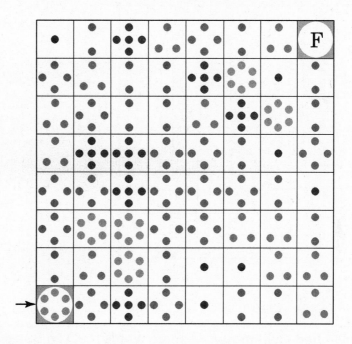

MATH ◆ SPATIAL

TRIANGULAR SQUARE

Directions for solving are on page 39.

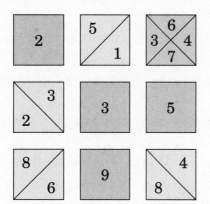

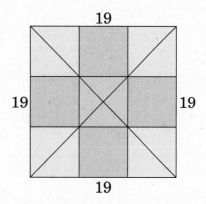

IN THE ABSTRACT

VISUAL ◆ SPATIAL

Directions for solving are on page 15.

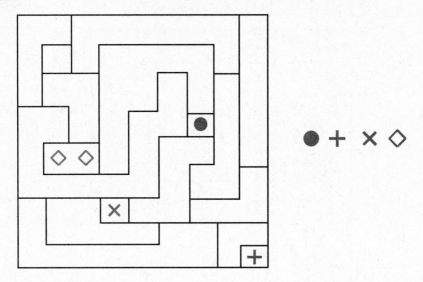

ASSOCIATIONS

LANGUAGE

Below, you'll find eight groups of three words that can be associated in some way with each other (example: mantel, fireplace, logs). Cross out each group as you find it. The initial letters of the remaining words will spell out the answer to the riddle:

HOW DOES A DOG STOP A DVD?

DEER HEAVEN SCARE EARNEST DROP WATERLESS USUAL

MAGENTA SEVEN DIVE FENNEL EBONY TON STINK

GRAPEFRUIT TRIBE MOOSE FRIGHTEN HEEL ROSEMARY

EEL PLUNGE POACH POUND AUNT SCARLET WEAVE DRY

SUPPLE CRIMSON BRASH TARRAGON UNDER OUNCE TIME

LEMON TRAIL STARTLE ELK ARID ONION LIME NEST

TARGET SHOOT

Directions for solving are on page 14.

1.

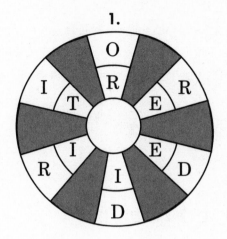

2.

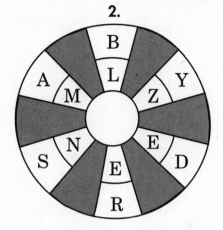

LANGUAGE

ELIMINATION

Directions for solving are on page 18.

OPPORTUNITY KAYAK HUNGRY LOST EERIE CANNOT
LIVID BE SPROUT MOUTH RECALLED NECTAR

Eliminate the word…

1. that, when its two vowels are replaced with a Y, spell another word.

2. that is composed of Roman numerals.

3. that is composed of state postal abbreviations.

4. that spells out a country when a letter is added.

5. that has more vowels than consonants.

6. that is spelled the same forwards as backwards.

7. that is composed of letters from the second half of the alphabet.

V COUNT

VISUAL

Directions for solving are on page 17. This time, see how many V's you can count in the sentence.

VERY VIVACIOUS VIVIAN VON VAVVER

VIEWED VARIOUS INNOVATIVE VIDEOS

INVOLVING THE PAVLOVIAN, EVASIVE

SURVIVAL OF EVOLVING BIVALVES

IN VILLAGES IN THE VICINITIES OF

VANCOUVER, TEL AVIV, AND VILLANOVA.

WORD WHEEL

LANGUAGE

Starting with the "A" at the arrow, see how many everyday words of three or more letters you can find going clockwise. Don't skip over any letters. For exam-ple, if you saw the letters C, A, R, E, D, you would score five words: CAR, CARE, CARED, ARE, RED. We formed 27 words.

SEVEN WORD ZINGER

Using each letter once, form seven everyday 3-letter words with the first letter coming from the center, the second from the middle, and the third from the outer circle. Your words may differ from ours.

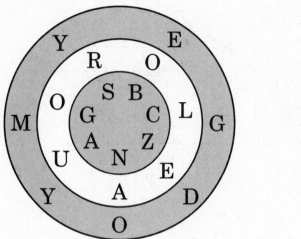

— — —

— — —

— — —

— — —

— — —

— — —

— — —

WORD VISIBILITY

Directions for solving are on page 18.

1. M I C M L E
   T O U K R T

2. P L R E I T
   C A P O N R

3. S T R L M E
   B O A I P K

4. S O L E U B
   R I C R N T

5. L A R M E W
   C O U P I T

6. T I K O N E
   L H R P E F

PATCH PUZZLE

LANGUAGE

Directions for solving are on page 21.

```
            H     G
         F     S     S
      S  L        T     D
      B     S  ░  ░  N     P
   C  R  P  ░  S  P  N     S
   R  N  ░  H  R  ░  R  W
M  W  ░  S  L  R  ░     C
P  N  ░     B  L  Y  ░  P  K
   P     N  S  ░  F  D  S
      Y  ░  ░  S  W  S
         S  T     T     S
         T     L     S
            G     M
```

EASY PICKINGS

LANGUAGE

Directions for solving are on page 24. When the puzzle is completed correctly, the remaining letters will spell out a humorous observation.

TC HE IC LS DR RA EC DN   GU TN SD EA RY

QT WU EI LC HV SE   MI UA SN KT   BA ED

AL CI SC RO IM AP OA DN BI SE AD   DB YO

MS OA GN WE FY .

BLOCK PARTY

WEEK 7

Directions for solving are on page 29.

HEXAGON HUNT

Directions for solving are on page 20.

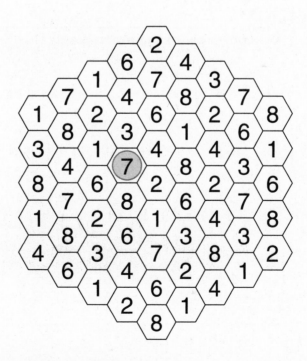

WHAT'S YOUR NUMBER? MATH ◆ LOGIC

Directions for solving are on page 15.

5	2	6	1
8	9	10	7
1	7	4	4
12	4	12	?

CODE WORD DECODING

Directions for solving are on page 21.

$\overline{1}$ $\overline{2}$ $\overline{3}$ $\overline{4}$ $\overline{5}$ $\overline{6}$ $\overline{7}$ $\overline{8}$ $\overline{9}$ $\overline{10}$ $\overline{11}$

T H 10   8 3 2 4 10 2   T H 10   9 11 8 3 6 1   5 7

K 6 5 W 8 10 1 4 10 ,   T H 10   8 5 6 4 10 2

T H 10   11 H 5 2 10 8 9 6 10   5 7

W 5 6 1 10 2 .

MAGNIFIND

Figure out which area of the drawing has been enlarged.

VISUAL

ALPHABET CIRCLE MAZE

Directions for solving are on page 26.

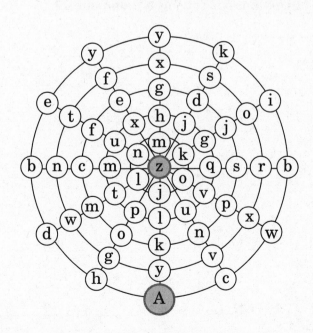

LICENSE PLATES

Each box contains six letters of the names of best-selling authors. The top three are a part of the first name and the bottom three are a part of the last name, in order.

1.
```
O H N
R I S
```

2.
```
E P H
K I N
```

3.
```
N O R
B E R
```

4.
```
N N E
R I C
```

5.
```
M E S
P A T
```

6.
```
A N I
S T E
```

DOVETAILED WORDS

Directions for solving are on page 22.

1. P O E N W G L U I N _____ _____

2. P U B R L U P E L E _____ _____

3. F E J B U R U L A Y R Y _____ _____

4. G H O N R E Y A D E P E W _____ _____

5. O N E G I G P O N L A N T _____ _____

ONLINE NETWORK

As on page 27, take the letters in the left-hand column along the paths (indicated by the lines) and place them in their proper boxes in the right-hand column. When done, you'll find a thought in the two groups by reading the letters in the right-hand columns from top to bottom.

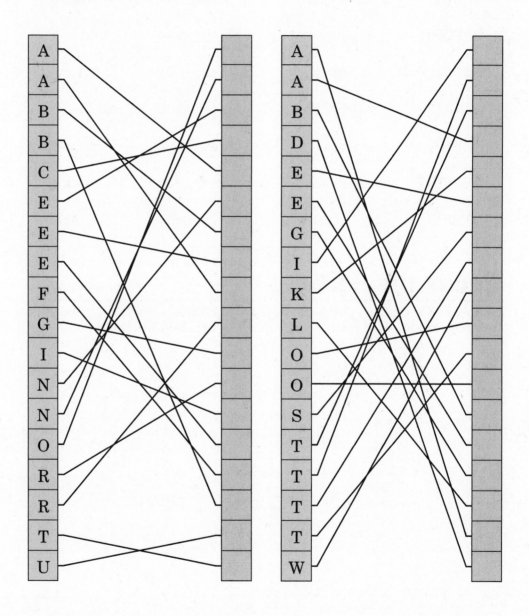

ANTONYMS QUIZ

Directions for solving are on page 16.

1. EFFICIENT   a. incompetent   b. direct   c. messy

2. ALOOF   a. modest   b. lazy   c. friendly

3. OPPOSE   a. support   b. tighten   c. fear

4. FRIVOLOUS   a. grumpy   b. expensive   c. serious

5. INNATE   a. acquired   b. seasonal   c. visual

6. PRESERVE   a. steam   b. sweeten   c. transform

7. PERSIST   a. request   b. abandon   c. stalk

8. DESPISE   a. perturb   b. cherish   c. quake

COUNT THE SQUARES

VISUAL ♦ SPATIAL

To solve this puzzle, write down the four letters that describe each square (a figure with four EQUAL sides) in the diagram below.

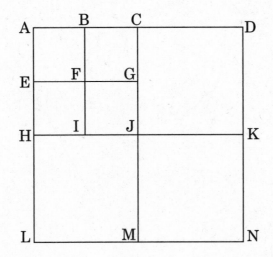

TRI, TRI AGAIN

WEEK 8

Directions for solving are on page 25.

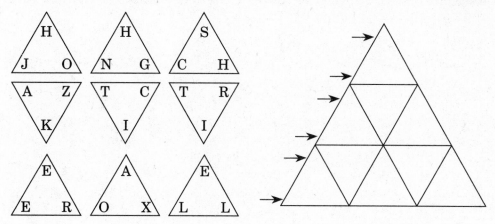

VISUAL

FRUIT-FOR-ALL

Find the row or column that contains five DIFFERENT fruits.

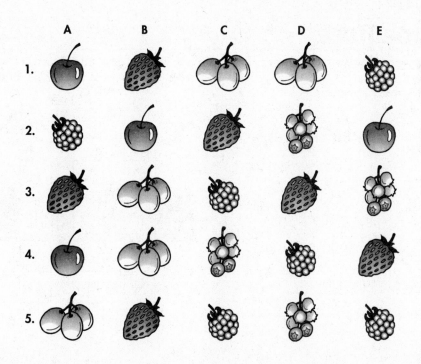

53

SHOES & SOCKS

VISUAL ◆ MATH

Examine the shoes and socks below for exactly three minutes and then answer the questions: 1. Which row contains the most SHOES? 2. Which row contains the most SOCKS? 3. Which row contains an equal number of SHOES and SOCKS?

SLIDE RULE

LANGUAGE

Slide each column of letters up or down in the box and form as many everyday 3-letter words as you can in the windows where POT is now. We formed 26 words.

Your list of words:

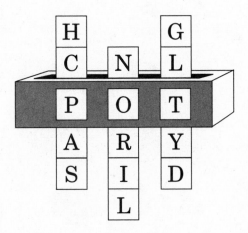

SKILLS TEST

Can you figure out the problem below?

Billy has ten marbles more than Bobby, who has six fewer than Buzz, who has fifteen more than Brenda. If the child with the fewest marbles has twenty, what is the total number of marbles owned by the four children?

SUDOKU

Directions for solving are on page 13.

4		8	1			9		
6		1		9				5
	7				5		2	
		4	7		1			
3	1			2			8	4
			6		4	5		
	9		3				1	
8				1		3		7
		5			7	8		9

SENTENCE TEASER

LOGIC

At the Logician's Sports Club, it has been observed that:

A. All the golfers have mustaches.

B. All the basketball players are tall.

C. All the people with mustaches are tall.

D. All the people with mustaches are wealthy.

On the basis of this information, determine which of the following people might be found at the Logician's Sports Club:

1. Frank the golf champion, who is very wealthy

2. Tom the basketball player, who has a hard time making ends meet

3. Christopher the golfer, who is over six feet tall

4. Arthur, a rather short fellow with a bushy mustache

WAYWORDS

LANGUAGE

Directions for solving are on page 10. This time, you'll be looking for a 10-word thought beginning with FEW.

AS	THEY	SEEM	ABLE
TIME	GOOD	PEOPLE	IN
FUNNY	AS	FEW	ADVANCE
PROPER	THINGS	ARE	LATE

WORD CHARADE

WEEK 8

Directions for solving are on page 29. This time, you'll be looking for a 6-letter word.

My first letter is surrounded only by letters from the first half of the alphabet.

My second letter only appears twice in each of two columns.

My third letter appears in the top half of the diagram, but not in the bottom half.

My fourth letter is surrounded by a state capital reading clockwise.

My fifth letter is the only vowel in one column.

My sixth letter appears only once in the diagram.

O	U	H	F	J	Z	D	Q
K	G	P	O	R	A	C	V
B	D	R	I	L	R	T	N
S	N	E	C	P	G	A	R
F	O	M	H	B	I	J	G
E	V	Q	G	S	L	N	K
V	I	T	C	F	H	Z	B
D	P	A	U	T	O	C	T

— — — — — —

DECODING

SYMBOL-ISM

**Directions for solving are on page 11.
For this puzzle, we've indicated that the ■ = N.**

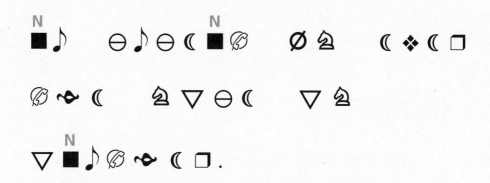

57

DEDUCTION PROBLEM

LOGIC

Spotty Sara, a beloved, bespotted pooch, just had a litter of similarly spotted puppies. Each puppy has as many spots as Spotty Sara had spotted puppies! Some time later, Spotty Sara gave birth to one final puppy, but this one has no spots at all! If each of the other puppies could donate one of its spots to the new puppy, would the new puppy have more or fewer spots than his already-spotted brothers and sisters?

IN THE ABSTRACT

VISUAL ◆ SPATIAL

Directions for solving are on page 15.

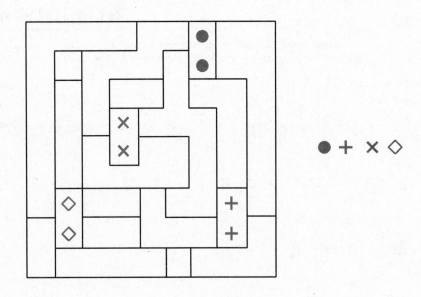

THE LINEUP

Directions for solving are on page 13.

IJFREEVDPHYSICIANSDWHULLPQHOGTIEXMBACKH

1. Which letter of the alphabet does not appear in the lineup?

2. What 10-letter word — with its letters in correct order and appearing together — can you find in the lineup?

3. Which letter of the alphabet appears exactly three times in the lineup?

4. What 6-letter word — with its letters in correct order and appearing together — can you find in the lineup?

5. Other than the answers to Questions 2 and 4, how many everyday words — with their letters in correct order and appearing together — of four or more letters can you find in the lineup?

LANGUAGE

SKILLS TEST

There are five 5-letter, noncapitalized, everyday words beginning with N and ending with H. Can you figure them out?

N _ _ _ H   N _ _ _ H   N _ _ _ H

N _ _ _ H   N _ _ _ H

ARROW MAZE

VISUAL

Directions for solving are on page 11.

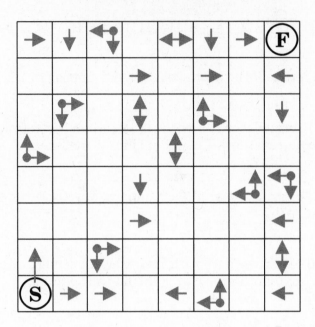

ALL IN A ROW

MATH

Directions for solving are on page 9. This time, look for the row with the most groups of consecutive numbers adding up to 11.

A. 5 5 1 6 2 7 1 2 1 8 4 9 2 7 3 2 6 9 1 2 4 3 1 8

B. 1 2 3 7 2 9 4 6 2 5 3 3 6 4 1 5 7 4 3 3 1 5 7 9

C. 9 9 7 6 2 1 1 1 7 8 1 1 4 3 2 5 8 1 3 7 2 4 5 7

WORD HUNT

WEEK
9

Directions for solving are on page 33. This time, you'll be searching for 4-, 5-, and 6-letter beverages (like COFFEE). We formed 8 words.

F	F	E	T	A
O	E	R	G	W
C	A	D	G	N
U	I	S	O	P
J	H	C	N	U

Your list of words:

ASSOCIATIONS

Below, you'll find eight groups of three words that can be associated in some way with each other (example: mantel, fireplace, logs). Cross out each group as you find it. The initial letters of the remaining words will spell out the answer to the riddle:

WHAT DO LAZY DOGS DO FOR FUN?

GORILLA PINE CAPABLE INDIGO LESSEN HOT FIRM ANKLE

EDAM DOWNPOUR STEAM ROTATE BABOON EASY PACE

WHIRL RIGID ANTENNA DIMINISH AZURE REAP

THUNDERSTORM KLUTZ SPIN ECHO REDUCE DRAMA BRIE

CLOUDBURST CHEER STIFF CHIMPANZEE AVID ELM ROPE

CHEDDAR BLUE SPRUCE SLEEK

61

FUN WITH FACTS AND FIGURES   MATH

Directions for solving are on page 14.

1. Take the years in a century and divide them by the value of the Roman numeral V.

2. Next, add the point value of a blackjack in gambling.

3. Now subtract the number of lives that cats traditionally have.

4. Divide by the number halfway between 12 and 20.

5. Add the number of letters in the name of the European nation that contains Madrid, Barcelona, and Seville.

Our answer is the number of Wonders of the ancient world.
Is yours?

MARCHING ORDERS   MATH ◆ LOGIC

Directions for solving are on page 22.

1.   FINISH

10	16	13	18	17	14
11	9	8	10	15	13
12	14	7	14	18	16
8	9	12	11	16	12
12	11	14	10	15	19
10	7	13	16	13	16

START

2.   FINISH

16	12	21	26	25	34
24	17	22	16	31	26
18	21	8	11	23	28
14	13	24	19	21	20
5	9	18	14	26	25
10	7	17	13	22	17

START

TARGET SHOOT

Directions for solving are on page 14.

1.

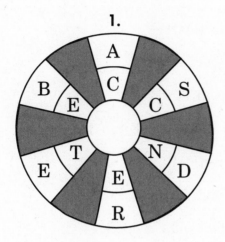

2.

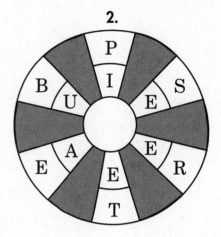

WORD VISIBILITY

Directions for solving are on page 18.
This time, you'll be looking for 6-letter words.

1. C A O H E M
   T H S D R W

2. S N C H L R
   A T U G O T

3. T R O S V L
   P I N M E I

4. U N D O R L
   E D C I K E

5. Y A S C N O
   C O D I A R

6. B I C K W T
   S A S L E P

ANIMAL CHARADES

LANGUAGE

In the Charade below, each line contains a clue to a letter of the alphabet. These letters, in the given order, will spell out the name of an animal. The animal's identity is also hinted at in the last sentence of the Charade.

My FIRST is in PANDA and in DROP;

My SECOND is in COYOTE and in CROP;

My THIRD is in LION but not in TIME;

My FOURTH is in MINK but not in LIME;

My FIFTH is in TIGER and in FEAR;

My SIXTH is in HYENA and in YEAR.

My WHOLE is a critter that looks like a horse,

But my noise is not a neigh, so I'm not, of course!

WORD WHEEL

LANGUAGE

Directions for solving are on page 44. Beginning with the "M" at the top of the wheel, we formed 30 words of three or more letters.

HEXAGON HUNT

Directions for solving are on page 20.

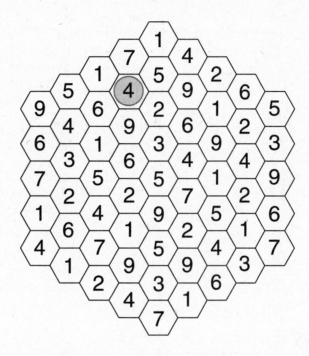

LANGUAGE

EASY PICKINGS

Directions for solving are on page 24. When the puzzle is completed correctly, the remaining letters will spell out an observation.

NM AI UT UN KR LE   GA LU WO AT YB SE

WP IU LN SL.

CARD SENSE

LOGIC

Directions for solving are on page 17.

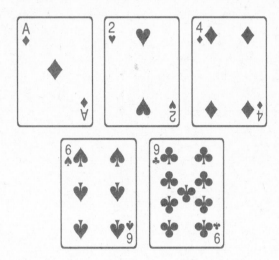

1. No two red cards are adjacent.

2. The six is somewhere above both diamonds.

3. The ace is not on the bottom.

X COUNT

VISUAL

Directions for solving are on page 17. This time, see how many X's you can count in the sentence.

XERXES FOXX EXAMINED HIS

VEXING EX-WIFE XAVIERA'S

EXPENSES, EXPLAINING THAT

EXTRA MIXERS, XYLOPHONES,

AND AXES EXHIBITED EXTREME,

EXOTIC EXORBITANCE.

ANAGRAM MAZE

WEEK
10

Directions for solving are on page 9.
This time, there are 19 words to anagram and the first word
you'll be anagramming is COAL.

1 KNOW	2 HUBS	3 FAST	4 CLAY	5 FEEL	6 COAL
7 UNDO	8 VINE	9 TERM	10 FOUL	11 CELL	12 LOUT
13 TINY	14 BARN	15 PIER	16 GOES	17 MILL	18 PIGS
19 MICE	20 WISH	21 CLAP	22 PALM	23 MIEN	24 FULL
25 WASP	26 TAPE	27 LIME	28 CLIP	29 FILE	30 LOOK
31 FIRE	32 BANG	33 SALT	34 BAKE	35 BALE	36 AFAR

BLOCK PARTY

Directions for solving are on page 29.

SLIDE RULE

LANGUAGE

**Directions for solving are on page 54.
This time, we formed 32 words.**

Your list of words:

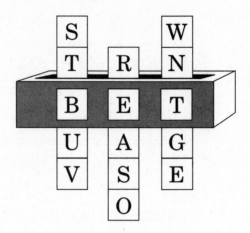

LICENSE PLATES

LANGUAGE

Each box contains six letters of the names of some cast members who appeared in "Ocean's Thirteen." The top three letters are part of the first name and the bottom three are part of the last name, in order.

1.
```
R A D
I T T
```

2.
```
A T T
D A M
```

3.
```
O R G
L O O
```

4.
```
L E N
K I N
```

5.
```
N D Y
A R C
```

6.
```
O T T
G O U
```

DOVETAILED WORDS

Directions for solving are on page 22.

1. B A S T R N A A W B E N R A R Y _____ _____

2. I S P T A A I L N Y _____ _____

3. R L O O B O I N N _____ _____

4. C E C A L R E R R O T Y _____ _____

5. B R O G O W L N D _____ _____

VISUAL ◆ SPATIAL

COUNT THE TRAPEZOIDS

Write down the four letters that describe each trapezoid (a four-sided figure with only two parallel sides). How many can you find?

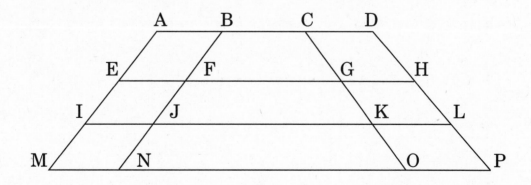

MAGNIFIND

VISUAL ◆ SPATIAL

Figure out which area of the drawing has been enlarged.

CODE WORD

DECODING

Directions for solving are on page 21.

$$\overline{1}\ \overline{2}\ \overline{3}\ \overline{4}\ \overline{5}\ \overline{6}\ \overline{7}\ \overline{8}\ \overline{9}\ \overline{10}$$

5 2 10 8   10 8 4   5 8 8   6 H I 4 G 5   9 5

6 H 8 Y   9 7 8   9 4 1   9 5 K   3 H Y.

2 6 H 8 7 5   1 7 8 9 10   6 H I 4 G 5   6 H 9 6

4 8 V 8 7   3 8 7 8   9 4 1   9 5 K   3 H Y

4 2 6.

ONLINE NETWORK

As on page 27, take the letters in the left-hand column along the paths (indicated by the lines) and place them in their proper boxes in the right-hand column. When done, you'll find a quote from French statesman Georges Clemenceau in the two groups.

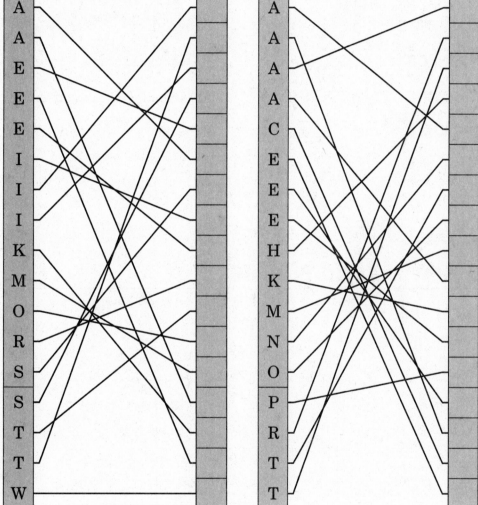

A
A
E
E
E
I
I
K
M
O
R
S
S
T
T
W

A
A
A
C
E
E
H
K
M
N
O
P
R
T
T

ANTONYMS QUIZ   LANGUAGE

Directions for solving are on page 16.

1. STAGNANT   a. cool   b. active   c. calm

2. GAUNT   a. plump   b. tall   c. sharp

3. ASHEN   a. chalky   b. awkward   c. rosy

4. SUBTLE   a. obvious   b. mobile   c. sensible

5. PRECIOUS   a. certain   b. worthless   c. profound

6. VAGUE   a. definite   b. soaked   c. brusque

7. PRIM   a. adept   b. rude   c. relaxed

8. BLAND   a. cultured   b. trite   c. tasty

WHAT'S YOUR NUMBER?   MATH ◆ LOGIC

Directions for solving are on page 15.

6	3	8
1	7	7
6	9	?

BULL'S-EYE LETTER

WEEK 11

Directions for solving are on page 8.

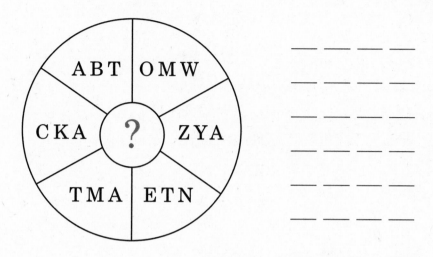

_____ _____ _____ _____

_____ _____ _____ _____

_____ _____ _____ _____

_____ _____ _____ _____

_____ _____ _____ _____

_____ _____ _____ _____

TRI, TRI AGAIN

Directions for solving are on page 25.

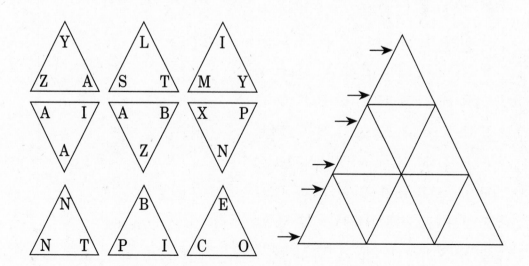

SKILLS TEST

LANGUAGE

Anagram each set of letters below to find the last name of a U.S. President.

NO MIDAS

TOE LOVERS

FED A GIRL

HOG WANTS IN

AIR HORNS

BRAVE NUN

ALPHABET SOUP

VISUAL ◆ LANGUAGE

Not every letter is in the diagram. When you spot a letter that is, cross it off the alphabet. Next, anagram the letters that are left to form the last name of an American author.

O	P	Q	B	J	K	E	F	Y	X	U	B
H	L	R	S	V	M	H	G	Z	P	L	J
B	C	X	Q	R	S	C	P	F	H	L	M
S	X	V	U	D	J	R	S	V	M	H	Z
L	R	S	V	M	H	J	K	F	E	Q	G
P	L	J	B	C	X	Q	R	S	C	P	V
F	H	L	M	S	X	V	U	D	J	R	S
H	G	Z	P	L	J	B	C	X	Q	H	J
F	Y	E	X	U	B	H	L	R	S	V	M
Q	R	S	C	P	V	F	H	L	M	S	X

A	J	S
B	K	T
C	L	U
D	M	V
E	N	W
F	O	X
G	P	Y
H	Q	Z
I	R	

Author:

_____

74

SUDOKU

WEEK 11

Directions for solving are on page 13.

	1	3				5		
	9	8	1		6			3
					9	1	7	6
	4		6					7
3	6			9			8	2
9					1		3	
8	7	9	5					
1			3		8	7	2	
		4				8	5	

LANGUAGE

WAYWORDS

Directions for solving are on page 10. This time, you'll be looking for a 6-word thought beginning with FORGIVING.

LIVING	ENDURE	YOU	RACE
PEACE	FREE	FINE	SET
KNOWS	ANOTHER	WILL	PLEASE
FORGIVING	THOSE	WHO	NEVER

ALPHABET CIRCLE MAZE

VISUAL

Directions for solving are on page 26.

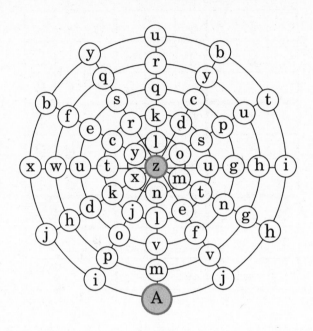

MAGIC NUMBER SQUARES

MATH

Directions for solving are on page 8.

1.

	7		51
		39	
35	27		
		59	

132

2.

72			
	52	48	
		32	56
24			

168

FRUIT CHARADES

In the Charade below, each line contains a clue to a letter of the alphabet. These letters, in the given order, will spell out the name of a fruit. The fruit's identity is also hinted at in the last sentence of the Charade.

My FIRST is in FIG and in GRAIN; _____

My SECOND is in PEAR and in BRAIN; _____

My THIRD is in ORANGE and in CLAN; _____

My FOURTH is in PLUM and in PLAN; _____

My FIFTH is in MELON and in MINE. _____

My WHOLE is a fruit grown on a vine.

_____

LOOK TO THE SKIES!

Find the row or column that contains five DIFFERENT sky sights.

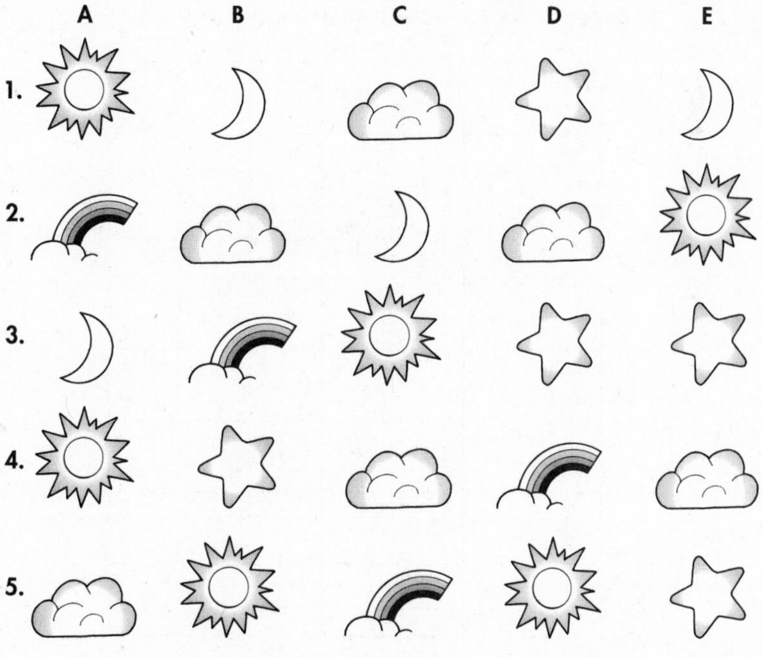

77

DEDUCTION PROBLEM

The local Department of Bureaucracy uses two different kinds of red tape — regular and extra-sticky. Each year, it begins with a fresh piece of each, and since most of what the department does requires extra gumming up, the extra-sticky piece was twice as long as the regular red tape at the beginning of this year. A new administration took over the office just a little while ago. It promised to cut down on the red tape, and it did — it cut six inches off each piece. Unfortunately, now the extra-sticky piece is three times as long as the regular red tape. How long was each piece originally?

ARROW MAZE

Directions for solving are on page 11.

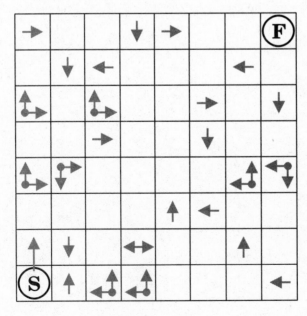

THE LINEUP

Directions for solving are on page 13.

QCSXSTREAKYBGAMEZWILDPHOSPHORUSXJIVENEX

1. Which letter of the alphabet does not appear in the lineup?

2. What 10-letter word — with its letters in correct order and appearing together — can you find in the lineup?

3. Which letter of the alphabet appears exactly three times in the lineup?

4. What 7-letter word — with its letters in correct order and appearing together — can you find in the lineup?

5. Other than the answers to Questions 2 and 4, how many everyday words — with their letters in correct order and appearing together — of four or more letters can you find in the lineup?

IN THE ABSTRACT

Directions for solving are on page 15.

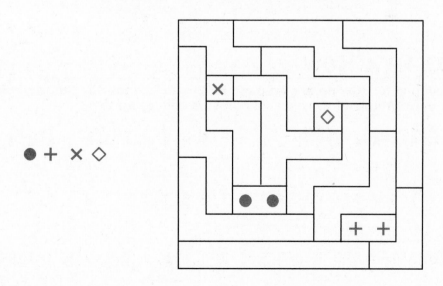

WORD CHARADE

VISUAL ◆ LANGUAGE

Find each letter in the diagram according to the instructions, and write each letter on its dash to spell out a 6-letter word.

My first letter has the same letter to its immediate left and immediate right.

My second letter appears exactly four times in the diagram.

```
O  T  R  D  V  Y  J  K
Y  V  H  T  L  N  S  G
H  G  A  E  U  F  T  X
N  D  W  C  T  A  P  R
B  K  T  I  Q  H  M  S
T  J  G  L  C  L  W  B
Y  N  F  O  M  T  A  Z
D  U  A  P  R  S  P  T
```

My third letter appears once in each row and column.

My fourth letter never appears to the immediate left or right or directly above or below my third letter.

My fifth letter is the fourth letter of a word reading from bottom to top in one of the columns.

My sixth letter is directly above an M and to the immediate left of an R.

— — — — — —

ALL IN A ROW

MATH

Directions for solving are on page 9. This time, look for the row with the most groups of consecutive numbers adding up to 13.

A. 6 6 6 5 4 4 6 1 2 5 4 3 7 8 2 3 7 4 3 7 3 6 2 3

B. 7 1 5 2 2 4 6 6 8 1 9 1 2 2 7 4 8 2 3 9 2 1 2 8

C. 9 9 7 5 3 5 9 2 3 2 2 1 3 3 9 2 2 2 2 6 4 1 9 7

80

SKILLS TEST

For each number below, form words by unscrambling the letters following the dashes and place them into position before and after the given letters.

EXAMPLE: _S_ _T_ _A_ C C _A_ _T_ _O_ TAATOS

1. __ __ F F __ __   ECOE

2. __ __ L L __   EHO

3. __ __ __ H H __ __ __   TOLDWI

4. __ __ __ __ G G __ __   BOATON

LANGUAGE ◆ SPATIAL

WORD HUNT

Directions for solving are on page 33. This time, you'll be searching for 5-letter names of flowers. We found eight, including LOTUS.

O	P	I	L	T
P	Y	A	U	A
E	S	N	D	C
L	O	I	A	R
T	U	S	T	E

Your list of words:

Y COUNT

VISUAL

Directions for solving are on page 17. This time, see how many Y's you can count in the sentence.

YES, YOUR AND MY YELLOWY

YEARBOOKS MAY WRYLY

WAYLAY US, YIELDING A FEY

YEARNING FOR YON YOUTH OF

YORE, YET SLY NAYSAYERS MAY

PORTRAY YESTERDAY AS MYTH.

SLIDE RULE

LANGUAGE

Slide each column of letters up or down in the box and form as many everyday 4-letter words as you can in the windows where HARD is now. We formed 45 words, including HARD.

Your list of words:

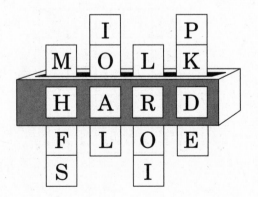

SUDOKU

WEEK 12

Directions for solving are on page 13.

		8	7	6		3	5	
	1							
4	6	3	1					2
5	8		3					9
		7		5		4		
6					2		1	7
8					9	1	2	4
							9	
	4	1		2	7	8		

SYMBOL-ISM

Directions for solving are on page 11.

COUNT THE RECTANGLES VISUAL ◆ SPATIAL

Write down the four letters that describe each rectangle (a four-sided figure). How many can you find?

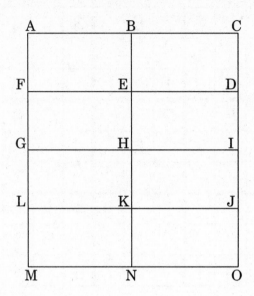

ASSOCIATIONS

LANGUAGE

Below, you'll find eight groups of three words that can be associated in some way with each other (example: mantel, fireplace, logs). Cross out each group as you find it. The initial letters of the remaining words will spell out the answer to the riddle:

WHAT DO SEA MONSTERS EAT?

CATSUP FALCON FOAM HELIUM SYCAMORE INK FAINT

STATUE DOG MAYONNAISE HAWK HANDKERCHIEF WITTY

CANINE ACTUAL MUSTARD DIM NINE SHAKE DREAM PALE

CEDAR HUMOROUS SHAPELY MAPLE HASTE METHANE

IMPEACH VIBRATE EAGLE PRIEST OXYGEN POOCH QUAKE

STAIN FUNNY

ANIMAL CHARADES

WEEK 13

Directions for solving are on page 64.

My FIRST is in HAMSTER and in START;   _____

My SECOND is in HARE and in CHART;   _____

My THIRD is in SABLE but not in MAZE;   _____

My FOURTH is in ZEBRA but not in DAZE;   _____

My FIFTH is in ERMINE and in MINT;   _____

My SIXTH is in SLOTH and in HINT.   _____

My WHOLE is a critter that burrows a hole   _____

But I'm not a gopher, certainly not a mole.

_____

HEXAGON HUNT

Directions for solving are on page 20.

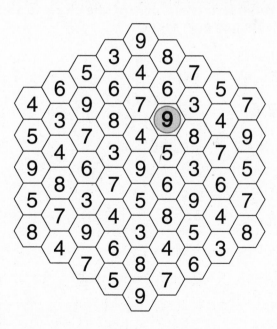

TARGET SHOOT

Directions for solving are on page 14.

1.

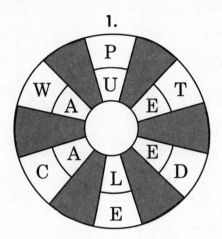

2.

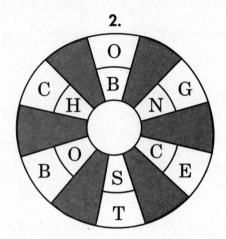

LICENSE PLATES

Each box contains six letters of the names of Major League baseball teams. The top three letters are part of the city and the bottom three are part of the team name, in order.

1.

T L A
A V E

2.

A G O
U B S

3.

D E T
G E R

4.

A T I
E D S

5.

M O R
O L E

6.

T O N
R O S

WORD VISIBILITY

Directions for solving are on page 18.

1. R I L P E R
   D O B L A Y

2. T R A V L T
   C H E D C E

3. S R I E N B
   D T R O A M

4. P R E M B T
   W A O L P S

5. E R A K G A
   O N I N L E

6. C U N D O E
   F A M T L Z

SEVEN WORD ZINGER

Directions for solving are on page 45.

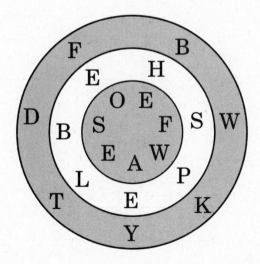

— — — —

— — — —

— — — —

— — — —

— — — —

— — — —

— — — —

BLOCK PARTY

VISUAL ◆ SPATIAL

Directions for solving are on page 29.

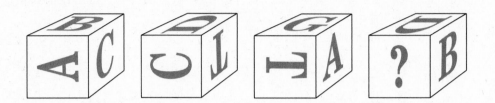

DOVETAILED WORDS

LANGUAGE

Directions for solving are on page 22.

1. W H R I E T D E   _____ _____

2. T O Y M A A T M O   _____ _____

3. F L A S M I T N O G R O K _____ _____

4. M E V R E C U N R U S Y   _____ _____

5. P O R A E N A G E R   _____ _____

BULL'S-EYE LETTER

WEEK 13

Directions for solving are on page 8.

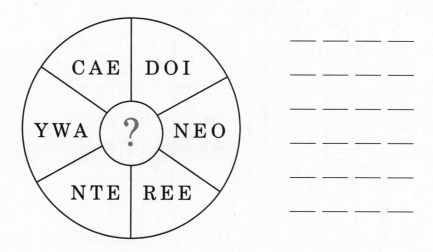

_ _ _ _ _

_ _ _ _ _

_ _ _ _ _

_ _ _ _ _

_ _ _ _ _

CODE WORD

Directions for solving are on page 21.

$$\overline{1}\ \overline{2}\ \overline{3}\ \overline{4}\ \overline{5}\ \overline{6}\ \overline{7}\ \overline{8}\ \overline{9}\ \overline{10}$$

4 6 10   8 10 1 4   2 7 Y   4 O   5 O N V 3 N 5 10

7   F O O 9   4 6 7 4   6 10   3 1   2 R O N G

3 1   4 O   9 10 4   6 3 M   6 7 V 10   6 3 1

O 2 N   2 7 Y .

SUDOKU

LOGIC

Directions for solving are on page 13.

6			7		9	4	5	
		5		4			7	
	4	7				3	9	
		4			6			3
	1		8	5	4		2	
7			2			9		
	5	1				8	3	
	7			3		5		
	6	8	4		5			2

MAGNIFIND

VISUAL ◆ SPATIAL

Figure out which area of the drawing has been enlarged.

ANAGRAM MAZE

WEEK 14

Directions for solving are on page 9.
This time, there are 19 words to anagram and the first word
you'll be anagramming is GOAT.

1 BODY	2 HUNT	3 GOAT	4 FROM	5 FADE	6 APES
7 PURR	8 OOZE	9 FIVE	10 PLUS	11 CUFF	12 FEAR
13 TUNA	14 BUSY	15 ACHE	16 VILE	17 FOIL	18 LOCO
19 SEAL	20 ALOE	21 WHIM	22 NEWS	23 SNAP	24 FURS
25 BARE	26 LAMP	27 WAIT	28 DECK	29 INTO	30 FALL
31 CULT	32 SIFT	33 ICON	34 KIDS	35 CREW	36 WINE

WHAT'S YOUR NUMBER?

Directions for solving are on page 15.

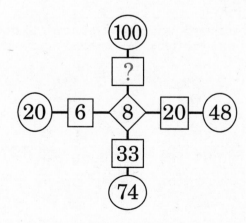

HOLE IN ONE

LOGIC

Twenty-four golfers entered a hole-in-one contest. Each golfer was given a ball with a different 4-digit number combination using the numbers 2, 4, 5, and 9 on it. Looking at the 23 balls still on the green, can you figure out what combination is on the ball that won the contest?

IN THE MONEY

MATH

How quickly can you convert each bag of money into dollars and cents and determine which one contains the greatest amount?

1. 84 dimes
2. 33 quarters
3. 848 pennies
4. 170 nickels

CROSS PATHS

Start at the arrow. There are two circles in that box, so move two boxes, either across or up. Each time you land in a box, move the number of dots in that box in only one direction, up, down, or across until you reach Finish (F). You may cross your own path, but do not retrace it.

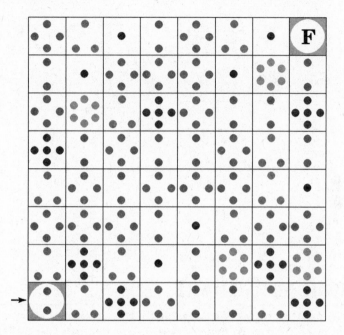

POP!

The balloons in a dart game are arranged so their letters spell out the word "CLICKED." To win, you must pop six different balloons with six different darts, but after each pop the remaining letters must spell out a new word reading across from left to right. Do not rearrange the balloons. Can you determine the order of the balloons to pop and the words formed? Your words may differ from ours.

93

IN THE BALANCE

Scales 1, 2, and 3 are perfectly balanced. Determine how many triangles it takes to balance scale 4.

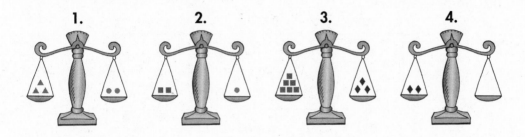

TRIANGULAR SQUARE

Place the nine numbered squares into the diagram so that the four numbers in each of the diagram's four large triangles equal the number outside of it. The patterns have to match and you may not rotate the squares.

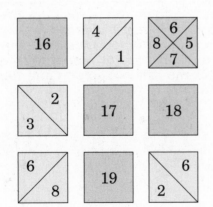

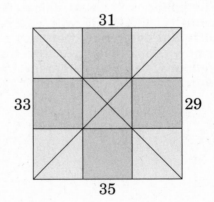

94

POP!

Directions for solving are on page 93. This time, you'll be using the letters in the word "ORANGES."

LOGIC

HOLE IN ONE

Directions for solving are on page 92. This time, the 4-digit number combination uses 3, 6, 7, and 8.

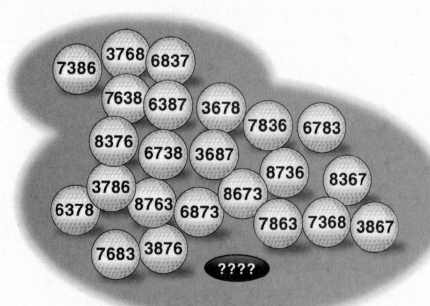

KEEP ON MOVING

VISUAL

The goal is to move from the shaded square to the asterisk. Since the shaded square has the number 2 in it, you must move two squares up, down, left, or right, but not diagonally. In the new square will be another number; move that number of squares up, down, left, or right, continuing in this way until you reach the asterisk. It's okay to cross your own path.

3	3	4	3	3	4
1	3	2	2	✳	1
2	1	4	3	2	3
3	3	3	1	3	1
2	1	1	2	3	2
1	2	2	3	4	4

OVERLAY

VISUAL ◆ SPATIAL

When you overlay the three diagrams in the top row, which of the three lettered diagrams, A, B, or C, will be formed?

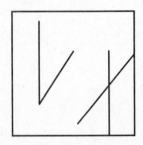
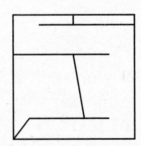
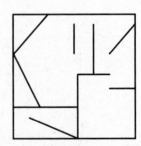

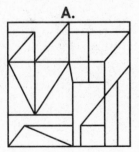
A.

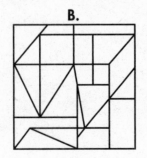
B.

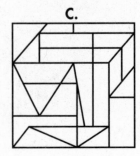
C.

SWITCHEROO

In each group, for the first word and its number equivalent given, determine what the number equivalent is for the second word.

1. BOSS is to 1577 as SOBS is to:
   (a) 1755 (b) 7715 (c) 7157 (d) 7517

2. RITE is to 6492 as TIER is to:
   (a) 9426 (b) 9624 (c) 9264 (d) 2649

3. THUS is to 3158 as SHUT is to:
   (a) 8351 (b) 8153 (c) 8513 (d) 8135

4. ACME is to 4271 as MACE is to:
   (a) 7421 (b) 7214 (c) 7412 (d) 1274

5. BEAR is to 5679 as BARE is to:
   (a) 7695 (b) 5769 (c) 5796 (d) 5967

6. KALE is to 8213 as LAKE is to:
   (a) 1238 (b) 8132 (c) 1283 (d) 1832

GOING IN CIRCLES

In each circle, insert one letter into each empty space to form an 8-letter word. Words may read either clockwise or counterclockwise and may begin with any letter in the circle.

1.
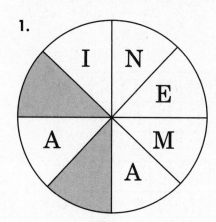

2.
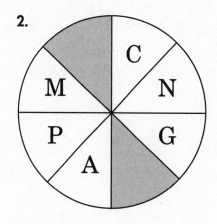

ANIMAL CHARADES

Each line contains a clue to a letter of the alphabet. These letters, in the given order, will spell out the name of an animal. The animal's identity is also hinted at in the last sentence of the Charade.

My FIRST is in OCELOT and in ABOUT; _____

My SECOND is in PORCUPINE and in SPOUT; _____

My THIRD is in PANTHER but not in TEACH; _____

My FOURTH is in MACKEREL but not in REACH; _____

My FIFTH is in CROCODILE and in SLEIGH; _____

My SIXTH is in WALLABY and in PRAY. _____

My WHOLE is a bird, although I don't quack;
   I'm also a country that borders Iraq.

_____

WORD HUNT

Find words by moving from one letter to any adjoining letter. You may start a word with any letter in the diagram. In forming a word you may return to a letter as often as you wish, but do not stand on a letter using it twice in direct succession. In this Word Hunt, you are searching for 4-letter words that are parts of the body. We found 11 words, including SOLE.

Your list of words:

P	M	H	I	N
A	L	C	E	H
F	C	E	A	S
A	O	S	L	N
N	J	O	T	D

RELATIONSHIPS QUIZ

WEEK 15

KENNEL is to DOG as STY is to PIG because a DOG lives in a KENNEL and a PIG lives in a STY. Each of the statements below is a relationship of some kind. Can you select the right word from the four following each?

1. LIZARD is to REPTILE as KANGAROO is to _____.
   (a) marsupial (b) Australia (c) fish (d) wallaby

2. LIBYA is to AFRICA as TAIWAN is to _____.
   (a) Asia (b) Europe (c) China (d) Taipei

3. HORSE is to PALOMINO as CAT is to _____.
   (a) kitten (b) throne (c) Manx (d) hyena

4. GLACIER is to ICE CUBE as OCEAN is to _____.
   (a) thimble (b) waves (c) continent (d) pond

5. POWER is to WATT as SOUND is to _____.
   (a) noise (b) decibel (c) clang (d) hearing

ANTONYMS QUIZ

An antonym is a word that is opposite in meaning to another word; for example, "cold" is the antonym of "hot." One of the words following each capitalized word is the antonym of that word.

1. PLACIDITY   a. lenity   b. agitation   c. affectation

2. NOBLE   a. loathsome   b. binding   c. endangered

3. PRETENTIOUS   a. primitive   b. blithe   c. modest

4. TORPID   a. flagrant   b. florid   c. active

5. ADMONISH   a. glorify   b. scuffle   c. burrow

6. EXPLICIT   a. dejected   b. vague   c. coarse

7. TREACHERY   a. allegiance   b. conveyance   c. replication

8. CORDIAL   a. prophetic   b. habitual   c. aloof

ROUND TRIP

When this puzzle has been completed correctly, you will have made a round trip through its set of dots. You must visit every dot exactly once, make no diagonal moves, and return to your starting point. Parts of the right path are shown; can you find the rest?

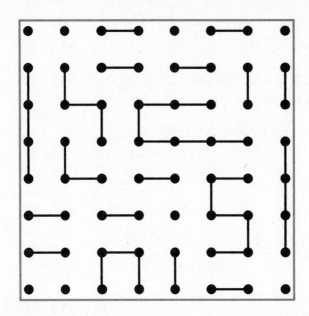

COMPOUND IT

LANGUAGE

Starting at #1, pick a word that will form a compound word with a word chosen in #2. Then with the word you've selected in #2, pick one from #3 to form another compound word. Continue in this manner to #10, so that you've formed nine compound words. In some instances more than one compound word can be formed, but there is only one path to get you to #10.

1. fox, hot, blue, fruit

2. house, hole, bird, cake

3. seed, plant, boat, walk

4. yard, out, bed, rich

5. spoken, fellow, sheet, work

6. ship, turn, shop, view

7. shape, lift, talk, table

8. pink, spoon, off, leaf

9. stage, shoot, beat, call

10. run, true, coach, simple

WORD CHARADE

Find each letter in the diagram according to the instructions, and write each letter on its dash to spell out a 6-letter word.

My first letter appears directly above a V and to the immediate right of an L.

My second letter does not appear in the diagram.

My third letter is the sixth letter in a row where the letters are in alphabetical order, from left to right, but not consecutive order.

My fourth letter is in the first column but not in the eighth column.

E	Z	R	V	P	K	G	Q
B	S	Q	F	W	O	C	G
Q	T	I	D	E	R	C	X
O	Z	F	H	L	P	N	J
X	J	Y	M	D	V	U	Q
W	L	B	D	U	I	E	B
G	I	K	N	P	R	T	W
J	U	M	I	E	X	C	E

My fifth letter is the fourth letter of a 6-letter word reading right to left in one of the rows.

My sixth letter is surrounded by eight consonants.

— — — — — —

SLIDE RULE

Slide each column of letters up or down in the box and form as many everyday 4-letter words as you can in the windows where FLEW is now. We formed 35 words, including FLEW.

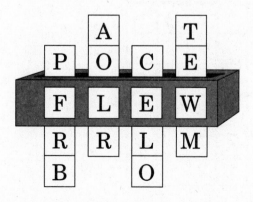

Your list of words:

SENTENCE TEASER

Read the four statements A–D, and assume that the statements are all true for the film library that contains only westerns and thrillers. Next, read statements 1–4, and, using the information received from statements A–D, try to determine whether the final four statements are true or false.

A. All the westerns are in color.

B. All the thrillers were made before 2000.

C. All the color films last more than 100 minutes.

D. All the movies made before 2000 last more than 100 minutes.

• • •

1. The film library has no 90-minute movies.

2. The film library has no thrillers in color.

3. The film library has no westerns made before 2000.

4. The film library has no color movies made before 2000.

SUDOKU

Place a number into each box so each row across, column down, and small 9-box square within the larger square (there are 9 of these) contains 1 through 9.

		6	3		2			4
		7	9	6	4			
3		9				2		1
6			4	8		7	3	
				7				
	2	8		3	6			9
1		4				6		5
			5	4	7	1		
5			6		1	3		

CODED PRESIDENTS

In this list of U.S. Presidents, we've replaced each consonant with an X and each vowel (including Y) with an O. Can you decode each Chief Executive's name?

1. OXXOXOX   XOXXOXX

2. XOXOXX   OXOXO

3. XOXX   XOOXXO   OXOXX

4. XOXOXX   XOOXOX

5. OXOXXOX   XXOXX

6. XOXXOX   XOX   XOXOX

7. XXOOXOXO   XOOXOXOXX

8. XOXX   XXOXXOX

9. XOXXOXX   XOXOX

10. XOXXOX   XOXXXOX

WORD WHEEL

Starting with the "S" at the arrow, see how many everyday words of three or more letters you can find going clockwise. Don't skip over any letters. For example, if you saw the letters C, A, R, E, D, you would form five words: CAR, CARE, CARED, ARE, RED. We found 36 words.

CIRCLE SEARCH

Move from circle to adjoining circle, horizontally and vertically only, to form 15 common, everyday words of at least three letters. Don't change the order of the letters in the circles that contain more than one letter. Proper names are not allowed.

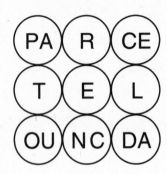

STACKED UP

VISUAL ◆ SPATIAL

The box on the left can be formed by three of the numbered boxes superimposed on top of each other; do not turn them in any way. Can you figure out which three work?

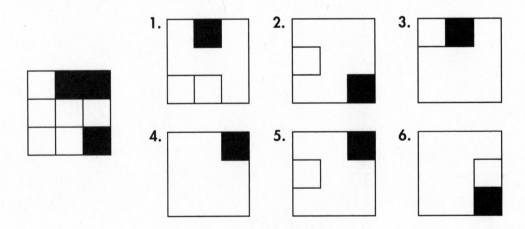

WHIRLIGIG

In each numbered section of the Whirligig are five letters. Anagram each group of letters so that when you add the "BAR" from the middle of the diagram to the front of each group, you will form twelve common 8-letter words.

1. _____
2. _____
3. _____
4. _____
5. _____
6. _____
7. _____
8. _____
9. _____
10. _____
11. _____
12. _____

RHYMING REPLACEMENTS

Each pair of words below will become a familiar phrase when you replace each word in capital letters with a word that rhymes with it. For example, CORK & SCENES would be replaced by the rhyming PORK & BEANS. Can you figure out all ten pairs?

1. MARS & WIPES
2. HOOP & BALLAD
3. CLOVER & POUT
4. SNACK & ZOO
5. MUTTONS & WOES
6. MOPE & DAUGHTER
7. SWING & SCREEN
8. GREET & HOUR
9. LONE & PRONE
10. BANK & SMILE

COUNT ON IT!

LANGUAGE

Use the given letters to fill in the familiar saying, one letter per dash. All the letters following 1 are the first letters of each word, the letters following 2 are the second letters of each word, etc. It is up to you to determine which letter goes where.

1. R O A C I Y   2. N T E F A O   3. N F S U F

4. T U E   5. S R   6. E

__ __ __ ,   __ __   __ __ __ __ __   __ __ __
1 2 3   1 2   1 2 3 4 5   1 2 3

__ __ __ __ ,   __ __ __ __ __ __ .
1 2 3 4   1 2 3 4 5 6

FILLING STATION

LANGUAGE

Place the given consonants on the dashes to form words. The vowels have already been placed for you, and as an additional help, each entry lists its category beside its given consonants.

1. H L L N N N P R T T (fictional character)

__ I __ __ __ E   O __ __ __ A __   A __ __ I E

2. K L N S T T W (actress)

__ A __ E   __ I __ __ __ E __

3. C H K M R S (thing)

__ __ A __ __ O __ __

4. D F H R T W Z Z (movie)

"__ __ E   __ I __ A __ __   O __   O __"

5. B G N R T (American city)

__ A __ O __   __ O U __ E

CARD SENSE

Five playing cards were shuffled and put in a pile, one on top of another. Using the clues, can you identify each card's position in the pile?

1. The ace is directly below the heart.

2. A spade is on top.

3. One red card is directly on top of the other.

4. The diamond is somewhere above the five.

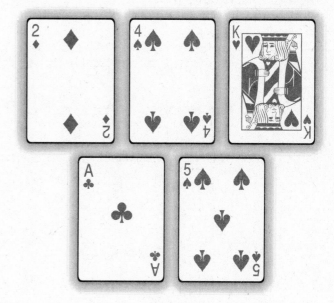

ALL IN A ROW

Which row below contains the most groups of consecutive numbers adding up to 12? Look carefully, because some groups may overlap. We've underlined an example of a group in each row to start you off.

A. 8 <u>3 5 4</u> 2 7 6 1 4 1 2 5 8 7 1 9 5 7 4 1 8 1 3 2

B. 2 1 1 3 6 4 5 1 6 3 <u>2 8 2</u> 9 8 4 1 1 7 6 5 1 7 3

C. 6 5 2 1 3 1 9 7 4 2 8 3 1 1 2 8 5 9 <u>4 2 6</u> 1 4 3

GRAND TOUR

Form a continuous chain of 5-letter words moving through the maze from START to FINISH. The second part of one word becomes the first part of the next word. This puzzle starts with BUR-RO-BOT (burro, robot).

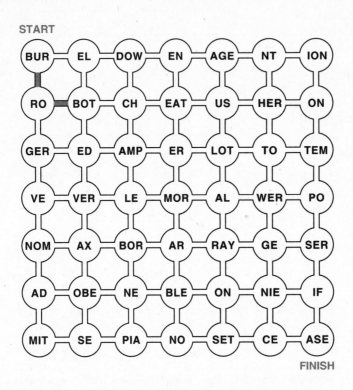

BLOCK PARTY

Study the different views of the block, and draw what should appear on the face that has a question mark.

VISION QUEST

Find the row or column that contains five DIFFERENT gardening tools.

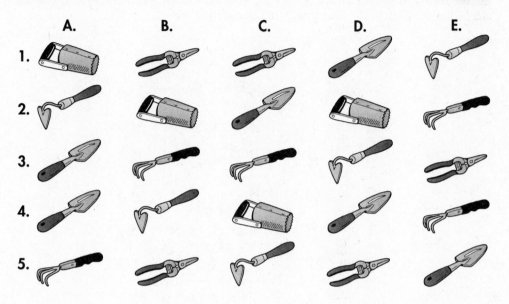

DECODING

LETTER, PLEASE

The numbers below stand for certain letters on the telephone dial. You will see that one number may stand for more than one letter — for example, 3 may be D, E, or F. By finding the correct letter for each number, you will have spelled out a thought.

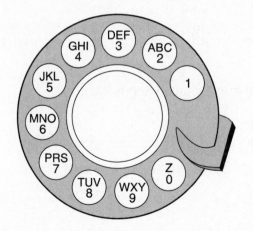

2   7766473

47   2   25683;

38534556368

47   7246.

HEXAGON HUNT

VISUAL

In this diagram of six-sided figures, there are 10 "special" hexagons. These 10 are special because the six numbers around each one are all different from each other and the center. We've circled one of the 10. Can you find the other 9?

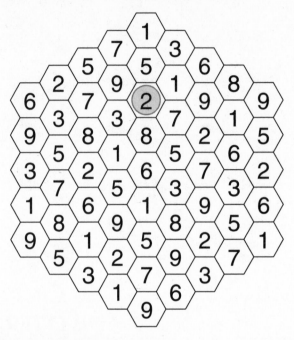

DEDUCTION PROBLEM

LOGIC

Jenny Doalot attends Night Sports Academy every evening of the week, Monday to Friday. Her schedule has her participating in a different sport each night. The five sports are aerobics, bowling, dance, fencing, and karate. From Jenny's exhausted statements below, can you determine the day on which she participates in each activity?

1. "I have my fencing class the day before I have karate."

2. "Dance is Friday's activity."

3. "Bowling and aerobics aren't scheduled on consecutive days."

4. "Aerobics and karate are scheduled earlier in the week than bowling."

MAGNIFIND

Figure out which areas of the drawing have been enlarged.

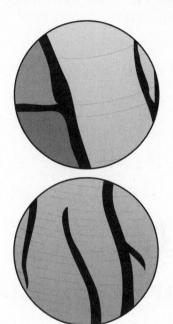

CROSS-UPS

Using only the letters given above each diagram, fill in the boxes in such a way that an everyday compound word is formed, one part reading across and the other part reading down. The letter already in the diagram is a letter shared by both parts of the word.

1. E F K L L R

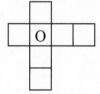

2. D K O R W W

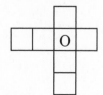

WEEK 17 · ASSOCIATIONS

LANGUAGE

You'll find eight groups of three words that can be associated in some way with each other (example: mantel, fireplace, logs). Cross out each group as you find it. The initial letters of the remaining words will spell out the answer to the riddle:

WHY COULDN'T THE TEDDY BEAR EAT DESSERT?

HEALTH MEETING CHEAT SIMPLE EXTRA STREAM

WISE WARRANT PLAIN JUDICIOUS BILK APPLE

SHAPE ASSEMBLY SELECT KANSAS CURRENT

PRUDENT SATISFY OKLAHOMA THIMBLE FIGURE

STRAIGHTFORWARD UNSURE CHIMPANZEE FLAG

SWINDLE CONGREGATION FRESH LEMUR FLOW

EVIDENCE MONKEY DENSE FORM IOWA

ALPHABET CIRCLE MAZE

VISUAL

Start at A at the bottom, continue through the alphabet only once, and finish at the Z in the center. You will pass through other letters when going from one letter to the next, but move in only one direction, either around a circle or along a spoke. Don't enter or cross through the Z until you are finished.

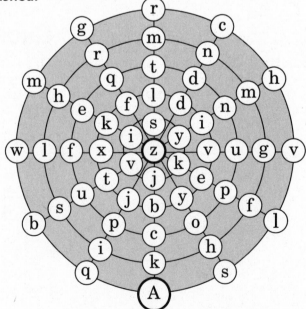

ONLINE NETWORK

In each two-column group, take the letters in the left-hand column along the paths (indicated by the lines) and place them in their proper boxes in the right-hand column. When done, for each puzzle you'll find three related words reading down the right-hand column.

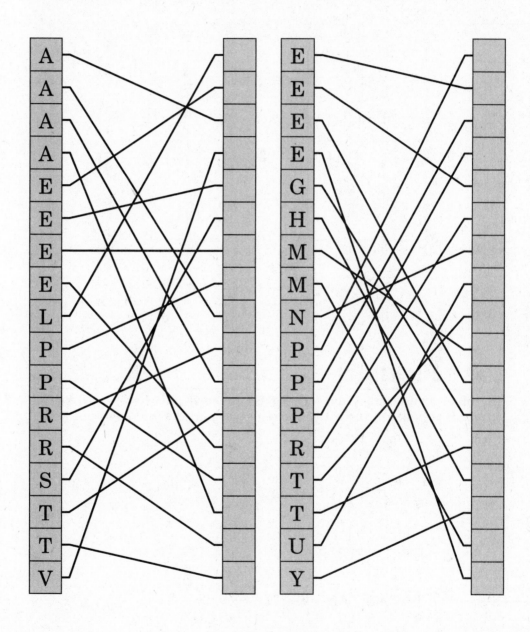

COUNTDOWN

VISUAL

Following the connecting lines, find the only route in this grid that passes through the numbers backward from 9 to 1 consecutively.

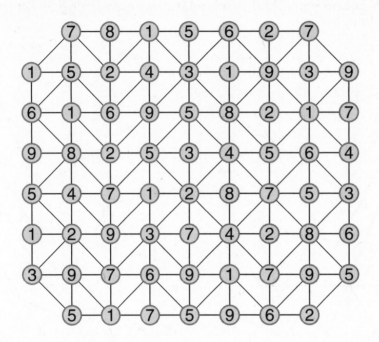

EASY PICKINGS

LANGUAGE

To solve, simply cross out one letter in each pair below. When the puzzle is completed correctly, the remaining letters will spell out a fact.

YO OH EU   WR NO AN ' TV

SM OI NR CK   RI FD   MA TE

EF IV ER SR ET   SY KO UH

TW NH TI VN KL.

LOOSE TILE

WEEK 17

The tray on the right seemed the ideal place to store the set of loose dominoes. Unfortunately, when the tray was full, one domino was left over. Determine the arrangement of the dominoes in the tray and which is the Loose Tile.

LANGUAGE

U.S. S's

The list below consists of the names of six U.S. states, but we've removed all of their letters except for the S's. Can you write one letter on each dash to complete the names of the states?

1. __ __ S S __ __ __ __ S __ __ __ S

2. __ __ S __ __ __ __ __ __ __ __ __ __

3. __ __ __ __ S __ __ __ __

4. __ __ __ __ S

5. __ __ S __ __ __ S __ __

6. __ __ __ S __ __

115

ELIMINATION

Cross off the capitalized words below according to the instructions given. The remaining words, in order, will form a thought.

SALE TRUTH COOL MAGICAL SHIPSHAPE IS WORDS KISS WORN WILL EDIFICE POWERFUL NOT MEET STRANGER AND NEUTRAL FEATHERWEIGHT BURN SAIL CHALICE THE WARN TONGUE THAN OR HONEYBUNCH MEAT EAR TELL FICTION

Eliminate the...

1. three compound words.

2. word that can be dialed on an old telephone as 6388725 (see page 109 for an illustration).

3. three pairs of words where, in each pair, the words sound the same.

4. three words formed only with letters from the first half of the alphabet.

5. word that contains, among others, the fifth, sixteenth, and twenty-third letters of the alphabet.

6. three words that form a phrase meaning "to reveal personal or confidential information."

7. five-word saying that means "veracity exists in a more aberrational state vis-à-vis invented narrative."

WHAT'S YOUR NUMBER?

Can you figure out the relationship of the four numbers in the first two squares and, based on that, what missing number goes into the space with the question mark?

6	4
10	8

16	11
27	22

80	60
27	?

ALPHABET SOUP

Cross off each letter from the alphabet list that appears in the larger group of letters. Then rearrange the letters not crossed out to form the name of a country.

F	O	W	K	O	F	K	W	F	R	F	W	K	N	O	R
U	D	N	O	F	R	U	N	W	P	Y	R	O	N	R	Y
Y	J	A	Q	W	K	F	Y	R	O	U	J	D	Z	G	N
S	K	Q	U	M	B	O	V	W	P	T	X	J	Q	D	K

A B C D E F G H I J K L M N O P Q R S T U V W X Y Z

Country: _____

LANGUAGE

SLIDE RULE

Slide each column of letters up or down in the box and form as many everyday 4-letter words as you can in the windows where SOAR is now. We formed 36 words, including SOAR.

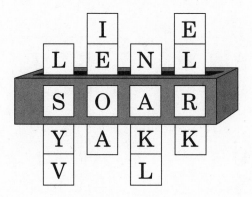

Your list of words:

IN THE ABSTRACT

VISUAL ◆ SPATIAL

Fill in each section with one of the four symbols so no sections containing the same symbol touch. Four sections are already complete.

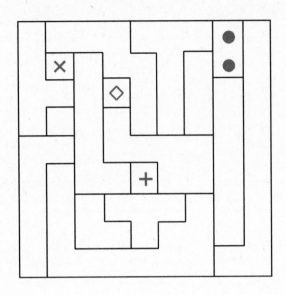

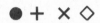

LICENSE PLATES

LANGUAGE

Each box contains six letters of a well-known American city and state. The top three are a part of the city and the bottom three are a part of the state, in order.

1.
```
U C S
R I Z
```

2.
```
L A N
F L O
```

3.
```
R O I
C H I
```

4.
```
I T T
S Y L
```

5.
```
A U S
X A S
```

6.
```
T T L
H I N
```

BULL'S-EYE LETTER

Add the SAME single letter to each group of three letters then rearrange the letters to form six everyday 4-letter words.

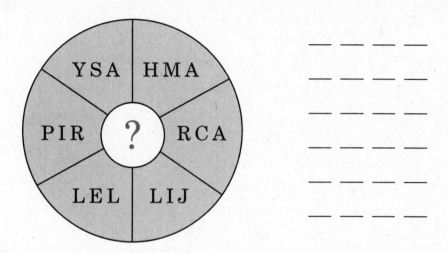

_ _ _ _

_ _ _ _

_ _ _ _

_ _ _ _

_ _ _ _

_ _ _ _

LOGIC

SUDOKU

Directions for solving are on page 102.

1	9	6			2			
2			1	7		6	8	
							2	9
9		5	6			2		1
	2		5		1		7	
3		7			8	4		5
8	4							
	6	1		9	5			3
			8			7	9	6

ANAGRAM MAZE

VISUAL ◆ LANGUAGE

The diagram contains 36 words, 19 of which are anagrams of other everyday words. Start at the top arrow and anagram DEER. While solving, move up, down, right, or left to the only adjacent word that can be anagrammed. Continue until you arrive at the bottom arrow. There is only one path through the maze.

1 VOLT	2 PULL	3 SOCK	4 WASP	5 TOED	6 DEER
7 MAKE	8 FARM	9 BUFF	10 CARS	11 MAZE	12 ZINC
13 ROAR	14 PERT	15 MYTH	16 FEAT	17 VEIL	18 BOLD
19 FOAL	20 TAPE	21 DROP	22 DUMB	23 NEON	24 CALM
25 CAFE	26 HIGH	27 ROBE	28 STUD	29 JINX	30 REAM
31 SKIN	32 FERN	33 CURL	34 LEAD	35 FORM	36 LAIN

SYMBOL-ISM

DECODING

This is simply a Cryptogram that uses symbols instead of letters to spell out a truism. Each symbol stands for the same letter throughout. For this puzzle, we've indicated that ∅ = M and ◕ = N.

THE LINEUP

WEEK 18

While scrutinizing the lineup of letters, can you answer the five questions correctly in five minutes or less?

WYBVFJSULKCOCONUTZMITTGPROMENADEQWHAT

1. Which letter of the alphabet does not appear in the lineup? _____

2. What 7-letter word — with its letters in correct order and appearing together — can you find in the lineup? _____

3. Which letter of the alphabet appears exactly three times in the lineup? _____

4. What 9-letter word — with its letters in correct order and appearing together — can you find in the lineup? _____

5. Other than the answers to Questions 2 and 4, how many everyday words — with their letters in correct order and appearing together — of four or more letters can you find in the lineup? _____

SKILLS TEST

Determine which box contains the most O's.

1.

```
X X O O O X X X
X X O X O X O O X
O X X X X O O X X
X X O X X O X X O
X X O O O O X O X
```

2.

```
O X X O O X O X O
O O X X O X X O X
X X O X O O X X O
X O X O X O X O X
X X X X X X O X O
```

WORD EQUATIONS

LANGUAGE

Determine the three defined words in each equation. The third word is formed when the second is written directly after the first; for example, for "for each + shape = act in a play," you would respond "per + form = perform."

1. in favor of + buyer's offer = prohibit

2. river blockade + grow mature = cause harm to

3. duel reminder + give permission to = shade of red

4. very slim + male monarch = reasoning

5. first-aid set + billfold bill = cute feline

STAR WORDS

VISUAL ◆ LOGIC

Only five of the eight words given will fit together in the diagram. Place them in the directions indicated by the arrows.

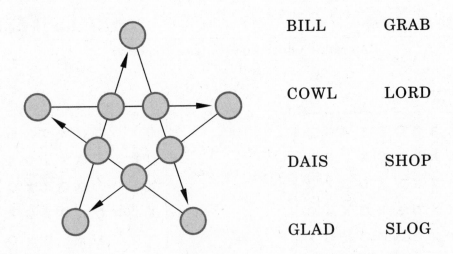

BILL   GRAB

COWL   LORD

DAIS   SHOP

GLAD   SLOG

WAYWORDS

WEEK 19

An 10-word thought can be found beginning with the word IT. Then, move to any adjacent box up, down, or diagonally for each following word.

ETERNITY	TAKES	IT	NEVER
A	FEELS	INTELLIGENT	ALWAYS
WOMAN	BRAVE	LOVE	PROVIDE
BRAVE	A	MAN	TO

MATH

FUN WITH FACTS AND FIGURES

This puzzle tests you on a lot of little facts and figures. Solve the quiz in the order given since each answer is used in the next statement. There are no fractions used here.

1. Take the number of vowels in the word CONCENTRATION and multiply it by the number of consonants in the word. _____

2. Next, subtract the number of seasons in a year. _____

3. Now divide by the number of letters in the name of the continent that contains Liberia, Chad, and Egypt. _____

4. Add the number of points awarded for a touchdown in football. _____

5. Subtract the number of men in a tub in a children's rhyme. _____

The answer is the number of squares in a tic-tac-toe board. Is yours?

TRI, TRI AGAIN

LANGUAGE ◆ SPATIAL

Fit the nine triangles into the big one so six everyday words are spelled out reading across the arrows. Do not rotate the triangles.

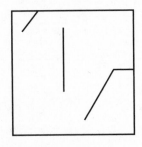

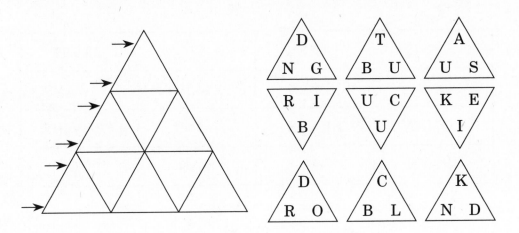

OVERLAY

VISUAL ◆ SPATIAL

When you overlay the three diagrams in the top row, which of the three lettered diagrams, A, B, or C, will be formed?

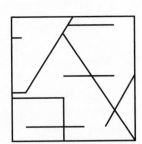

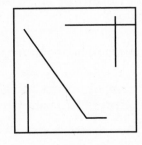

A.	B.	C.

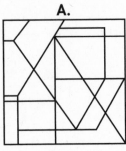

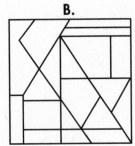

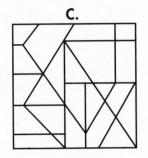

124

ANTONYMS QUIZ

Directions for solving are on page 99.

1. BRAZEN   a. bashful   b. impoverished   c. frail

2. ABSTRUSE   a. verdant   b. perpetual   c. uncomplicated

3. BEDRAGGLED   a. resultant   b. meticulous   c. testy

4. LAVISH   a. frugal   b. liberated   c. ideological

5. JOVIAL   a. rotund   b. cognitive   c. sullen

6. VOLUBLE   a. reticent   b. comparable   c. lucid

7. RESOLUTE   a. radiant   b. flexible   c. gauche

8. MENACING   a. crucial   b. gentle   c. livid

LETTER, PLEASE

Directions for solving are on page 109.

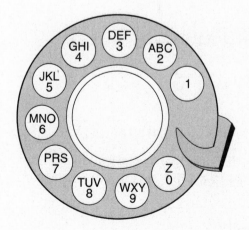

259297 73636237

86 23 42779

2322873 968 63837

5669 946'7

3255464 46 5683

9484 9687 76453.

ARROW MAZE

VISUAL

Starting at the S and following the arrow up, see if you can find your way to F. When you reach an arrow, you MUST follow its direction and continue in that direction until you come to the next arrow. When you reach a two-headed arrow, you can choose either direction. It's okay to cross your own path.

P COUNT

VISUAL

Here's an eye exam that's also an P exam! First, read the sentence below. Next, go back and read the sentence again, but this time count all of the P's. How many are there?

PRECIOUS PENELOPE PAPPADOPOULIS

PICKED PURPLE POPPIES AND PRETTY

PINK PANSIES, PERHAPS PREPARING

FOR HER PAL PIPPA P. PEPPARD'S

POPULAR PAJAMA PARTY.

COUNT TO TEN

Examine the diamonds and pearls and then answer these questions: 1. Which row contains the most diamonds? 2. Which row contains the most pearls? 3. Which row contains an equal number of diamonds and pearls?

1.

2.

3.

4.

5.

6.

7.

8.

9.

10.

BLOCK PARTY

Directions for solving are on page 108.

CARD SENSE

LOGIC

Five playing cards were shuffled and put in a pile, one on top of another. Using the clues, can you identify each card's position in the pile?

1. The colors alternate, top to bottom.

2. The seven is above both the king and the two.

3. Neither diamond is on top of the stack.

QUICK FILL

LANGUAGE

Determine the 10-letter word from the clues. All the letters in the word are listed.

A C D I I N O R T Y

1. In the alphabet, letter 3 is immediately before letter 1.

2. Letter 10 is from the second half of the alphabet.

3. Letter 8 is a vowel.

4. Letters 4, 6, and 7, in order, spell out a word for a 2,000-pound weight.

5. In the alphabet, letter 2 is nine letters before letter 9.

6. Letter 5 appears elsewhere in the word.

$$\overline{1} \quad \overline{2} \quad \overline{3} \quad \overline{4} \quad \overline{5} \quad \overline{6} \quad \overline{7} \quad \overline{8} \quad \overline{9} \quad \overline{10}$$

CIRCLE MATH

Each overlapping circle is identified by a letter having a different number value from 1 to 9. Where some circles overlap, there is a number: It is the SUM of the values of the letters in those overlapping circles. Can you figure out the correct values for the letters? As a starting help, G = 8.

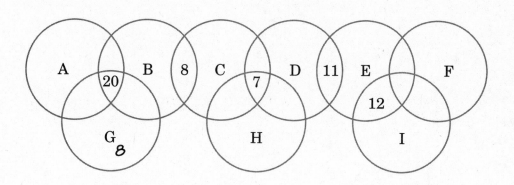

RINGERS

Each Ringer is composed of five rings. Use your imagination to rotate the rings so that you spell out four 5-letter words reading from the outside to the inside when all five rings are aligned correctly.

1.

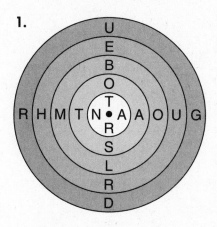

2.

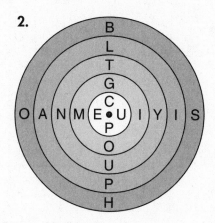

COUNT ON IT!

LANGUAGE

Solving directions are on page 106.

1. B C T T M S   2. H O P R A O   3. O E O O N O
4. K I Y T   5. S H L

$\overline{1}\ \overline{2}\ \overline{3}$ $\overline{1}\ \overline{2}\ \overline{3}\ \overline{4}$ $\overline{1}\ \overline{2}\ \overline{3}\ \overline{4}\ \overline{5}$

$\overline{1}\ \overline{2}\ \overline{3}\ \overline{4}\ \overline{5}$ $\overline{1}\ \overline{2}\ \overline{3}$ $\overline{1}\ \overline{2}\ \overline{3}\ \overline{4}\ \overline{5}$.

IN THE ABSTRACT

VISUAL ◆ SPATIAL

Directions for solving are on page 118.

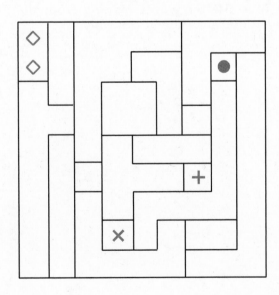

MARCHING ORDERS

Using a different two-step sequence of addition and/or subtraction, can you make your way from Start to Finish in each puzzle? We've started the first one for you using the sequence –2 and +5; continue this sequence to reach Finish. You will not cross your own path or pass through any square twice.

1. FINISH ↑

18	23	21	22	25	27
17	20	14	26	23	29
14	16	15	17	24	18
13	10	8	12	11	12
12	5	11	14	9	11
8	6	9	7	10	8

↑ START

2. FINISH ↑

17	15	18	21	19	22
11	14	16	17	20	18
12	16	15	13	14	17
9	8	10	12	19	11
5	3	7	6	8	12
6	4	8	10	9	11

↑ START

RELATIONSHIPS QUIZ

Directions for solving are on page 99.

1. FLY is to PLANE as DRIVE is to _____.
   (a) road   (b) jet   (c) captain   (d) car

2. DENMARK is to KRONE as CHILE is to _____.
   (a) peso   (b) Argentina   (c) dollar   (d) euro

3. DECK is to CARD as ALPHABET is to _____.
   (a) school   (b) child   (c) block   (d) letter

4. KOUFAX is to PITCH as PHELPS is to _____.
   (a) cycle   (b) shoot   (c) swim   (d) run

5. AVARICE is to GREED as NONPLUS is to _____.
   (a) minus   (b) perplex   (c) calm   (d) inscribe

RING LOGIC

LOGIC

Complete the diagram by drawing in the links between the rings using the statements. Assume that all the rings in the picture are locked rigidly into position and cannot be moved in any direction. Consider yourself a true ringmaster if you can find the solution in under six minutes!

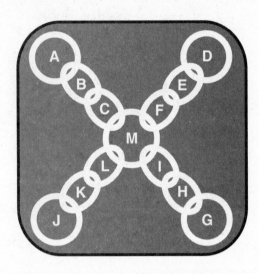

1. The pattern looks the same even when it's rotated like a wheel.

2. Rings B and C are each linked twice.

3. The top right side of ring H is in front of ring I.

CIRCLE SEARCH

LANGUAGE

Directions for solving are on page 104. Here you're looking to form 17 words of at least three letters.

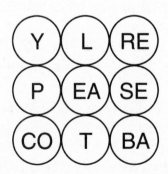

ANIMAL CHARADES

Directions for solving are on page 98.

My FIRST is in SWAN and in CROWN; _____

My SECOND is in FALCON and in DROWN; _____

My THIRD is in TURTLE but not in RUST; _____

My FOURTH is in DOVE but not in DUST; _____

My FIFTH is in LEMUR and in LEND; _____

My SIXTH is in PARTRIDGE and in FRIEND; _____

My SEVENTH is in SQUIRREL but not in RELATE; _____

My EIGHTH is in PENGUIN but not in EIGHT; _____

My NINTH is in GRASSHOPPER and in SHAME. _____

My WHOLE is a furry carnivore and a Michigan native's nickname, say no more!

_____

SKILLS TEST

John is older than James, and Jack is younger than Jeremy. Jeremy is older than James, but he is younger than John. Who is the oldest?

MISSING DOMINOES

VISUAL ◆ LOGIC

In this game use all 28 dominoes that are in a standard set. Each one has a different combination from 0-0, 0-1, 0-2, to 6-6. Domino halves with the same number of dots lie next to each other. To avoid confusion we have used an open circle to indicate a zero. Can you fill in the missing white dominoes to complete the board?

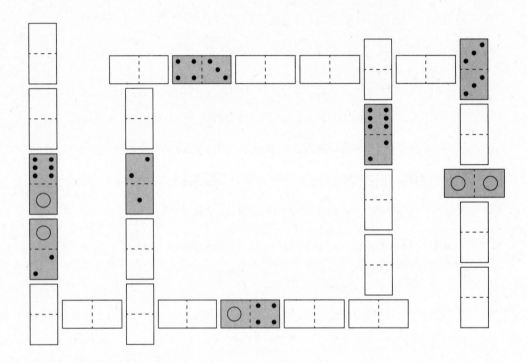

DOMINOES

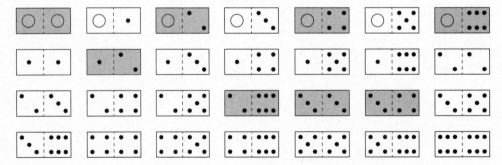

SEVEN WORD ZINGER

WEEK 21

Using each letter once, form seven everyday 3-letter words with the first letter coming from the center, the second from the middle, and the third from the outer circle. Your words may differ from ours.

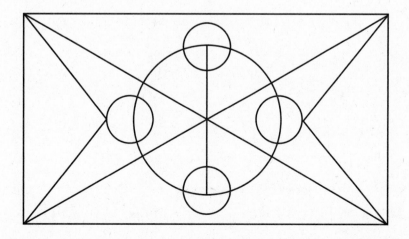

W O
U O
A I
E A F E L W
R D
G L N
B A
N

— — —

— — —

— — —

— — —

— — —

— — —

— — —

VISUAL ◆ LOGIC

ON THE LINE

Can you trace this figure without lifting your pencil from the paper, crossing, or retracing your own path?

TARGET SHOOT

LANGUAGE

Find the two letters which, when entered into the center circle of each target, will form three 6-letter words reading across.

1.

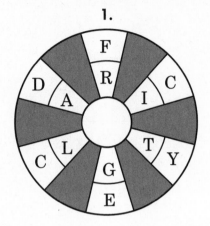

2.

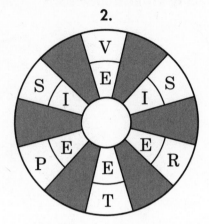

NEXT TO NOTHING

VISUAL ◆ LANGUAGE

In the first row, the Y is next to the number zero and the W is next to the letter O. Circle all of the letters next to zeroes then scramble the circled letters to spell out a man's name.

Y0	WO	KO	JO
HO	EO	AO	C0
LO	DO	I0	SO
RO	U0	BO	MO
FO	GO	Q0	ZO
XO	N0	PO	VO

136

WORD HUNT

Directions for solving are on page 98. This time, you'll be searching for 23 4-letter words that begin with W (such as WAND).

E	D	N	M	W
E	A	R	T	E
K	W	Y	P	N
H	I	F	L	O
P	M	D	E	W

Your list of words:

SUDOKU

Directions for solving are on page 102.

8	2		7			1		4
3					5	7	2	
		5	2					
	7			4	2		9	1
		2		5		4		
1	5		9	7			3	
					3	2		
	6	3	1					5
2		1			9		4	7

137

STACKED UP

VISUAL ◆ SPATIAL

Directions for solving are on page 104.

1.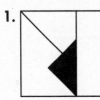

2.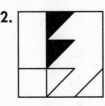

3.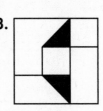

4.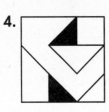

5.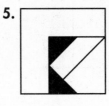

6.

DOVETAILED WORDS

LANGUAGE

Two related words, with their letters in the correct order, are combined in each row of letters. Can you find both words?

1. R B A O I O S S E T   _____ _____

2. F S R N O O S W T   _____ _____

3. J F O U R N E G S L E T   _____ _____

4. P S E L T I I G H T T E   _____ _____

5. P B A A N M D B O A O   _____ _____

ROUND TRIP

Directions for solving are on page 100.

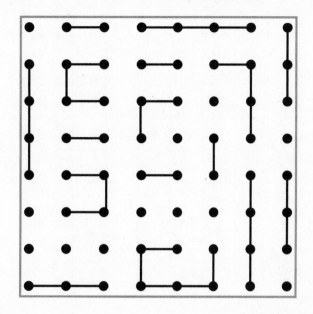

SQUARE LINKS

Write one letter in each empty box so that an everyday 8-letter word is spelled out around each gray box. Each word may read either clockwise or counterclockwise, and may start at any of its letters.

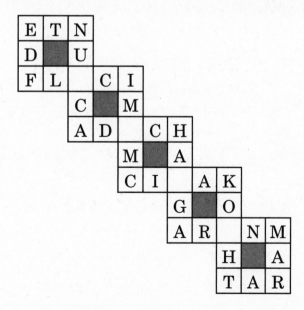

ARROW MAZE

VISUAL

Solving directions are on page 126.

CODE WORD

DECODING

Decipher a quote and the Code Word's eleven letters, represented by the numbers 1 through 11. So, if the Code Word were "THUNDERCLAP," 1 in the quote would be T, 2 would be H, etc.

$$\overline{1}\ \overline{2}\ \overline{3}\ \overline{4}\ \overline{5}\ \overline{6}\ \overline{7}\ \overline{8}\ \overline{9}\ \overline{10}\ \overline{11}$$

M 5 2 11 7 F L I F 4 ' 3 F 5 I L 1 8 4 3 5 8 4 M 4 2

6 10 7 D I D 2 7 9 8 4 5 L I Z 4 10 7 6 C L 7 3 4

9 10 4 11 6 4 8 4 9 7 3 1 C C 4 4 D I 2 G 6 10 4 2

9 10 4 11 G 5 V 4 1 P .

KEEP ON MOVING

WEEK
21

Directions for solving are on page 96. Here, start in the shaded square with the number 4.

3	1	✳	4	4	4
2	3	4	3	2	4
5	1	2	1	4	1
2	3	3	3	1	1
1	3	5	2	2	3
4	3	3	1	5	4

VISUAL ◆ LANGUAGE

WORD CHARADE

Directions for solving are on page 101.

My first letter is the only letter from the first half of the alphabet in one of the columns.

My second letter only appears immediately above or below wherever my first letter appears.

My third letter appears more often than any other letter in one of the rows.

My fourth letter appears more often than any other letter in one of the columns.

My fifth letter always has a vowel to its immediate left and right wherever it appears.

My sixth letter appears only in the top half of the diagram.

C	W	Z	N	U	T	G	Y
W	U	H	A	R	G	V	T
Q	T	D	F	B	E	M	S
N	R	L	D	F	Q	T	Z
F	B	U	H	I	G	Y	E
D	Q	V	M	O	S	B	L
I	Y	B	I	H	I	R	G
Z	S	R	C	W	G	A	N

—— —— —— —— —— ——

HEXAGON HUNT

VISUAL

Directions for solving are on page 110.

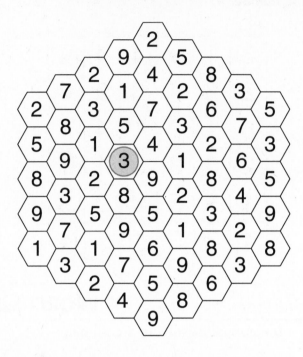

GOING IN CIRCLES

LANGUAGE

Directions for solving are on page 97.

1.

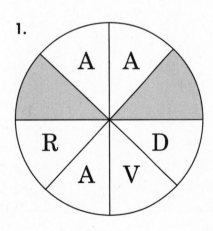

2.

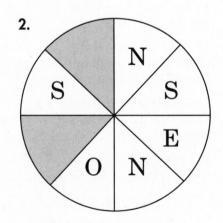

WHAT'S YOUR NUMBER?

WEEK 22

Can you figure out the relationship of the numbers in the first three figures and, based on that, what missing number goes into the space with the question mark?

6	2	8	4
5	7	9	11
3	4	2	?
91	57	145	89

LANGUAGE

ELIMINATION

Directions for solving are on page 116. Once again, the remaining words will form a thought.

A GREEN CHIP AMBULATORY PRESSURE STUN
VERBALIZE BAY IS PSYCHO COMMUNICABLE WHAT
OFF GRAND COCONUT TURNS EXPRESS VERTIGO
RAPIDS COAL THE LITTLE SURMOUNT INTO
ARTICULATE CABDRIVER ROCK DIAMONDS
REPRESENTATION OLD NOTORIOUS BLOCK

Eliminate the...

1. three one-word Alfred Hitchcock movie titles.

2. six-word phrase that means "a person much like his or her parent."

3. three different verbs that mean "put into words."

4. word that begins with four consecutive letters, in some order, of the alphabet.

5. six words that form three two-word names of U.S. cities.

6. words of five syllables each.

7. three words that end with the same three letters.

ANAGRAM MAZE

VISUAL ◆ SPATIAL

Directions for solving are on page 120. This time, there are 17 words to anagram and the first word you'll be anagramming is SHUT.

1 SHUT	2 KEEP	3 DOES	4 IOTA	5 CULT	6 OOZE
___	___	___	___	___	___
7 FIVE	8 HUNT	9 RAID	10 PURE	11 PLUS	12 ALOE
___	___	___	___	___	___
13 PURR	14 BAKE	15 GOAT	16 WHIM	17 DECK	18 WINE
___	___	___	___	___	___
19 MODE	20 REAR	21 WAIT	22 FOIL	23 FALL	24 INTO
___	___	___	___	___	___
25 VEER	26 KNOW	27 KEEN	28 SOWN	29 EDIT	30 CREW
___	___	___	___	___	___
31 EARN	32 ANTS	33 BOWL	34 WREN	35 DAWN	36 DOOR
___	___	___	___	___	___

EASY PICKINGS

LANGUAGE

To solve, simply cross out one letter in each pair below. When the puzzle is completed correctly, the remaining letters will spell out a fact.

YE OC OU CR   ES MN RI LT ED

HA EN DL OP SE   YS EO UN   SA NF DF

KO NT HA EW CR HS   EA RN TO UO NS DA

GY OG BU.

ASSOCIATIONS

Directions for solving are on page 112.

WHAT HAS WHEELS AND FLIES?

OSLO ALASKA ANT RED GRAVITY ENERGY TERMITE

ARTIFICIAL REMARKABLE REBEL BEETLE MANAGE

BATTERY GREEN DIRECT ANVIL PEP QUICK GUEST

COPENHAGEN EGG FANTASTIC SPEEDY TURNIP

BLUE SUPERVISE ROUND FAST DELICATE UPSET

HELSINKI FINE CANOPY VIGOR DAINTY KALE

EXTRAORDINARY

MATH

ALL IN A ROW

Directions for solving are on page 107. This time, look for the most groups of consecutive numbers adding up to 13.

A. 9 1 4 3 8 1 2 6 4 5 7 2 3 6 1 8 2 2 1 7 1 9 4 1

B. 2 3 6 5 2 1 5 6 8 3 4 2 1 1 4 9 3 7 2 6 1 3 1 9

C. 1 7 3 4 8 5 1 4 3 2 3 8 6 9 2 4 5 3 1 6 6 4 7 3

TARGET SHOOT

LANGUAGE

Find the two letters which, when entered into the center circle of each target, will form three 6-letter words reading across.

1.

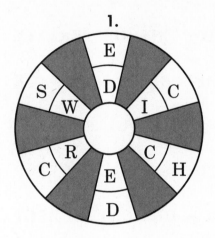

2.

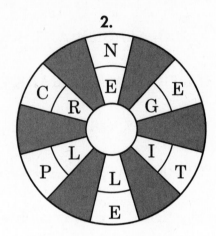

IN THE ABSTRACT

VISUAL ◆ SPATIAL

Fill in each section with one of the four symbols so no sections containing the same symbol touch. Four sections are already complete.

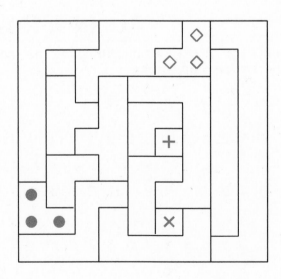

146

COUNTDOWN

Following the connecting lines, find the only route in this grid that passes through the numbers backward from 9 to 1 consecutively.

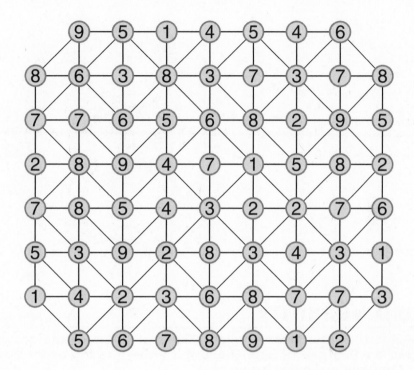

EASY PICKINGS

To solve, simply cross out one letter in each pair below. When the puzzle is completed correctly, the remaining letters will spell out an old Japanese proverb.

TN AO   UT EU AK LC HG   GI SL   TW AO

WL EI LA SR NG .

SEVEN WORD ZINGER

LANGUAGE

Using each letter once, form seven everyday 3-letter words with the first letter coming from the center, the second from the middle, and the third from the outer circle. Your words may differ from ours.

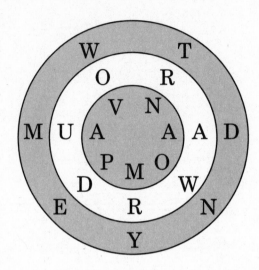

— — —

— — —

— — —

— — —

— — —

— — —

WORD VISIBILITY

LANGUAGE

There are six 5-letter words below. The first letter of the answer is found in the first pair of letters, and it is either the top or the bottom letter. Continue across each pair.

For example, the word GIRL would be found thus: G A R L
                                               I̶ I T X̶

1. B R M W H
   T I R C T

2. G R I E M
   C L E R N

3. P H E A T
   S C I N B

4. P L V F G
   R O A N E

5. H A K L T
   F B U D P

6. W R L J E
   J U I T Y

148

ANAGRAM MAZE

WEEK
23

The diagram contains 36 words, 21 of which are anagrams of other everyday words. Start at the top arrow and anagram LONE. Move up, down, right, or left to the only adjacent word that can be anagrammed. Continue until you arrive at the bottom arrow. There is only one path through the maze.

1 DIAL	2 EGOS	3 ORBS	4 VETO	5 LONE	6 FANG
7 RULE	8 GLEE	9 HERE	10 FURY	11 KIWI	12 FORK
13 DIVA	14 TELL	15 CORK	16 MEAN	17 METE	18 RING
19 CALK	20 GAPE	21 RUBY	22 BAND	23 BALD	24 WAKE
25 LOLL	26 BODY	27 ROOF	28 STAB	29 IRKS	30 APES
31 FILM	32 STAR	33 COLA	34 ANTE	35 LAVA	36 LESS

LANGUAGE

CIRCLE SEARCH

Move from circle to adjoining circle, horizontally and vertically only, to form 12 common, everyday words of at least three letters. Don't change the order of the letters in the circles that contain more than one letter. Proper names are not allowed.

149

ONLINE NETWORK

In each two-column group, take the letters in the left-hand column along the paths (indicated by the lines) and place them in their proper boxes in the right-hand column. When done, you'll find a thought in the two groups by reading the letters in the right-hand columns from top to bottom.

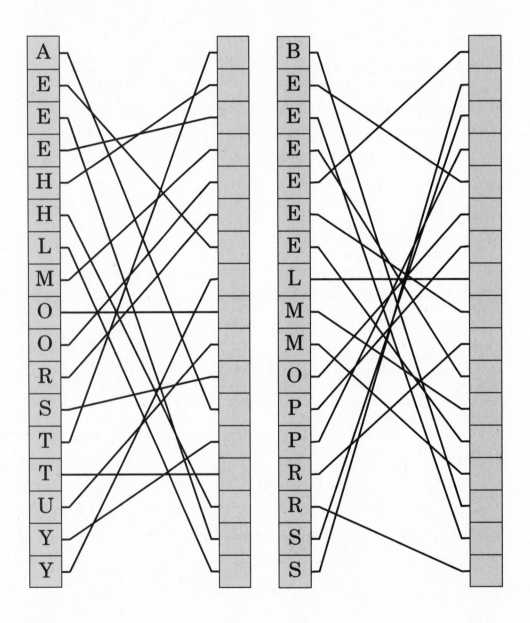

SUDOKU

Place a number into each box so each row across, column down, and small 9-box square within the larger square (there are 9 of these) contains 1 through 9.

			1		8		3	2
	8	7						5
				4	2	9		6
	6			9		2		
		8	3	2	7	4		
		1		8			9	
8		3	2	1				
4						3	2	
5	7		9		3			

CODE WORD

Decipher a quote and the Code Word's eleven letters, represented by the numbers 1 through 11. So, if the Code Word were "FORMULATING," 1 in the quote would be F, 2 would be O, etc.

$$\overline{}\ \overline{}\ \overline{}\ \overline{}\ \overline{}\ \overline{}\ \overline{}\ \overline{}\ \overline{}\ \overline{}\ \overline{}$$

1 2 3 4 5 6 7 8 9 10 11

10 H 2   1 3 5 B 8 2 M   W 9 10 H   10 H 9 4

C 5 U 6 10 3 11   9 4   10 H 7 10   10 5 5   M 7 6 11

1 2 5 1 8 2   G 5   7 3 5 U 6 D   4 7 11 9 6 G ,

" 10 H 2   1 3 5 B 8 2 M   W 9 10 H   10 H 9 4

C 5 U 6 10 3 11 . . . "

MAGIC NUMBER SQUARES

WEEK 23

Fill in the empty boxes so these groups add up to the number below each diagram: 1. each row; 2. each column; 3. both diagonals; 4. the four center squares; 5. the four corner squares; 6. each quarter of the diagram. A number will be used only once per diagram.

1.

	16	15	
13			
9	11		
	4		

38

2.

8	30		
	18	26	
34			
	24		

92

MAGNIFIND

VISUAL ◆ SPATIAL

Figure out which area of the drawing has been enlarged.

STAR WORDS

WEEK 23

Only five of the eight words given will fit together in the diagram. Place them in the directions indicated by the arrows.

DIET   REAP

LEAP   TART

PACT   TIER

PROD   TOIL

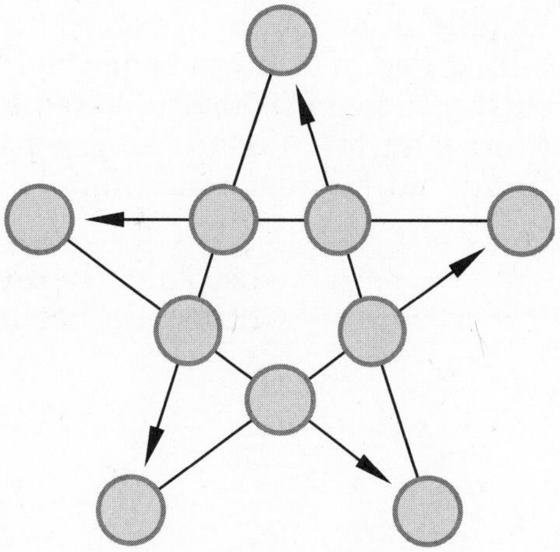

MATH

FUN WITH FACTS AND FIGURES

This puzzle tests you on five little facts and figures. Solve the quiz in the order given since each answer is used in the next statement. There are no fractions used here.

1. Take the number of sides on a rectangle and multiply it by the number of inches in a foot.

2. Next, add the number of doughnuts in half a dozen.

3. Now divide by the value of the Roman numeral XXVII.

4. Add the number of quarters in $2.50.

5. Subtract the number of people who perform in a quartet.

Our answer is the number on the black billiards ball.
Is yours?

DEDUCTION PROBLEM

LOGIC

Three friends invested in the stock market recently. One of the three made off with $10,000, a second lost the same amount, and the third friend broke even.

In talking about their experiences afterwards, the man who made a killing lied in order to keep the IRS off his back, the man who lost his shirt also lied because he hated to admit that he'd been a fool, but the third man told the truth. From the following two statements, try to figure out how each man fared.

Lee said, "Leroy broke even."
Leo said, "Lee made $10,000."

RELATIONSHIPS QUIZ

LANGUAGE

KENNEL is to DOG as STY is to PIG because a dog lives in a kennel and a pig lives in a sty. Each of the statements below is a relationship of some kind. Can you select the right word from the four given?

1. GRAY is to BLACK as PINK is to _____.
   (a) white   (b) red   (c) blue   (d) rose

2. DIRT is to HILL as SAND is to _____.
   (a) desert   (b) beach   (c) rock   (d) dune

3. ICE is to SKATE as WATER is to _____.
   (a) shore   (b) wave   (c) ski   (d) ocean

4. DRESS is to FABRIC as PANCAKE is to _____.
   (a) flour   (b) waffle   (c) griddle   (d) syrup

5. SNOW is to BLIZZARD as WIND is to _____.
   (a) rain   (b) frost   (c) gale   (d) tide

TRI, TRI AGAIN

WEEK 24

Fit the nine triangles into the big one so six everyday words are spelled out reading across the arrows. Do not rotate the triangles.

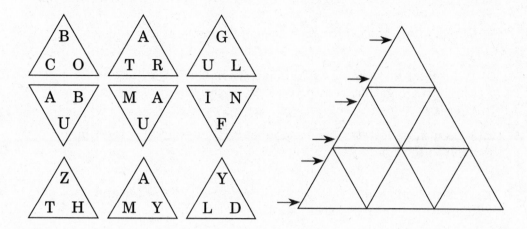

ALL IN A ROW

MATH

Which row below contains the most groups of consecutive numbers adding up to 12? Look carefully, because some groups may overlap. We've underlined an example of a group in each row to start you off.

A. 4 3 3 2 1 8 2 5 5 1 1 6 9 8 1 <u>2 6 4</u> 5 1 7 2 4 9

B. 1 1 1 4 <u>9 3</u> 2 2 1 4 6 5 2 5 8 1 1 2 4 1 3 3 4 8

C. 7 3 3 6 7 8 1 4 1 1 1 4 <u>9 2 1</u> 8 5 4 3 7 4 6 1 1

THE LINEUP

While scrutinizing the lineup of letters below, can you answer the five given questions correctly in five minutes or less?

SKILTQWSVFRAGMENTPUDENYDRYINGOHSZBNCITEJT

1. Which letter of the alphabet does not appear in the lineup?

2. What 8-letter word — with its letters in correct order and appearing together — can you find in the lineup?

3. Which three letters of the alphabet appear exactly three times each in the lineup?

4. What 6-letter word — with its letters in correct order and appearing together — can you find in the lineup?

5. Other than the answers to Questions 2 and 4, how many everyday words — with their letters in correct order and appearing together — of four or more letters can you find in the lineup?

WHAT'S YOUR NUMBER?

Can you figure out the sequence of numbers in the boxes below and what missing numbers go into the spaces with the question marks?

14	13	15	12	?
28	29	27	30	?

STACKED UP

WEEK 24

The box on the left can be formed by three of the numbered boxes superimposed on top of each other; do not turn them in any way. Can you figure out which three work?

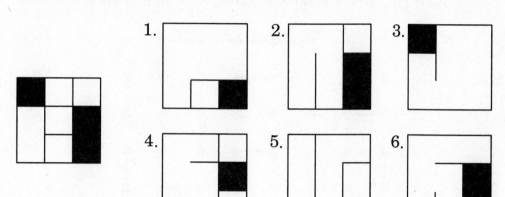

GOING IN CIRCLES

In each circle, insert one letter into each empty space to form an 8-letter word. Words may read either clockwise or counterclockwise and may begin with any letter in the circle.

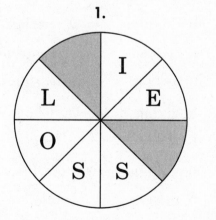

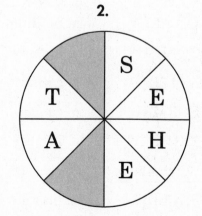

ROUND TRIP

VISUAL ◆ LOGIC

When this puzzle has been completed correctly, you will have made a round trip through its set of dots. You must visit every dot exactly once, make no diagonal moves, and return to your starting point. Parts of the right paths are shown; can you find the rest?

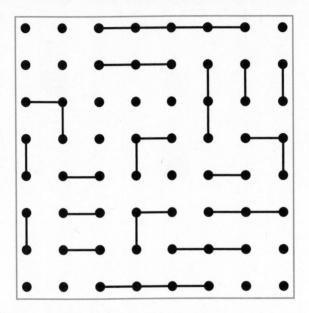

ANTONYMS QUIZ

LANGUAGE

An antonym is a word that is opposite in meaning to another word; for example, "cold" is the antonym of "hot." One of the words following each capitalized word is the antonym of that word.

1. COMPLEX	a. defunct	b. simplistic	c. divisible
2. INVALID	a. binding	b. muddy	c. average
3. COPIOUS	a. homely	b. scarce	c. mysterious
4. NAÏVE	a. careless	b. evident	c. worldly
5. FORMAL	a. casual	b. divine	c. rickety
6. TRUNCATE	a. relapse	b. forbid	c. lengthen
7. SPORADIC	a. recurrent	b. foreign	c. exclusive
8. FALLIBLE	a. impulsive	b. unerring	c. idle

RING LOGIC

Complete the diagram below by drawing in the links between the rings using the statements below. Assume that all the rings in the picture are locked rigidly into position and cannot be moved in any direction. Consider yourself a true ringmaster if you can find the solution in under six minutes!

1. Five rings are linked to ring C and only E is linked to the front of C.

2. Five rings are linked to ring L and only I and M are linked to the front of L.

3. The right sides of B, E, and F are to the front.

4. The left sides of H and M are to the front.

5. B is linked twice.

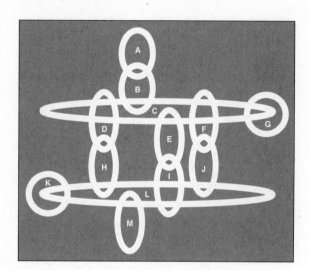

DECODING

SYMBOL-ISM

This is simply a Cryptogram that uses symbols instead of letters to spell out a truism. Each symbol stands for the same letter throughout. For this puzzle, we've already indicated that the ⚃ = S.

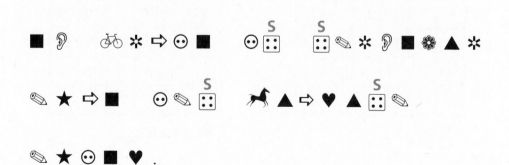

SKILLS TEST

Each of the letter groups below is the name of a flower with all of its vowels and **THE SAME** single **CONSONANT** missing. The missing consonant, which may appear more than once in each name, is the same for all eight. Can you figure them out?

MGN	Y	Z	NDR
GDS	CM	DH	VT

MARCHING ORDERS

MATH ◆ LOGIC

Using a different two-step sequence of addition and subtraction, can you make your way from Start to Finish in each puzzle? We've started the first one for you using the sequence -4 and +5; continue this sequence to reach Finish. You will not cross your own path or pass through any square twice.

1. FINISH ↑

12	11	7	12	16	11
13	6	9	8	14	15
7	10	5	13	12	10
9	12	8	7	9	14
3	4	11	6	12	11
8	5	10	7	16	13

↑ **START**

2. FINISH ↑

20	17	26	20	30	26
11	23	27	29	23	32
16	14	20	24	19	25
7	12	10	11	17	10
4	3	6	9	8	16
8	2	11	5	14	7

↑ **START**

PATCH PUZZLE

WEEK 25

Place the correct vowel (a, e, i, o, or u) into each blank space in the diagram, and you will have a finished crossword with words reading across and down.

B		D			C		G		S	M		G
	N		S			W					R	N
S	C		T			L	L			R		
S	H	R		B	S			R	R		S	T
			F				T		C			
C	R		F	T		N		G	H	T	L	Y
	H				C		N			Y		
T	H		N	K		D		R		P		N
				R		G		M				
S	P	R		T			N		B	L		
T			L			S	S		G	R		Y
	G	L			L		T				V	
W			D		S		Y			G		S

PROGRESSION

Can you figure out the sequence of letters in each diagram below and what missing letter goes into the space with the question mark?

1.

A	D	G
G	K	O
O	T	?

2.

B	F	J	P	?

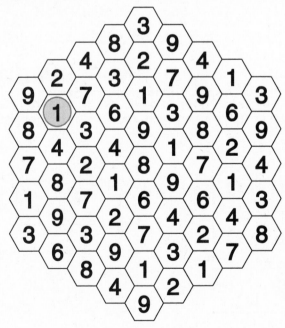

R COUNT

VISUAL

Here's an eye exam that's also a R exam! First, read the sentence below. Next, go back and read the sentence again, but this time count all of the R's. How many are there?

RICHARD RUPERT REVEALED

THAT REVERED ARBITRATOR

ROBERT ROPER RARELY DRIVES

HIS RED ROADSTER WITHOUT

HIS FURRY TERRIER RORY.

HEXAGON HUNT

VISUAL

In this diagram of six-sided figures, there are 10 "special" hexagons. These 10 are special because the six numbers around each one are all different from each other and the center. We've circled one of the 10. Can you find the other 9?

GRAND TOUR

WEEK 25

Form a continuous chain of 5-letter words moving through the maze from START to FINISH. The second part of one word becomes the first part of the next word. This puzzle starts with ME-TAL-ON (metal, talon).

START

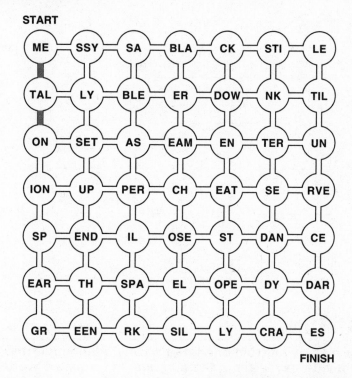

FINISH

ANIMAL CHARADES

In the Charade below, each line contains a clue to a letter of the alphabet. These letters, in the given order, will spell out the name of an animal. The animal's identity is also hinted at in the last sentence of the Charade.

My FIRST is in BELUGA and in GAMBLE;

My SECOND is in CARIBOU but not in RAMBLE;

My THIRD is in COBRA and in BROKE;

My FOURTH is in MOCCASIN but not in INVOKE;

My FIFTH is in SARDINE and in MAGAZINE;

My SIXTH is in RABBIT but not in RAVINE.

My WHOLE is a feline, but I'm no stray;

I like to hunt rats and other small prey.

WEEK 25

U.S. Y's

LANGUAGE

The list below consists of the names of six U.S. states, but we've removed all of their letters except for the Y's. Can you write one letter on each dash to complete the names of the states?

1. ___ ___ ___   Y ___ ___ ___

2. ___ ___ ___ ___ ___ ___ ___ Y

3. ___ Y ___ ___ ___ ___ ___

4. ___ ___ ___ ___ ___ Y ___ ___ ___ ___ ___ ___

5. ___ ___ ___   ___ ___ ___ ___ ___ Y

6. ___ ___ ___ Y ___ ___ ___ ___

WORD HUNT

LANGUAGE ◆ SPATIAL

Find words by moving from one letter to any adjoining letter. You may start a word with any letter in the diagram. In forming a word you may return to a letter as often as you wish, but do not stand on a letter using it twice in direct succession. In this Word Hunt, you are searching for Major League Baseball team nicknames of four or more letters (such as METS). We found 10 nicknames.

Your list of words:

C	A	N	G	M
S	T	R	E	I
W	N	D	S	T
G	I	A	P	R
R	E	L	S	O

RINGERS

Each Ringer is composed of five rings. Use your imagination to rotate the rings so that you spell out four 5-letter words reading from the outside to the inside when all five rings are aligned correctly.

1.

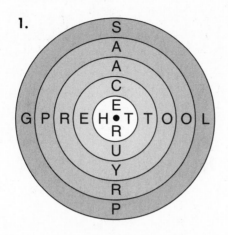

2.

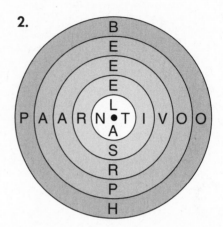

LANGUAGE

ELIMINATION

Cross off the capitalized words below according to the instructions given. The remaining words, in order, will form a truism.

HE CIVIC WHO LIVED WRESTLES BANISH BEGINS WITH CRAFTWORK ME INTESTINES STRENGTHENS SETTLE ME

Eliminate the word…

1. in which every letter appears exactly twice.

2. that spells another word for "fiend" when read backwards.

3. that contains a number spelled out within its letters together and in order.

4. that is composed entirely of Roman numerals.

5. that forms a U.S. city when a vowel is added somewhere within it.

6. whose letters are in alphabetical (but not consecutive) order.

7. that can be tapped out on a telephone pad as 226474.

LICENSE PLATES

Each box contains six letters of a U.S. capital city and the state. The top three are a part of the capital city and the bottom three are a part of the state, in order.

1.

```
G O M
B A M
```

2.

```
L U L
W A I
```

3.

```
F O R
C U T
```

4.

```
T O P
S A S
```

5.

```
I C H
V I R
```

6.

```
A S H
S E E
```

WAYWORDS

A 6-word thought can be found beginning with the word FRIENDS. Then, move to any adjacent box up, down, or diagonally for each following word.

RECENT	OF	SPELL	JUST
STANDARD	BEST	LIVING	SEEK
PURE	YOUR	CONCLUDE	INSPIRE
FINAL	BREAK	RAISE	FRIENDS

COUNT THE SQUARES

To solve this puzzle, write down the four letters that describe each square (a figure with four EQUAL sides) in this figure. We found 17 squares; how many can you locate?

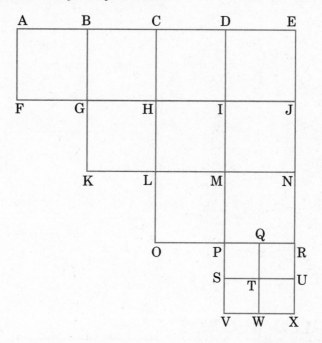

CIRCLE MATH

MATH

Each overlapping circle is identified by a letter having a different number value from 1 to 9. Where some circles overlap, there is a number: It is the SUM of the values of the letters in those overlapping circles. Can you figure out the correct values for the letters? As a starting help, I = 9.

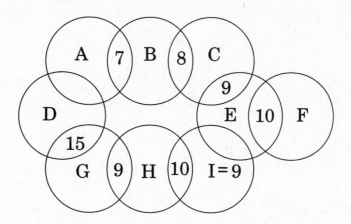

BULL'S-EYE LETTER

LANGUAGE

Add the SAME single letter to each group of three letters, then rearrange the letters to form six everyday 4-letter words.

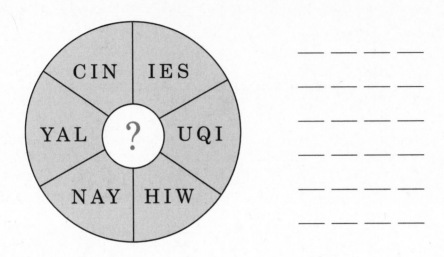

— — — —

— — — —

— — — —

— — — —

— — — —

— — — —

DOVETAILED WORDS

LANGUAGE

Two related words, with their letters in the correct order, are combined in each row of letters. Can you find both words? In a line like POBOOXDELER, or POboOxDeLEr, you can see the two words POODLE and BOXER.

1. S K P A I N L A E C H   _____ _____

2. S P A F R I R O N W C H   _____ _____

3. P E L E M O A N C H   _____ _____

4. C I S R Q C U A L R E E   _____ _____

5. B L A G R A C K Y   _____ _____

SKILLS TEST

How many different combinations of quarters, dimes, and nickels, all together and separately, will equal 40¢?

VISUAL ◆ SPATIAL

LOOSE TILE

The tray on the right seemed the ideal place to store the set of loose dominoes. Unfortunately, when the tray was full, one domino was left over. Determine the arrangement of the dominoes in the tray and which is the Loose Tile.

ARROW MAZE

Starting at the S and following the arrow leading out of it, see if you can find your way to F. When you reach an arrow, you MUST follow its direction and continue in that direction until you come to the next arrow. When you reach a two-headed arrow, you can choose either direction. It's okay to cross your own path.

ASSOCIATIONS

Below, you'll find eight groups of three words that can be associated in some way with each other (example: mantel, fireplace, logs). Cross out each group as you find it. The initial letters of the remaining words will spell out the answer to the riddle:

WHAT SOUNDS LIKE A BEVERAGE BUT IS IMPOSSIBLE TO DRINK?

DALMATIAN BARN WALK SHY BASSET ASSET CIRCLE LAGER

KNIGHT STALE BLOODHOUND INLET DIME MEEK STROLL

NEGATIVE TRITE TRIANGLE AMBLE GRAPE PINKIE BEER

STAIN SQUARE NICKEL THUMB TIMEWORN ORCHID

BASHFUL DESERT QUARTER ALE AMPLE FINGER

MISSING DOMINOES

WEEK
26

In this game you use all 28 dominoes that are in a standard set. Each one has a different combination from 0-0, 0-1, 0-2, to 6-6. Domino halves with the same number of dots lie next to each other. To avoid confusion we have used an open circle to indicate a zero. Can you fill in the missing white dominoes to complete the board?

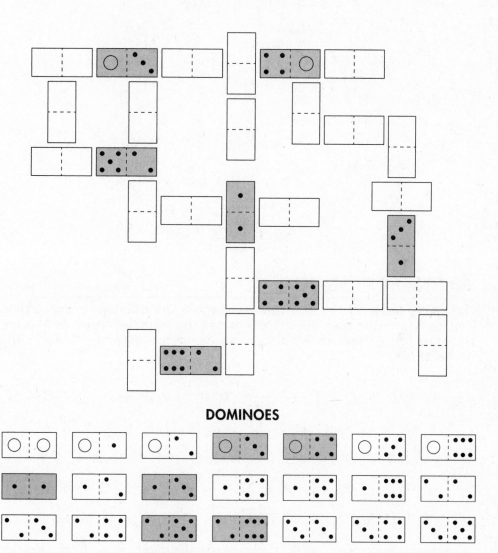

DOMINOES

WORD WHEEL

LANGUAGE

Starting with the "M" at the arrow, see how many everyday words of three or more letters you can find going clockwise. Don't skip over any letters. For example, if you saw the letters C, A, R, E, D, you would score five words: CAR, CARE, CARED, ARE, RED. We formed 28 words.

ALPHABET SOUP

LANGUAGE ◆ VISUAL

Not every letter of the alphabet appears in the diagram below. When you spot a letter that does, cross it off the alphabet provided. Next, anagram the letters that do not appear in the diagram to form the name of a movie.

```
D L P F Q I U D C M X B X Z P O Y T D L

K Q M G Q O H D L K E N M C B X V X M

G E N C Q Y D H I B R T Q P L F D K U I Z

C H B E P O L M R U Y X Z H P E G Q K L

D Y U R P Q B Y T L M N D Y F T O M Q N

L O F R T Y V Z C U O M E Y H T X C L F
```

A B C D E F G H I J K L M N O P Q R S T U V W X Y Z

OVERLAY

WEEK 27

When you overlay the three diagrams in the top row, which of the three lettered diagrams, A, B, or C, will be formed?

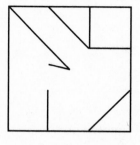
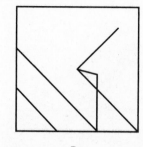
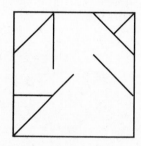

A.   **B.**   **C.**

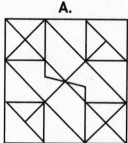
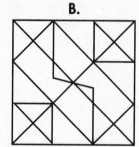
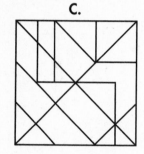

SLIDE RULE

Slide each column of letters up or down in the box and form as many everyday 3-letter words as you can in the windows where SIT is now. We formed 15 words.

Your list of words:

HOLE IN ONE

LOGIC

Twenty-four golfers entered a hole-in-one contest. Each golfer was given a ball with a different 4-digit number combination using the numbers 1, 2, 3, and 4 on it. Looking at the 23 balls still on the green, can you figure out what combination is on the ball that won the contest?

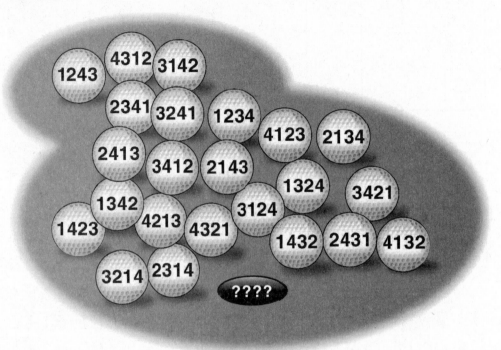

IN THE MONEY

MATH

How quickly can you convert each bag of money into dollars and cents and determine which one contains the greatest amount?

1. 720 pennies

2. 40 quarters

3. 205 nickels

4. 115 dimes

CROSS PATHS

Start at the arrow. There are six circles in that box, so move six boxes, either across or up. Each time you land in a box, move the number of dots in that box in only one direction, up, down, or across. You may cross your own path, but do not retrace it.

POP!

The balloons in a dart game are arranged so their letters spell out the word "PARTIED." To win, you must pop six different balloons with six different darts, but after each pop the remaining letters must spell out a new word reading across from left to right. Do not rearrange the balloons. Can you determine the order of the balloons to pop and the words formed? Your words may differ from ours.

175

HOLE IN ONE

LOGIC

Directions for solving are on page 174. This time, the 4-digit number combination uses 5, 6, 7, and 8.

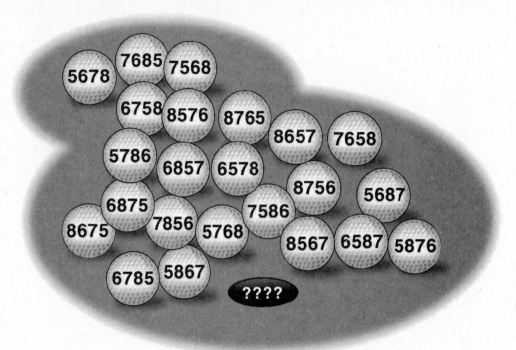

IN THE BALANCE

MATH ◆ LOGIC

Scales 1, 2, and 3 are perfectly balanced. Determine how many triangles it takes to balance scale 4.

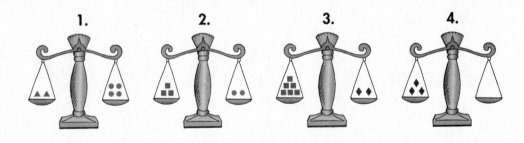

TRIANGULAR SQUARE

WEEK 27

Place the nine numbered squares into the diagram so that the four numbers in each of the diagram's four large triangles equal the number outside of it. The patterns have to match and you may not rotate the squares.

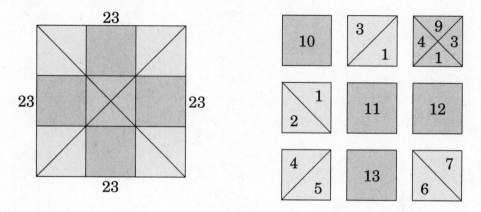

CROSS PATHS

Solving directions are on page 175. This time, the box at the arrow has three circles so your first move has to be three boxes across or up.

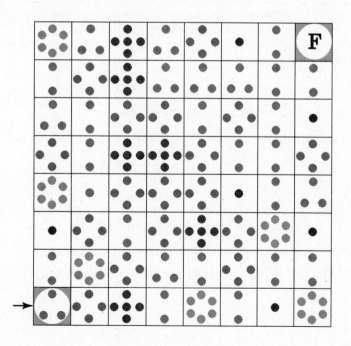

CREEPY CRAWLIES

VISUAL

Find the row or column that contains five DIFFERENT insects.

	A	B	C	D	E
1.					
2.					
3.					
4.					
5.					

SENTENCE TEASER

LOGIC

Read the four statements A–D below, and assume that these statements are all true. Next, read statements 1–4 and, using the information received from statements A–D, try to determine if the final four statements are true or false.

A. Plants that grow fast have flowers in summer.

B. Summer flowers have a strong scent.

C. Plants that grow fast have flowers that do not last very long.

D. Strongly scented flowers do not last long.

• • •

1. If a plant grows fast, one can be sure its flowers will have a strong scent and they won't last long.

2. Summer flowers do not last long.

3. Strongly scented flowers can only be found on plants that grow fast.

4. Flowers that do not last long always have a strong scent.

PRESIDENTIAL MONOGRAMS

WEEK 28

The list below consists of the names of 10 U.S. Presidents, but we've removed all of their letters except for their initials. Can you write one letter on each dash to complete the names of the Chief Executives?

1. R __ __ __ __ __   R __ __ __ __ __
2. B __ __ __   C __ __ __ __ __ __
3. A __ __ __ __ __ __   L __ __ __ __ __ __
4. F __ __ __ __ __ __ __   R __ __ __ __ __ __ __ __ __
5. J __ __ __ __ __ __   C __ __ __ __ __ __
6. G __ __ __ __ __   F __ __ __
7. B __ __ __ __ __ __   O __ __ __ __ __
8. G __ __ __ __ __ __   W __ __ __ __ __ __ __ __ __ __
9. H __ __ __ __ __ __ __   H __ __ __ __ __ __
10. H __ __ __ __ __   T __ __ __ __ __ __

BATS & BALLS

Examine the bats and balls below and then answer these questions: 1. Which row contains the most BATS? 2. Which row contains the most BALLS? 3. Which row contains an equal number of BATS and BALLS?

1.
2.
3.
4.
5.
6.
7.
8.
9.

ON THE LINE

VISUAL ◆ LOGIC

Can you trace this figure without lifting your pencil from the paper, crossing, or retracing your own path?

DEDUCTION PROBLEM

LOGIC

Arthur, Bert, Cecil, David, and Frank took an algebra test last week, receiving grades of A, B, C, D, and F, in some order. No two boys had the same grade. In discussing the test results, all but one of the boys lied; the only one who told the truth was the boy who got a C.

Arthur said, "I got the B, and Cecil didn't get an A."

Bert said, "Cecil got the A."

Cecil said, "Arthur didn't get a D."

David said, "I didn't get the F."

Frank said, "I don't know what grade I got!"

Who got which grade, and who's telling the truth?

SKILLS TEST

WEEK 28

Form five everyday 5-letter words that begin with "GLO." Words ending in "s" are fine, but do not form plurals or present-tense verbs ending in "s."

glo ___ ___   glo ___ ___   glo ___ ___

glo ___ ___   glo ___ ___

LANGUAGE ◆ VISUAL

WORD CHARADE

Find each letter in the diagram according to the instructions, and write each letter on its dash to spell out a 6-letter word.

My first letter is directly above an N and to the immediate left of a V.

My second letter appears in the diagram, but not in the first or last row, or the first or last column.

My third letter is directly below a J and to the immediate right of a K.

My fourth letter appears in every row without a vowel.

My fifth letter is the second letter of the longest word that reads downwards in one column.

My sixth letter is the fifth letter in a row that has an equal number of vowels and consonants.

S	D	B	J	T	F	C	V
G	F	T	N	L	S	B	J
H	G	M	I	M	K	H	R
Z	B	J	D	A	B	G	E
P	K	S	H	L	V	T	M
V	I	A	I	N	P	D	A
L	C	G	V	A	S	F	R
H	N	J	G	L	T	M	K

___ ___ ___ ___ ___ ___

ALPHABET CIRCLE MAZE

VISUAL

Start at A at the bottom, continue through the alphabet only once, and finish at the Z in the center. You will pass through other letters when going from one letter to the next, but move in only one direction, either around a circle or along a spoke. Don't enter or cross through the Z until you are finished.

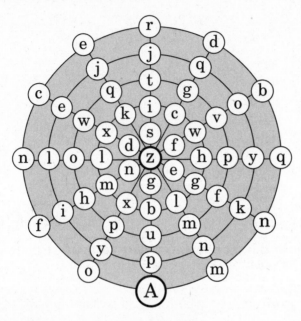

WHAT'S YOUR NUMBER?

MATH ◆ LOGIC

Can you figure out the sequence of numbers in the figures below and what missing numbers go into the spaces with the question marks?

1.

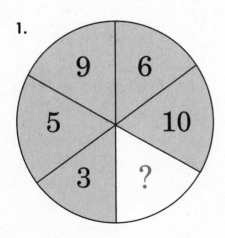

2.

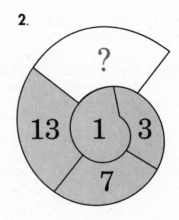

TIPS OF THE ICEBERG

This chart shows the gratuities each waiter earned on a recent breakfast shift at the Iceberg Diner. All you have to do is some careful addition and then answer the following questions:

1. Who made the most in total tips?
2. Who made the least?
3. Which two waiters made exactly the same amount?

EMPLOYEE	TIP 1	TIP 2	TIP 3	TIP 4	TIP 5
Al	$1.10	$1.20	$1.75	$1.05	$3.35
Brenda	$1.45	$4.10	$0.20	$1.00	$1.65
Charlie	$1.75	$1.20	$1.50	$1.10	$1.10
Dena	$1.30	$0.20	$0.75	$2.00	$1.10
Ed	$1.15	$0.20	$1.00	$1.00	$1.00
Flora	$1.10	$3.40	$1.00	$0.75	$1.30
Greta	$1.00	$1.15	$1.05	$1.00	$3.00
Hank	$1.15	$1.15	$1.15	$1.00	$1.00
Inez	$1.15	$1.00	$1.00	$1.00	$1.30
Jack	$1.15	$1.10	$1.30	$1.55	$1.35

ANAGRAM MAZE

LANGUAGE ◆ SPATIAL

Directions for solving are on page 149. This time, there are 21 words to anagram and the first word you'll be anagramming is ROCK.

1 ROCK	**2** LAIN	**3** BUFF	**4** PLIE	**5** SAGE	**6** HOSE
7 HOWL	**8** SAME	**9** MEMO	**10** VAST	**11** QUIT	**12** ARCH
13 LAPS	**14** FLUE	**15** JOLT	**16** ABET	**17** PRAY	**18** TOGA
19 BRAN	**20** CAVE	**21** KEEN	**22** FLIT	**23** BEET	**24** THUS
25 PROD	**26** BLOW	**27** IDLE	**28** COMA	**29** FOOT	**30** HARE
31 KNOW	**32** CELL	**33** WAGE	**34** BANK	**35** MALT	**36** SALT

TARGET SHOOT

LANGUAGE

Directions for solving are on page 146.

1.

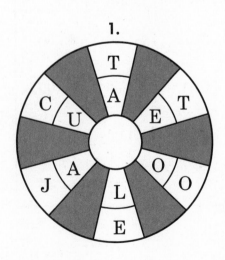

2.

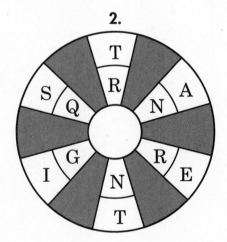

SUDOKU

WEEK
29

Directions for solving are on page 151.

				1	6	9		
3				1	6	9		
		4	9			2	7	3
	5		4				1	
			6	9		1		4
	1	3				5	9	
4		2		8	1			
	4				2		5	
8	2	1			5	7		
		6	1	7				2

CODE WORD

Directions for solving are on page 151.

$$\overline{1}\ \overline{2}\ \overline{3}\ \overline{4}\ \overline{5}\ \overline{6}\ \overline{7}\ \overline{8}\ \overline{9}\ \overline{10}\ \overline{11}$$

F 4 3 K 11   9 8 K 10   1 5 10 D 6 9   F 4 5   P 8 9 6 10 7 1 10

W 2 10 7   9 2 10 Y   8 5 10   11 6 M P 3 Y   P U 9 9 6 7 G

4 F F   D 4 6 7 G   11 4 M 10 9 2 6 7 G   9 2 8 9   6 11

U 7 P 3 10 8 11 8 7 9 .

KEEP ON MOVING

VISUAL

The goal is to move from the shaded square to the asterisk. Since the shaded square has the number 1 in it, you must move one square up, down, left, or right, but not diagonally. In the new square will be another number; move that number of squares up, down, left, or right, continuing in this way until you reach the asterisk. It's okay to cross your own path.

1	4	2	4	2	3
2	2	2	3	4	1
5	4	1	3	1	4
3	2	5	4	3	2
3	5	1	*	3	2
3	2	2	3	1	3

MAGIC NUMBER SQUARES

MATH

Directions for solving are on page 152.

1.

	26		13
	19		24
		22	
			25

82

2.

26			
	38		18
70		50	
		42	

176

CARD SENSE

Five playing cards — the six and queen of diamonds, the six of hearts, the king of spades, and the jack of clubs — were shuffled and put in a pile, one on top of another. Using the information in the clues below, can you identify each card's position in the pile?

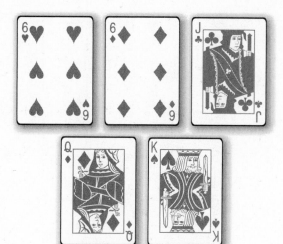

1. No two face cards are adjacent.

2. The bottom card is not black.

3. At least one diamond is above the king.

EASY PICKINGS

To solve, simply cross out one letter in each pair below. When the puzzle is completed correctly, the remaining letters will spell out an observation.

SC HU IC CS DE RS SC   GI TS   SA

QJ WO UE LR NV SE YF ,   MN OA ST   BA

DL CE SC RT IM AN OA DT BI SO NX.

COUNTDOWN

VISUAL

Directions for solving are on page 147.

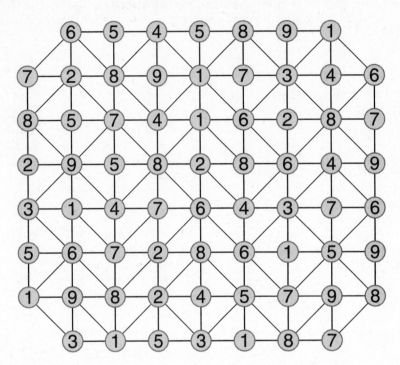

BLOCK PARTY

VISUAL ◆ SPATIAL

Study the different views of the block, and draw what should appear on the face that has a question mark.

SEVEN WORD ZINGER

WEEK
29

Directions for solving are on page 148.

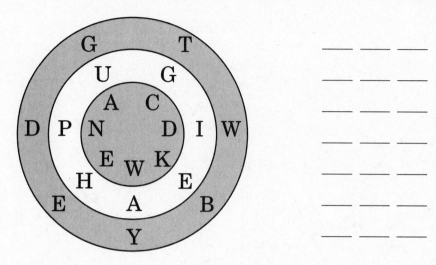

— — — —

— — — —

— — — —

— — — —

— — — —

— — — —

— — — —

DECODING

SYMBOL-ISM

Directions for solving are on page 159.
For this puzzle, we've indicated that the 👢 = B.

▲ ◆ ⊗ ❄ ↙ ⊖ ,   ❄ ▷   ○ ◆ ▲ ▷   👢❄   (B)

👢❄ ▷ ▷ ❄ ⊗   ▷ ≋   ⇊ ■ ≋ ⊗   ▲ ≋ ○ ❄   (B)

▨ ★   ▷ ✿ ❄   ↺ ◆ ❄ ▲ ▷ ❄ ≋ ■ ▲   ▷ ✿ ☎ ■

☎ ↙ ↙   ▨ ★   ▷ ✿ ❄   ☎ ■ ▲ ⊗ ❄ ⊗ ▲ .

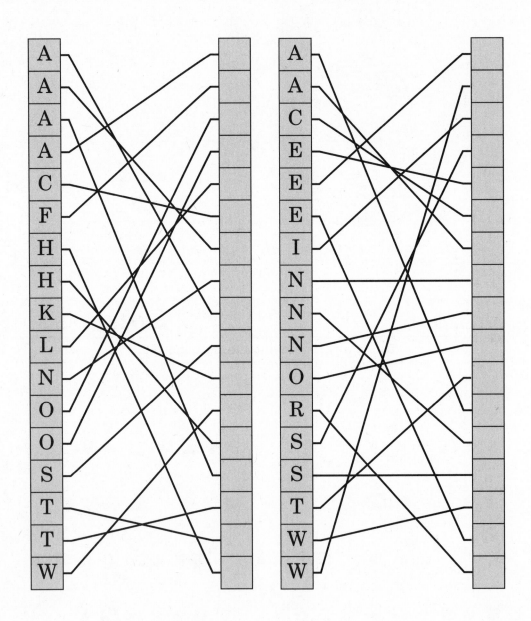

IN THE ABSTRACT

Directions for solving are on page 146.

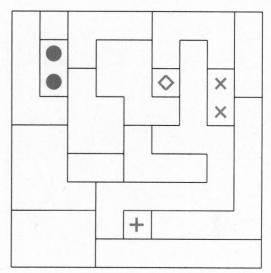

LANGUAGE

WORD VISIBILITY

Directions for solving are on page 148.

1. G A P L T
   P U I R B

2. L A W D M
   C O N V Y

3. V L R C K
   B A O D E

4. S T C I R
   H U R G P

5. C O U E M
   J I B S T

6. M U A T N
   C R T F E

MAGNIFIND

VISUAL ◆ SPATIAL

Figure out which area of the drawing has been enlarged.

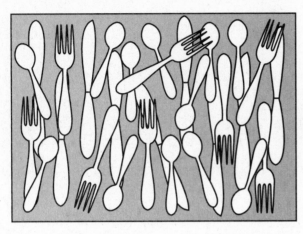

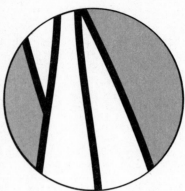

CIRCLE SEARCH

LANGUAGE

Directions for solving are on page 149.
Here you're looking to form 21 words.

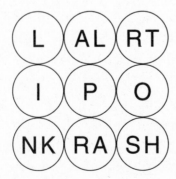

STAR WORDS

Directions for solving are on page 153.

EARL   KILT

FLAT   LEAF

FLEE   TEAK

KALE   TREK

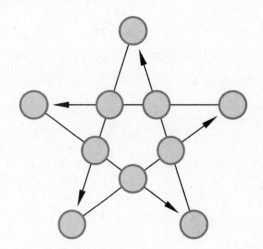

TRI, TRI AGAIN

Directions for solving are on page 155.

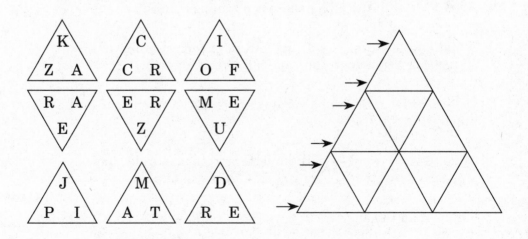

GOING IN CIRCLES

LANGUAGE

Directions for solving are on page 157.

1.

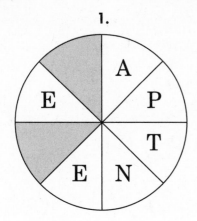

2.

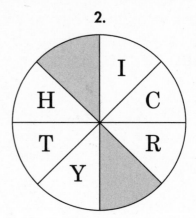

THE LINEUP

LANGUAGE

While scrutinizing the lineup of letters below, can you answer the five given questions correctly in five minutes or less?

JACKMBOPXWRAFFLEZEDITJKCYLINDERJESTHVQG

1. Which letter of the alphabet does not appear in the lineup?

2. What 8-letter word — with its letters in correct order and appearing together — can you find in the lineup?

3. Which letter of the alphabet appears exactly three times in the lineup?

4. What 6-letter word — with its letters in correct order and appearing together — can you find in the lineup?

5. Other than the answers to Questions 2 and 4, how many everyday words — with their letters in correct order and appearing together — of four or more letters can you find in the lineup?

STACKED UP

The box on the left can be formed by three of the numbered boxes superimposed on top of each other; do not turn them in any way. Can you figure out which three work?

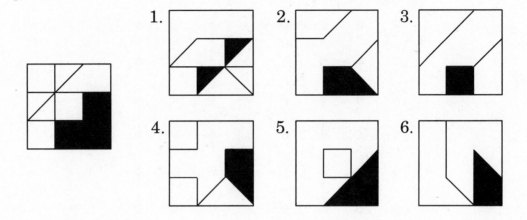

MATH

FUN WITH FACTS AND FIGURES

Directions for solving are on page 153.

1. Take the number of tentacles on an octopus and multiply it by the number of golden rings in "The Twelve Days of Christmas."

2. Next, subtract the number of days in July.

3. Now add the number of letters in the name of the U.S. state that contains Los Angeles, San Francisco, and San Diego.

4. Add the "loneliest number" of song.

5. Divide by the number of front tires on a car.

Our answer is the number of frames in a regular game of bowling. Is yours?

ROUND TRIP

VISUAL ◆ LOGIC

When this puzzle has been completed correctly, you will have made a round trip through its set of dots. You must visit every dot exactly once, make no diagonal moves, and return to your starting point. Parts of the right paths are shown; can you find the rest?

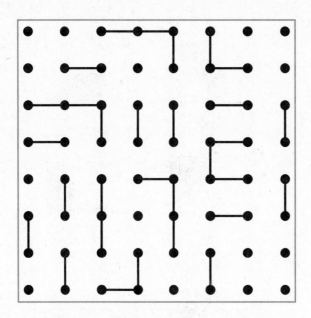

ALL IN A ROW

MATH

Directions for solving are on page 155. This time, look for the row with the most groups of consecutive numbers adding up to 14.

A. 7 2 2 1 5 5 4 6 1 3 9 6 7 2 8 3 9 2 6 8 1 2 4 5

B. 9 1 3 5 4 6 2 2 8 7 7 3 2 6 1 4 6 1 2 7 8 1 2 4

C. 1 4 7 2 6 3 7 8 4 2 1 2 9 9 1 2 7 3 1 2 6 6 7 5

196

Directions for solving are on page 165.

1.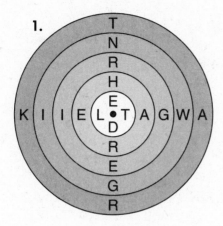

2.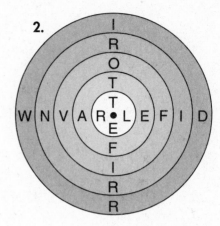

LANGUAGE   **RELATIONSHIPS QUIZ**

Directions for solving are on page 154.

1. BEE is to SWARM as QUAIL is to _____.
   (a) drove (b) covey (c) pride (d) bird

2. CHICAGO is to CUBS as HOUSTON is to _____.
   (a) Mets (b) Mounties (c) Expos (d) Astros

3. LAWYER is to CASE as POET is to _____.
   (a) ode (b) novel (c) family (d) typewriter

4. OUNCE is to PINT as PINT is to _____.
   (a) cup (b) yard (c) gill (d) peck

5. FAHRENHEIT is to THIRTY-TWO as CELSIUS is to _____.
   (a) zero (b) thirty (c) fifty (d) seventy

S COUNT

VISUAL

Directions for solving are on page 162. This time, see how many S's you can count in the sentence.

IN SUSAN SUSSMAN'S DISMISSIVE

ASSESSMENTS, SOME BUSINESS

ACCESSORIES SUCH AS SCISSORS

AND STAPLERS SHOULD

BE SEEN AS UNESSENTIAL, SILLY,

AND SENSELESS POSSESSIONS.

MARCHING ORDERS

MATH ◆ LOGIC

Directions for solving are on page 160.

1. FINISH

17	15	16	20	32	36
14	11	12	21	31	35
7	10	9	25	26	31
5	7	6	12	27	30
2	3	5	10	16	24
0	1	8	11	13	19

START

2. FINISH

16	19	20	33	35	38
14	18	15	24	30	36
12	8	10	14	28	33
6	5	9	13	25	27
4	3	7	15	23	24
0	2	5	18	20	22

START

RING LOGIC

Complete the diagram by drawing in the links between the rings using the statements below. Assume that all the rings in the picture are locked rigidly into position and cannot be moved in any direction. Consider yourself a true ringmaster if you can find the solution in under six minutes!

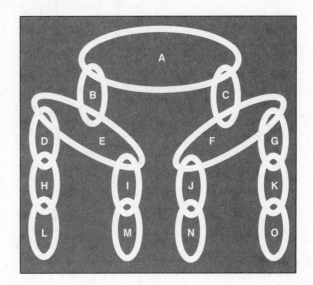

1. The right side of rings C, G, H, I, and O are to the front.

2. The pattern is symmetrical left to right.

ANTONYMS QUIZ

Directions for solving are on page 158.

1. ROTUND   a. thin   b. righteous   c. angry

2. MODERATE   a. famous   b. foreign   c. excessive

3. OPAQUE   a. translucent   b. boring   c. threatening

4. DESTITUTE   a. plausible   b. kind   c. wealthy

5. LETHARGIC   a. hungry   b. energized   c. ludicrous

6. SCRUMPTIOUS   a. colorful   b. disgusting   c. clever

7. SHRILL   a. low   b. costly   c. obscure

8. LABORED   a. apparent   b. fair   c. effortless

HEXAGON HUNT

VISUAL

Directions for solving are on page 162.

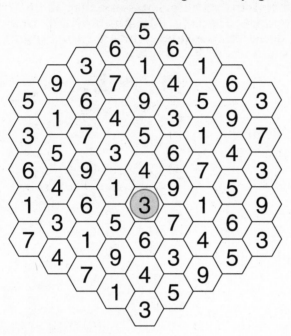

ANIMAL CHARADES

LANGUAGE

Directions for solving are on page 163.

My FIRST is in WOLF and in FLOOD;

My SECOND is in TURKEY but not in THUD;

My THIRD is in TROUT and in COURT;

My FOURTH is in PORCUPINE but not in RESORT;

My FIFTH is in KOALA and in TRACK;

My SIXTH is in HAMSTER but not in HAYSTACK;

My SEVENTH is in COPPERHEAD and in STAMPEDE.

My WHOLE is a hunter with plenty of speed.

GRAND TOUR

WEEK 31

Directions for solving are on page 163. This time, you'll be look-ing for a chain of 4-letter words, start-ing with GA-TE-ST (gate, test).

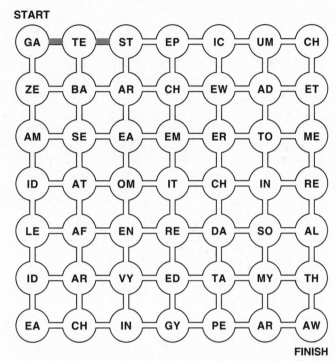

START

GA — TE — ST — EP — IC — UM — CH
ZE — BA — AR — CH — EW — AD — ET
AM — SE — EA — EM — ER — TO — ME
ID — AT — OM — IT — CH — IN — RE
LE — AF — EN — RE — DA — SO — AL
ID — AR — VY — ED — TA — MY — TH
EA — CH — IN — GY — PE — AR — AW

FINISH

LANGUAGE

LICENSE PLATES

Each box contains six letters of a diva singer's name. The top three are a part of the first name and the bottom three are a part of the last name, in order.

1.
```
A N E
A C K
```

2.
```
C E L
I O N
```

3.
```
I N A
R N E
```

4.
```
I A H
C A R
```

5.
```
T I N
G U I
```

6.
```
Y O N
O W L
```

BULL'S-EYE LETTER

LANGUAGE

Directions for solving are on page 168.

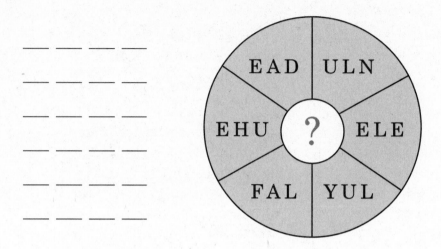

— — — —

— — — —

— — — —

— — — —

— — — —

WAYWORDS

LANGUAGE

Directions for solving are on page 166. This time, you'll be looking for a 7-word thought beginning with EXPERIENCE.

IS	LEARNING	BELIEVE	RICH
CREATES	EXPERIENCE	WHAT	PLEASURE
FOR	THAT	NOT	DO
TIMES	EVER	TO	FIRST

LOGIC

CARD SENSE

Directions for solving are on page 187.

1. The top card is not black.

2. The queen is below the spade.

3. The ace is adjacent to the diamond.

4. The six is above the jack.

MATH ◆ LOGIC

WHAT'S YOUR NUMBER?

Can you figure out the sequence of numbers in the diagrams below and what missing numbers go into the spaces with the question marks?

1.

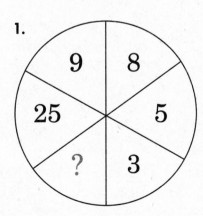

2.

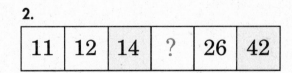

11	12	14	?	26	42

ELIMINATION

Directions for solving are on page 165.
Once again, the remaining words will form a truism.

MAGNUM YOUTH HEART ADO WILL TALK NEVER LIGHT
RETURN TORN ONCE IT GRANGE IS MINIMIZING GONE

Eliminate…

1. the word that can precede "house," "year," "headed," and "weight."

2. the word that contains a mammal with its letters together and in order.

3. the two words that can be joined together to make another word.

4. the word that spells a fruit when its first letter is changed to another letter.

5. the word that can follow "pillow," "small," and "baby."

6. the word that contains the same letter four times.

7. the word that forms another word when its first letter is moved to the end.

CIRCLE MATH

Directions for solving are on page 167. To help start you off, the letter B equals 2.

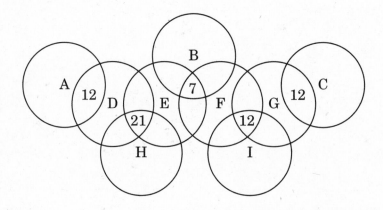

PATCH PUZZLE

Directions for solving are on page 161.

L	S			S	H			S	N		G
	R			W		Y		H		L	
P	N	S			D			R			M
			C	Y			N		N	E	S
	T	H		R	S		D		N		
W			R	Y		C		C	K	P		T
	L		S	H		N	K			R	
S	N		R	T		D		T		C	K	S
				R		N		C		S	T
P	D		L			Y		T			
	P		S		P	L			R		S
W		N	T			H		N		N	
S		T	S		W		N		G		N

PROGRESSION

Which of the numbered figures, 1 through 4, replaces the question mark?

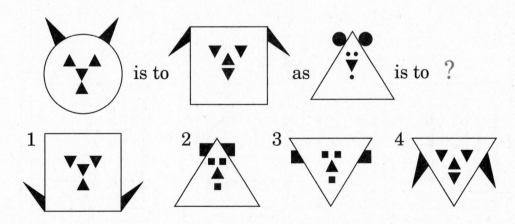

205

WORD HUNT

LANGUAGE ◆ SPATIAL

Directions for solving are on page 164. This time, you'll be searching for 4-letter words where each begins and ends with the same letter (such as AREA). We found 19 words.

Your list of words:

D	A	R	P	U
I	E	O	M	L
N	A	B	T	I
O	U	L	C	A
T	A	H	I	K

OVERLAY

VISUAL ◆ SPATIAL

Directions for solving are on page 173.

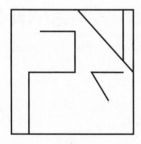

A.

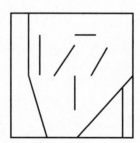

B.

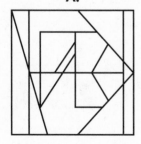

C.

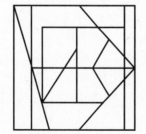

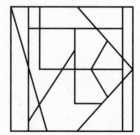

SUDOKU

Directions for solving are on page 151.

7	3		4		1			
	1	4	9					7
				2		3	1	4
		2	8	3			7	
6								3
	9			7	2	1		
9	2	8		1				
3					8	4	9	
			2		5		3	1

WORD WHEEL

Directions for solving are on page 172. Beginning with the "W" at the top of the wheel, we formed 34 words of three or more letters.

207

WORD CHARADE

VISUAL ◆ LANGUAGE

Directions for solving are on page 181.

My first letter is the only letter repeated three times in one of the rows.

My second letter appears more times than any other letter.

B	F	Q	T	W	T	J	G
Q	A	P	E	L	C	E	J
D	I	L	A	I	B	F	M
A	J	W	B	Q	L	A	D
M	E	R	M	J	P	F	Q
G	C	L	A	C	I	E	C
D	T	E	D	G	M	R	B
I	A	G	F	R	T	E	A

My third letter appears only in the bottom four rows.

My fourth letter is directly above an I and to the immediate left of an F.

My fifth letter appears twice as many times in the bottom four rows as in the top four rows.

My sixth letter is the first and last letter of one of the columns.

__ __ __ __ __ __

DOVETAILED WORDS

LANGUAGE

Directions for solving are on page 168.

1. S P O F O R O K N   _____ _____

2. P E R A P A S E R E R   _____ _____

3. C O L A B R I N O E E T   _____ _____

4. C U P S I H I L O L O W N   _____ _____

5. C O W H E R A N T   _____ _____

MISSING DOMINOES

In this game you use all 28 dominoes that are in a standard set. Each one has a different combination from 0-0, 0-1, 0-2, to 6-6. Domino halves with the same number of dots lie next to each other. To avoid confusion we have used an open circle to indicate a zero. Can you fill in the missing white dominoes to complete the board?

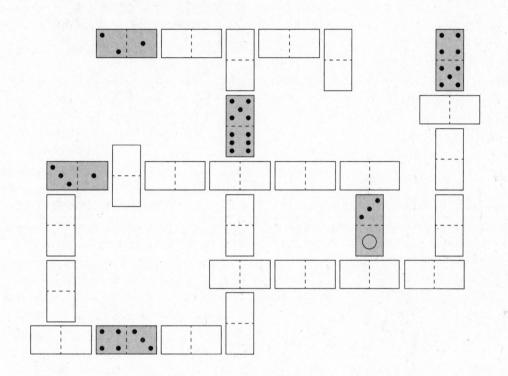

DOMINOES

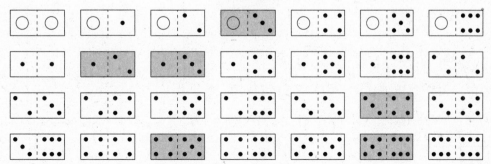

WEEK 32

SLIDE RULE   LANGUAGE

Directions for solving are on page 173.
This time, we formed 33 words.

Your list of words:

ALPHABET SOUP   VISUAL ◆ LANGUAGE

Not every letter is in the diagram. When you spot a letter that is, cross
it off the alphabet. Next, anagram the letters that are left to form the
name of a world capital.

B N E W Q U Y C V Z X T
M L O U W Q V C X H G T
K J N E Y U W L Q M N D
V U Y M L K E W Y F J H
W F L K Y O D X Z Y J T
Q X Z U Y T L K M N W C
G N E W Q L K Y U O N V
V M E W L K F G Y T H Z
U V M Q L O Y F C Z M N
D T E Q L J U K M B N X

A	J	S
B	K	T
C	L	U
D	M	V
E	N	W
F	O	X
G	P	Y
H	Q	Z
I	R	

210

BACON & EGGS

Examine the bacon and eggs below and then answer these questions: 1. Which row contains the most BACON? 2. Which row contains the most EGGS? 3. Which row contains an equal number of BACON and EGGS?

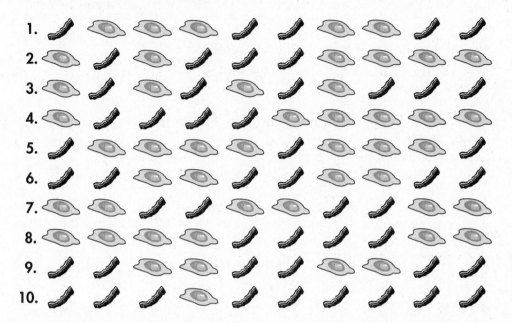

ASSOCIATIONS

Below, you'll find eight groups of three words that can be associated in some way with each other (example: mantel, fireplace, logs). Cross out each group as you find it. The initial letters of the remaining words will spell out the answer to the riddle:

WHAT EYEGLASSES DO UNDERCOVER AGENTS WEAR?

ROBIN START COLD CHEMISTRY PALE LAND CARDINAL

YANK CALM LAKE BIOLOGY LARK FOOL BREATHE FOOT

OVAL SOOTHE POND EARTH CANASTA NIPPY RESPIRE

ALIEN PHYSICS SOIL LETHAL INHALE INCH STREAM

SENTENCE BRISK YARD EASE

211

SENTENCE TEASER

LOGIC

Directions for solving are on page 178.
This teaser is about a pet show.

A. Only ten prizes were distributed, and all were awarded to cats.

B. All the dogs had names beginning with consonants.

C. All the animals with pedigrees received a prize.

D. All the animals with pedigrees had names beginning with consonants.

• • •

1. None of the prize-winning animals had names beginning with a consonant.

2. Some dogs had pedigrees.

3. A cat named Katkin, without a pedigree, could have won first prize.

4. A cat named Kingkat, without a pedigree, could have come in last place.

TOOL BOX

VISUAL

Find the row or column that contains five DIFFERENT tools.

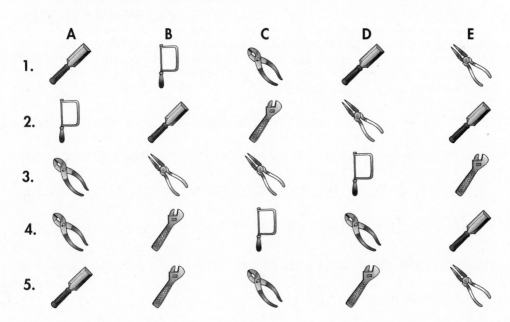

ALPHABET CIRCLE MAZE

Directions for solving are on page 182.

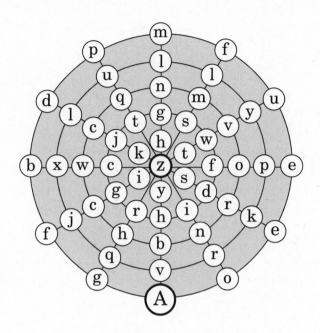

MATH ◆ LOGIC

WHAT'S YOUR NUMBER?

Can you figure out the relationship of the numbers in the boxes below and what missing number goes into the space with the question mark?

KEEP ON MOVING

VISUAL

Directions for solving are on page 186.
It's okay to cross your own path.

2	4	1	4	3	2
2	5	4	1	1	3
3	1	✳	2	4	3
5	4	4	**3**	2	3
3	2	1	5	2	4
4	1	3	4	3	1

ON THE LINE

VISUAL ◆ LOGIC

Can you cross all the lines between the dots by drawing one continuous line without crossing or retracing your own path?

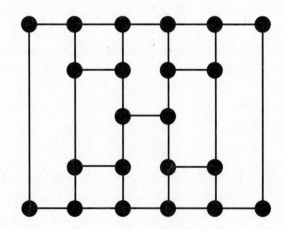

ARROW MAZE

Directions for solving are on page 170.

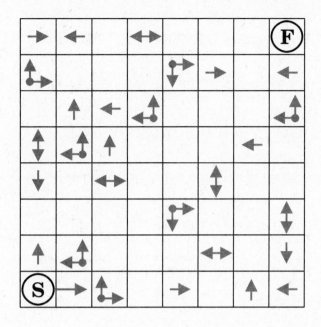

VISUAL ◆ SPATIAL

COUNT THE RECTANGLES

Write down the four letters that describe each rectangle (a four-sided figure). We found 32 rectangles; how many can you find?

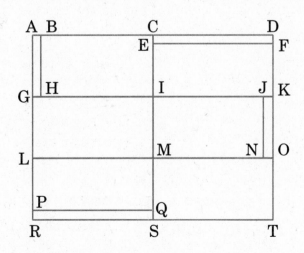

215

T COUNT

VISUAL

Directions for solving are on page 162. This time, see how many T's you can count in the sentence.

TO TELL THE TRUTH, THAT

TATTLETALE TIM TRITT'S

THIRTY-TWO TEETH WERE

INTERMITTENTLY SPATTERED

WITH TOMATO PASTE AND

ITTY-BITTY POTATOES.

DEDUCTION PROBLEM

LOGIC

Five brothers won different amounts of money in the state lottery during one month's time. Richard won less than Herbert. Carl won more than Paul. Leo won more than Richard. Herbert won more than Leo. Carl won less than Richard. Can you tell in what order, from the least amount to the most amount of money, the brothers won?

SKILLS TEST

To figure out each equation below, you may use addition, subtraction, multiplication, division, and fractions.

1. Arrange three 4's to equal 11.

2. Arrange six 6's to equal 37.

LOGIC

SUDOKU

Directions for solving are on page 151.

			2					7
5		6		3		4		
2	7				6	3		
			1				3	9
	6		8		7		5	
8	2				5			
		2	5				9	4
		7		1		5		3
3					4			

LOOSE TILE

VISUAL ◆ SPATIAL

The tray on the left seemed the ideal place to store the set of loose dominoes. Unfortunately, when the tray was full, one domino was left over. Determine the arrangement of the dominoes in the tray and which is the Loose Tile.

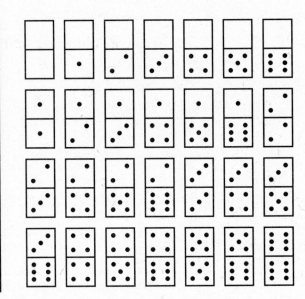

BLOCK PARTY

VISUAL ◆ SPATIAL

Directions for solving are on page 188.

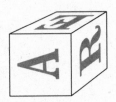 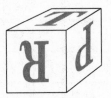  

CARD SENSE

WEEK
34

Directions for solving are on page 187.

1. The five is not on top.

2. The spade is immediately above the jack.

3. The diamonds are not adjacent.

4. The six is somewhere above the heart, but is not on top.

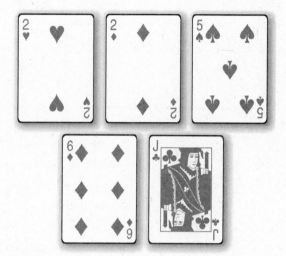

LANGUAGE ◆ SPATIAL

TRI, TRI AGAIN

Directions for solving are on page 155.

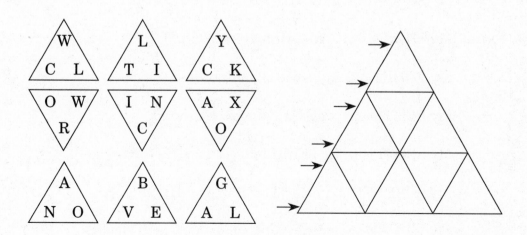

IN THE ABSTRACT

VISUAL ◆ SPATIAL

Directions for solving are on page 146.

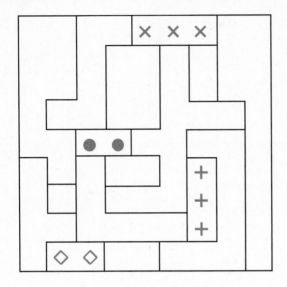

ANIMAL CHARADES

LANGUAGE

Directions for solving are on page 163.

My FIRST is in GORILLA and in INDIGO;

My SECOND is in ECHIDNA but not in CHATEAU;

My THIRD is in JAGUAR and in GROUP;

My FOURTH is in PARROT but not in STOOP;

My FIFTH is in MASTIFF and in FINESSE;

My SIXTH is in CATFISH but not in SORCERESS;

My SEVENTH is in PANTHER and in HENPECK.

My WHOLE is a critter with a most distinctive neck.

TIPS OF THE ICEBERG

We're back at the Iceberg Diner. After doing some careful addition, answer the following questions:

1. Who made the most in total tips?
2. Who made the least?
3. Which two waiters made exactly the same amount?

EMPLOYEE	TIP 1	TIP 2	TIP 3	TIP 4	TIP 5
Al	$2.10	$1.80	$1.85	$1.30	$2.95
Brenda	$1.25	$1.10	$0.65	$1.00	$1.65
Charlie	$0.75	$1.70	$1.70	$1.70	$1.80
Dena	$1.90	$1.80	$0.85	$2.00	$1.10
Ed	$1.45	$0.80	$1.15	$1.85	$1.00
Flora	$1.80	$2.25	$1.05	$0.95	$1.90
Greta	$1.80	$1.05	$1.15	$1.10	$4.00
Hank	$1.85	$1.45	$1.25	$4.50	$1.05
Inez	$1.10	$3.20	$2.10	$2.00	$1.90
Jack	$2.25	$1.30	$1.90	$1.35	$1.95

HEXAGON HUNT

VISUAL

Directions for solving are on page 162.

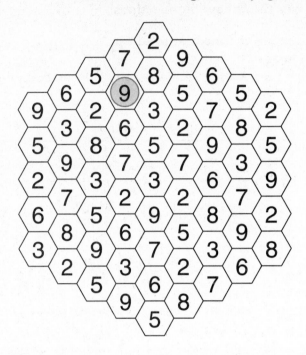

TARGET SHOOT

LANGUAGE

Directions for solving are on page 146.

1.

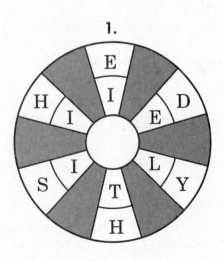

2.

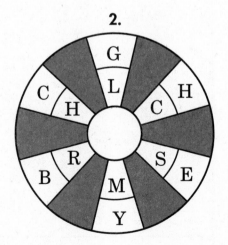

ANAGRAM MAZE

Directions for solving are on page 149.
This time, there are 19 words to anagram and the first word
you'll be anagramming is WHAT.

1 SILO	**2** CAFE	**3** LEFT	**4** DUMB	**5** FERN	**6** WHAT
7 DAME	**8** HIGH	**9** ROSE	**10** CAPE	**11** ZINC	**12** BLOT
13 ACTS	**14** HATE	**15** CURL	**16** AUNT	**17** BOSS	**18** KILN
19 JINX	**20** MODE	**21** EDIT	**22** ROAR	**23** VOLT	**24** PERT
25 MYTH	**26** YOKE	**27** WAYS	**28** PULL	**29** FARM	**30** MAKE
31 NAME	**32** PEAT	**33** FORM	**34** SOCK	**35** BOLD	**36** MAZE

MAGIC NUMBER SQUARES

Directions for solving are on page 152.

1.

	7		51
		39	
35	27		
		59	

132

2.

72			
	52	48	
		32	56
24			

168

FUN WITH FACTS AND FIGURES   MATH

Directions for solving are on page 153.

1. Take the maximum number of Xs that could be found in a completed, stalemated tic-tac-toe diagram and multiply it by the number of states in the U.S.

2. Next, divide by the number halfway between 10 and 40.

3. Now add the number of seconds in a minute.

4. Divide by the number of cents in three dimes and a nickel.

5. Add the number of letters in the name of the South American nation whose capital is Lima.

Our answer is the number of flags that have flown over Texas. *Is yours?*

WORD HUNT   LANGUAGE ◆ SPATIAL

Directions for solving are on page 164. This time, you'll be searching for 4- and 5-letter states and cities (such as RENO). We found five states and seven cities.

Your list of words:

A	M	P	A	D
U	T	W	I	H
L	I	M	O	R
S	A	N	E	D
T	U	H	V	O

SEVEN WORD ZINGER

Directions for solving are on page 148.

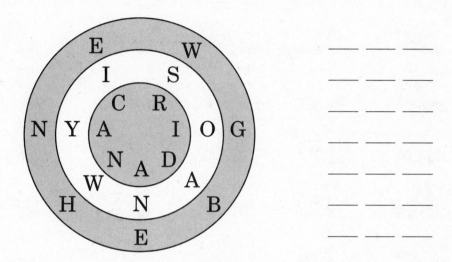

— — — — —

— — — — —

— — — — —

— — — — —

— — — — —

— — — — —

— — — — —

VISUAL ◆ SPATIAL

MAGNIFIND

Figure out which area of the drawing has been enlarged.

SHOE MANIA

VISUAL

Find the row or column that contains five DIFFERENT shoes.

	A	B	C	D	E
1.					
2.					
3.					
4.					
5.					

DOVETAILED WORDS

LANGUAGE

Directions for solving are on page 168.

1. W A P T E L R U M E M L O N _____ _____

2. J U S I O D C E A _____ _____

3. P I B E I N G E K _____ _____

4. S H W A A W N K _____ _____

5. S A P L E P P T E R _____ _____

226

SUDOKU

Directions for solving are on page 151.

2					4	8	3	
		4					1	
	3			5		4		
	8		3			5		1
3			5		7			6
4		6			1		8	
		9		3			5	
	6					3		
	7	3	9					4

LANGUAGE

BULL'S-EYE LETTER

Directions for solving are on page 168.

ATI · ITE · EON · ? · NIJ · AWY · EAP

_ _ _ _
_ _ _ _
_ _ _ _
_ _ _ _
_ _ _ _
_ _ _ _

MAGNIFIND

Figure out which area of the drawing has been enlarged.

ALL IN A ROW

MATH

Which row below contains the most groups of consecutive numbers adding up to 10? Look carefully, because some groups may overlap. We've underlined an example of a group in each row to start you off.

A. 1 3 <u>8 2</u> 1 1 6 9 4 1 3 3 5 7 2 1 8 4 2 1 5 1 1 6

B. 7 1 1 1 3 8 1 4 5 2 1 2 3 9 1 4 <u>7 3</u> 2 1 2 3 4 5

C. 5 2 5 3 2 1 <u>5 2 3</u> 1 3 1 8 4 9 2 7 5 2 6 2 1 1 4

IN THE ABSTRACT

Fill in each section with one of the four symbols so no sections containing the same symbol touch. Four sections are already complete.

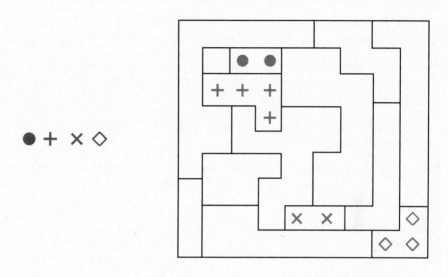

LANGUAGE

EASY PICKINGS

To solve, simply cross out one letter in each pair. When the puzzle is completed correctly, the remaining letters will spell out a fact.

ST HN TE   BC AI GP SG TE ES TV

OC MI TN YT   IW DN

MA BI CK HE IS VG AF YN   IB OS

DA EG JT AR NO IH GT.

THE LINEUP

While scrutinizing the lineup of letters, can you answer the five questions correctly in five minutes or less?

UPLGFZJINXMILEWABBREVIATECLIBERTYKHJOLTQST

1. Which letter of the alphabet does not appear in the lineup? _____

2. What 10-letter word — with its letters in correct order and appearing together — can you find in the lineup? _____

3. Which letter of the alphabet appears exactly three times in the lineup? _____

4. What 7-letter word — with its letters in correct order and appearing together — can you find in the lineup? _____

5. Other than the answers to Questions 2 and 4, how many everyday words — with their letters in correct order and appearing together — of four or more letters can you find in the lineup? _____

QUICK FILL

Determine the 10-letter word from the clues. All the letters in the word are listed.

C E E F I L N O R T

1. Letter 7 is a consonant and letter 2 is a vowel.

2. In the alphabet, letter 1 is six letters after letter 4.

3. Letters 6, 9, 8, and 10, in order, spell out a word that is an item of pocket change.

4. In the alphabet, letter 5 is immediately before letter 3.

$$\overline{1} \quad \overline{2} \quad \overline{3} \quad \overline{4} \quad \overline{5} \quad \overline{6} \quad \overline{7} \quad \overline{8} \quad \overline{9} \quad \overline{10}$$

COUNTDOWN

Following the connecting lines, find the only route in this grid that passes through the numbers backward from 9 to 1 consecutively.

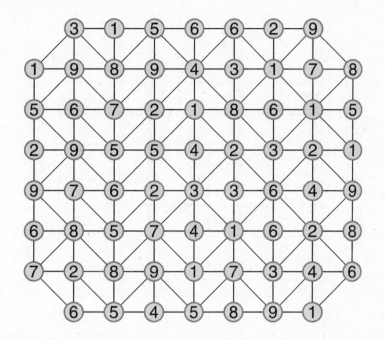

DECODING

CODE WORD

Decipher a quote and the Code Word's eleven letters, represented by the numbers 1 through 11. So, if the Code Word were "THUNDERCLAP," 1 in the quote would be T, 2 would be H, etc.

$$\overline{1}\ \overline{2}\ \overline{3}\ \overline{4}\ \overline{5}\ \overline{6}\ \overline{7}\ \overline{8}\ \overline{9}\ \overline{10}\ \overline{11}$$

10 H 2 G U 11 W H 5 C 5 6 4 10 7 6 10 8 11 8 5 4 2 4

7 10 1 5 K 2 3 7 6 D 4 10 9 8 8 K 2 2 1 4 5 6

1 8 7 11 9 6 G W 9 8 8 6 2 V 2 3 8 7 C K F 5 3

F 3 9 2 6 D 4 .

SUDOKU

LOGIC

Place a number into each box so each row across, column down, and small 9-box square within the larger square (there are 9 of these) contains 1 through 9.

4	9	5	1				8	
				4			9	5
8	2				3			
5				6		9	1	
		9	3		5	7		
	7	1		8				6
			4				3	1
2	3			5				
	1				8	6	5	2

GOING IN CIRCLES

LANGUAGE

In each circle, insert one letter into each empty space to form an 8-letter word. Words may read either clockwise or counterclockwise and may begin with any letter in the circle.

1.

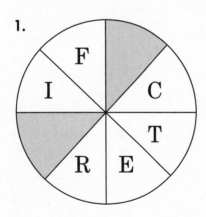

2.

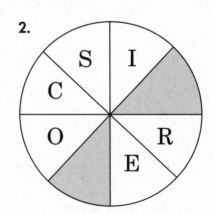

TRI, TRI AGAIN

Fit the nine triangles into the big one so six everyday words are spelled out reading across the arrows. Do not rotate the triangles.

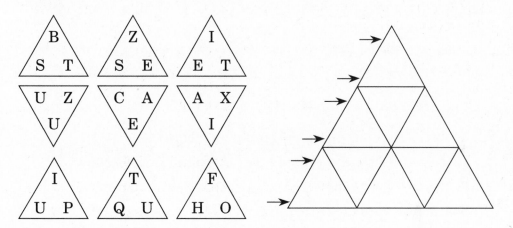

ANIMAL CHARADES

Each line contains a clue to a letter of the alphabet. These letters, in the given order, will spell out the name of an animal. The animal's identity is also hinted at in the last sentence of the Charade.

My FIRST is in LLAMA and in MUSTARD;   _____

My SECOND is in HALIBUT and in CUSTARD;   _____

My THIRD is in PORPOISE but not in POINT;   _____

My FOURTH is in MINK but not in ANOINT;   _____

My FIFTH is in CARDINAL and in RANGE;   _____

My SIXTH is in RACCOON and in STRANGE;   _____

My SEVENTH is in TURTLE but not in SPUR.   _____

My WHOLE is a rodent with glossy brown fur.

_____

233

ELIMINATION

LANGUAGE

Cross off the capitalized words below according to the instructions given. The remaining words, in order, will form a thought.

SLEEPING NOMINATE JOYFULLY COUSIN STRANGE GRAND LIVE TURN ANIMAL EACH MOTHER COUNTER CABINET MOMENT DOGS LAD OF CANYON PIE EVERY UNCLE FARM DAY FEDERAL

Eliminate…

1. words that are names of family members.

2. the word that can precede "part," "point," and "productive."

3. the two words that form an Arizona tourist attraction.

4. the two words that turn the following into a saying: "Let ___ ___ lie."

5. each word that begins with three consecutive letters of the alphabet, in some order.

6. the two words that form the title of a George Orwell novel.

7. the three words that can be formed from the word PRUDENTIAL.

LICENSE PLATES

LANGUAGE

Each box contains six letters of the first and last name of a noted artist of the past. The top three are a part of the first name and the bottom three are a part of the last name, in order.

1.

A U D
N E T

2.

A R C
G A L

3.

V A D
D A L

4.

M A N
O C K

5.

B L O
C A S

6.

G I A
K E E

ARROW MAZE

Starting at the S and following the arrow up, see if you can find your way to F. When you reach an arrow, you MUST follow its direction and continue in that direction until you come to the next arrow. When you reach a two-headed arrow, you can choose either direction. It's okay to cross your own path.

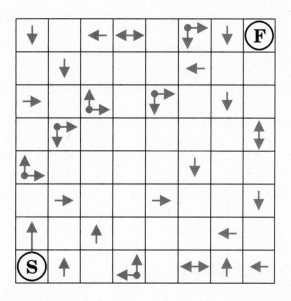

BLOCK PARTY

Study the different views of the block, and draw what should appear on the face that has a question mark.

ASSOCIATIONS
LANGUAGE

You'll find eight groups of three words that can be associated in some way with each other (example: mantel, fireplace, logs). Cross out each group as you find it. The initial letters of the remaining words will spell out the answer to the riddle:

WHAT DO YOU CALL A FELINE GYMNAST?

TERRIER ODOR ADJECTIVE INDIA SHREWD INQUIRE

NAVY BEAGLE PLATO CUNNING ANCHOR PAKISTAN

ARISTOTLE CHOOSY GAMBLE SMELL ROMANCE

MAXIM RISK FOXY ORGANIZE SOCRATES HAZARD

CAPTIVE ASK ADAGE SCENT AVENUE POODLE NEPAL

PROVERB TEST QUESTION

BULL'S-EYE LETTER
LANGUAGE

Add the SAME single letter to each group of three letters and then rearrange the letters to form six everyday 4-letter words.

— — — —

— — — —

— — — —

— — — —

— — — —

— — — —

PCA YCA

LPE **?** ASL

IWP CEO

TIPS OF THE ICEBERG

The chart shows the gratuities each waiter or waitress earned on a recent breakfast shift at the Iceberg Diner. All you have to do is some addition and then answer the following questions:

1. **Who made the most in total tips?**
2. **Who made the least?**
3. **Which two waitpersons made exactly the same amount?**

EMPLOYEE	TIP 1	TIP 2	TIP 3	TIP 4	TIP 5
Al	$0.70	$3.20	$3.20	$2.70	$1.05
Brenda	$1.10	$1.80	$1.25	$1.05	$1.00
Charlie	$1.10	$2.10	$1.10	$1.10	$1.90
Dena	$1.10	$0.85	$1.05	$1.00	$1.80
Ed	$2.05	$2.90	$1.00	$1.00	$2.75
Flora	$1.25	$1.40	$4.80	$0.55	$1.70
Greta	$0.90	$0.90	$0.35	$5.60	$1.00

VISION QUEST

VISUAL

Find the row or column that contains five DIFFERENT lizards.

	A.	B.	C.	D.	E.
1.					
2.					
3.					
4.					
5.					

SKILLS TEST

VISUAL ◆ LOGIC

Which figure does not belong in this group?

| 1 | 2 | 3 | 4 | 5 |

ONLINE NETWORK

In each two-column group, take the letters in the left-hand column along the paths (indicated by the lines) and place them in their proper boxes in the right-hand column. When done, for each puzzle you'll find three related words reading down the right-hand column.

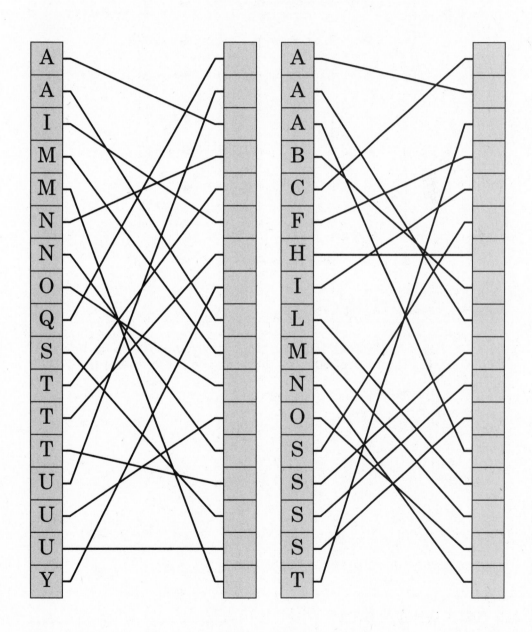

ROUND TRIP

VISUAL ◆ LOGIC

When this puzzle has been completed correctly, you will have made a round trip through its set of dots. You must visit every dot exactly once, make no diagonal moves, and return to your starting point. Parts of the right path are shown; can you find the rest?

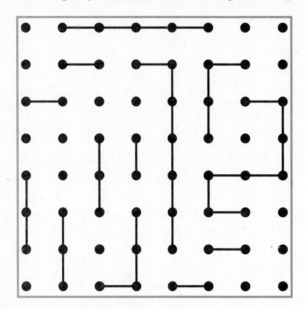

DOVETAILED WORDS

LANGUAGE

Two related words, with their letters in the correct order, are combined in each row of letters. Can you find both words? In a line like POTEORDRLEIER, or POteOrDrLEier, you can see the two words POODLE and TERRIER.

1. S C H L U I D T E E   _____ _____

2. B I N F A A B N Y T   _____ _____

3. C I A N N C D E L N S E E   _____ _____

4. W O A T L T E R R U S   _____ _____

5. G A R R N U E B T Y   _____ _____

CARD SENSE

Five playing cards were shuffled and put in a pile, one on top of another. Using the clues, can you identify each card's position in the pile?

1. The spade is somewhere above both diamonds.

2. The heart is somewhere above both eights.

3. The seven is directly above the club.

4. The five is not on the bottom.

WORD HUNT

Find words by moving from one letter to any adjoining letter. You may start a word with any letter in the diagram. In forming a word you may return to a letter as often as you wish, but do not stand on a letter using it twice in direct succession. In this Word Hunt, you are searching for 4-letter words with the letter Z. We found 18 words, including FAZE.

G	M	F	Q	U
D	A	L	I	S
H	E	Z	H	W
S	Y	R	O	D
T	E	N	M	O

Your list of words:

TARGET SHOOT

Find the two letters which, when entered into the center circle of each target, will form three 6-letter words reading across.

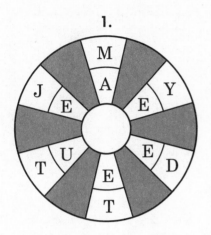

1.

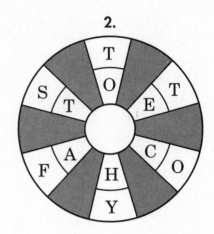

2.

OVERLAY

When you overlay the three diagrams inn the top row, which of the three lettered diagrams, A, B, or C, will be formed?

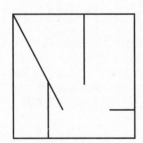

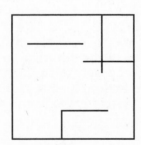

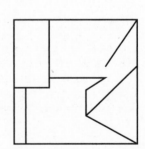

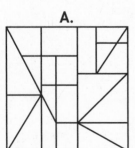

A.

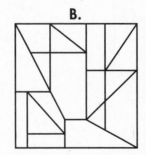

B.

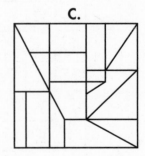

C.

WAYWORDS

An 10-word thought can be found beginning with the word THE. Then, move to any adjacent box up, down, or diagonally for each following word.

THE	LIKE	SMILE	REACH
WHAT	SECRET	TO	HAPPINESS
CARE	YOU	OF	IS
SHOUT	DO	STREAM	CONTEND

P Count

First read the sentence below. Next, go back and read the sentence again, but this time count all of the P's. How many are there?

THE PROPER PREPPY'S PAPA

INAPPROPRIATELY PRESUPPOSED

THAT PEPPY PEOPLE POPULATING

THE PHILIPPINES PLAYED PURPLE

PANPIPES PERPETUALLY.

WORD CHARADE

VISUAL ◆ SPATIAL

Find each letter in the diagram according to the instructions, and write each letter on its dash to spell out a 6-letter word.

My first letter appears to the immediate right of a U and the immediate left of a K.

My second letter appears in a row in which every other letter is part of the word THUNDER.

Y	B	L	P	T	L	N	X
S	O	H	W	F	O	K	U
I	M	P	T	I	E	N	T
D	J	R	G	U	C	L	H
E	A	U	M	K	X	F	D
O	S	I	V	Q	T	B	L
A	U	E	C	K	U	I	O
R	H	O	N	U	D	T	E

My third letter is surrounded by eight vowels.

My fourth letter, when inserted somewhere in the eight letters in one of the rows, forms a 9-letter word that means "showing restlessness."

My fifth letter only appears in the first, third, fifth, and seventh columns.

My sixth letter appears in the sixth column, but not in the eighth column.

— — — — — —

WHAT'S YOUR NUMBER?

MATH ◆ LOGIC

Can you figure out the sequence of the numbers in the boxes and what missing number goes into the box with the question mark?

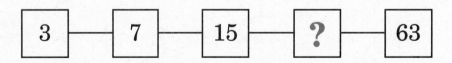

3 — 7 — 15 — ? — 63

MISSING DOMINOES

WEEK
38

In this game you use all 28 dominoes that are in a standard set. Each one has a different combination from 0-0, 0-1, 0-2, to 6-6. Domino halves with the same number of dots lie next to each other. To avoid confusion we have used an open circle to indicate a zero. Can you fill in the missing white dominoes to complete the board?

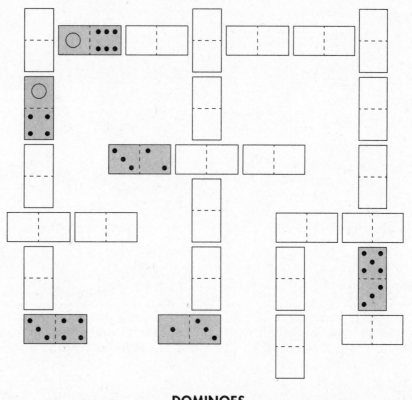

DOMINOES

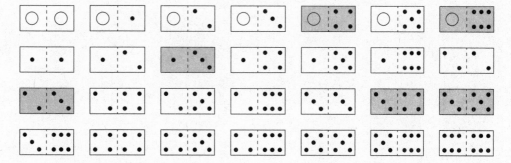

COUNT THE TRIANGLES

VISUAL ◆ SPATIAL

To solve this puzzle, write down the three letters that describe each triangle (a 3-sided figure) in this diagram. We found 24 triangles; how many can you locate?

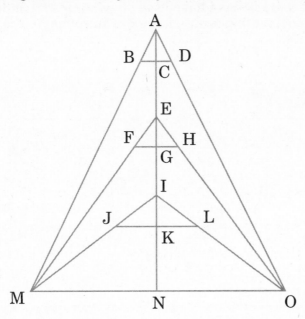

RINGERS

LANGUAGE ◆ SPATIAL

Each Ringer is composed of five rings. Use your imagination to rotate the rings so that you spell out four 5-letter words reading from the outside to the inside when all five rings are aligned correctly.

1.

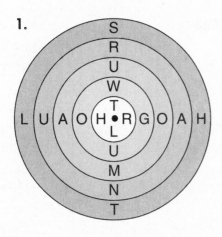

2.

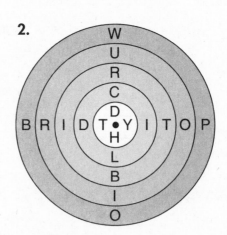

RING LOGIC

Complete the diagram by drawing in the links between the rings using the statements. Assume that all the rings in the picture are locked rigidly into position and cannot be moved in any direction. Consider yourself a true ringmaster if you can find the solution in under six minutes!

1. The pattern is symmetrical from left to right.

2. Exactly two rings are linked only once. Every other ring is linked at least twice.

3. The right side of ring E is in front of ring J.

4. The bottom of ring G is to the front.

5. The right side of ring M is to the front.

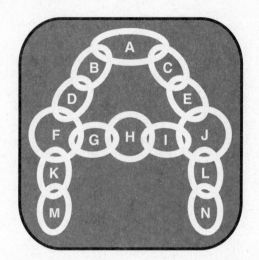

CIRCLE SEARCH

Move from circle to adjoining circle, horizontally and vertically only, to form 14 common, everyday words of at least three letters. Don't change the order of the letters in the circles. Proper names are not allowed.

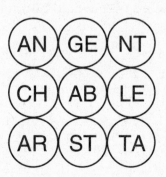

GRAND TOUR

LANGUAGE ◆ VISUAL

Form a continuous chain of 5-letter words moving through the maze from START to FINISH. The second part of one word becomes the first part of the next word. This puzzle starts with RE-NEW-EL (renew, newel).

START

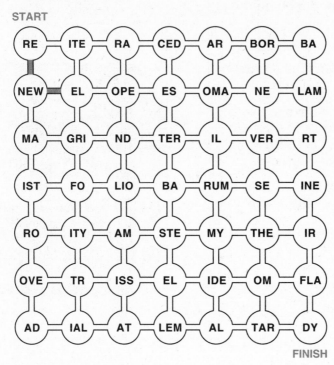

FINISH

WORD VISIBILITY

LANGUAGE ◆ LOGIC

There are six 5-letter words below. The first letter of the answer is found in the first pair of letters, and it is either the top or the bottom letter. Continue across each pair.

For example, the word GIRL would be found thus: G A R L
                                                   L I T X

1. T U P I G
   G A L E P

2. R O G B M
   V U H I Y

3. N I S U E
   A E A L K

4. E U I S H
   M V W C T

5. C A E V E
   G R N O L

6. H L B N T
   P O A O R

248

ANAGRAM MAZE

WEEK 39

The diagram contains 36 words, 19 of which are anagrams of other everyday words. Start at the top arrow and anagram POEM. While solving, move up, down, right, or left to the only adjacent word that can be anagrammed. Continue until you arrive at the bottom arrow. There is only one path through the maze.

1 FLAP	2 ROVE	3 BLOW	4 POEM	5 MARK	6 MELT
7 LAST	8 CONE	9 BOLD	10 GREW	11 CUFF	12 WING
13 DONE	14 FOUR	15 THUG	16 EVER	17 GELS	18 RIDE
19 KALE	20 LACY	21 TEND	22 ARCH	23 ROAD	24 TACO
25 JIVE	26 EYES	27 WHIM	28 WAIT	29 CULT	30 LIES
31 WILD	32 CITY	33 BARD	34 ABUT	35 LILT	36 DOES

COUNT ON IT!

Use the given letters to fill in the familiar saying, one letter per dash. All the letters following 1 are the first letters of each word, the letters following 2 are the second letters of each word, etc. It is up to you to determine which letter goes where.

1. C U W S A T   2. N A M O P H   3. F D E K E
4. L F E   5. E L   6. E

$\overline{1}\ \overline{2}\ \overline{3}\ \overline{4}$ $\overline{1}\ \overline{2}$ $\overline{1}\ \overline{2}\ \overline{3}$ $\overline{1}\ \overline{2}\ \overline{3}\ \overline{4}\ \overline{5}$

$\overline{1}\ \overline{2}\ \overline{3}$ $\overline{1}\ \overline{2}\ \overline{3}\ \overline{4}\ \overline{5}\ \overline{6}.$

ALPHABET SOUP

VISUAL ◆ LANGUAGE

Cross off each letter from the alphabet list that appears in the larger group of letters. Then rearrange the letters not crossed out to form the name of a gemstone.

```
V  E  M  V  G  N  M  V  T  Z  E  M  G  N  Z  V

G  N  Z  R  M  X  I  N  Q  Z  H  M  R  E  G  C

M  R  E  C  W  G  Z  N  I  V  C  J  R  K  M  N

F  Q  S  J  M  N  U  G  D  Y  F  W  R  G  Z  B
```

A B C D E F G H I J K L M N O P Q R S T U V W X Y Z

Gemstone: _____

FUN WITH FACTS AND FIGURES

MATH

This puzzle tests you on a lot of little facts and figures. Solve the quiz in the order given since each answer is used in the next statement. There are no fractions used here.

1. Take the number of the paws on a dog and multiply by the number of cents in a quarter. _____

2. Next, add the value of the Roman numeral CIII. _____

3. Now, subtract the number of Dalmatians in a classic Disney movie title. _____

4. Divide by the number of musicians in a trio. _____

5. Add the value of a pair of dice that shows snake eyes. _____

Our answer is the number of inches in a yard. *Is yours?*

W COUNT

Here's an eye exam that's also an W exam! First, read the sentence below. Next, go back and read the sentence again, but this time count all of the W's. How many are there?

WHILE WEARY WHOLESALER WILLY

W. WEDGWORTH WOKE UP FROM

DROWSING AT TWO TWENTY-TWO,

WILLY'S WEIRD WEIMARANERS

WEBSTER AND WALLY WOOFED,

BOWWOWED, AND GROWLED WILDLY.

LANGUAGE

SLIDE RULE

Slide each column of letters up or down in the box and form as many everyday 3-letter words as you can in the windows where TAN is now. We formed 50 words, including TAN.

Your list of words:

SQUARE LINKS

LANGUAGE

Write one letter in each empty box so that an everyday 8-letter word is spelled out around each black box. Each word may read either clockwise or counter-clockwise, and may start at any of its letters.

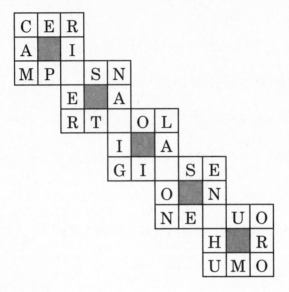

CIRCLE MATH

MATH

Each overlapping circle is identified by a letter having a different number value from 1 to 9. Where some circles overlap, there is a number: It is the SUM of the values of the letters in those overlapping circles. Can you figure out the correct values for the letters? As a starting help, E = 1.

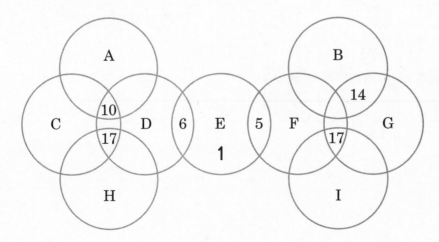

252

LANGUAGE

SEVEN WORD ZINGER

Using each letter once, form seven everyday 3-letter words with the first letter coming from the center, the second from the middle, and the third from the outer circle. Your words may differ from ours.

Y P
O E
N T
O N B G I Y
S A K
U H
T I H
E N

— — —

— — —

— — —

— — —

— — —

— — —

— — —

LANGUAGE

WORD EQUATIONS

Determine the three defined words in each equation. The third word is formed when the second is written directly after the first; for example, for "for each + shape = act in a play," you would respond "per + form = perform."

1. brainstorm + numbered agenda items = dreamer

2. bring in from another country + picnic pest = crucial

3. Olympics award + roaring feline = round piece of veal

4. light-switch position + drink cubes = work space

5. matched group + golf peg = small sofa

WAYWORDS

LANGUAGE

A 7-word thought can be found beginning with the word YOU. Then, move to any adjacent box up, down, or diagonally for each following word.

FORGET	YOU	LISTENING	PURCHASE
ENTERTAIN	PRETEND	GENERATE	BY
GRACE	A	NEVER	JUST
PRIMARY	BATCH	BORE	FRAGILE

ANTONYMS QUIZ

LANGUAGE

An antonym is a word that is opposite in meaning to another word; for example, "cold" is the antonym of "hot." One of the words following each capitalized word is the antonym of that word.

1. YOUTHFUL   a. palpable   b. mature   c. gratuitous

2. COGENT   a. irrelevant   b. plush   c. sappy

3. VIGILANT   a. careless   b. legitimate   c. coarse

4. DEXTEROUS   a. lapsed   b. humane   c. bungling

5. TEMPERATE   a. scanty   b. agitated   c. fallacious

6. FATIGUE   a. forge   b. countervail   c. exhilarate

7. DIPLOMATIC   a. miniature   b. tactless   c. peculiar

8. FLEET   a. sluggish   b. tolerant   c. opposed

STACKED UP

The box on the left can be formed by three of the numbered boxes superimposed on top of each other; do not turn them in any way. Can you figure out which three work?

1.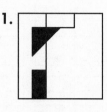

2.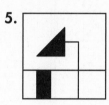

3.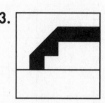

4.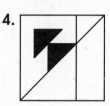

5.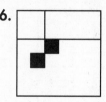

6.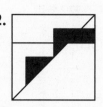

LOGIC

SUDOKU

Directions for solving are on page 232.

	8				5		1	9
	1	7	2	6				4
5					8			
	7	8	6					2
2			1	3	4			8
6				7	9	5		
		2						6
4			9	2	7	8		
7	9		4			2		

LOOSE TILE

The tray on the left seemed the ideal place to store the set of loose dominoes. Unfortunately, when the tray was full, one domino was left over. Determine the arrangement of the dominoes in the tray and which is the Loose Tile.

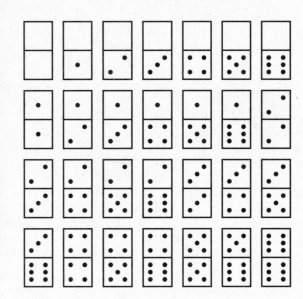

COMPOUND IT

Starting at #1, pick a word that will form a compound word with a word chosen in #2. Then with the word you've selected in #2, pick one from #3 to form another compound word. Continue in this manner to #10, so that you've formed nine compound words. In some instances more than one compound word can be formed, but there is only one path to get you to #10.

1. pole, under, power, earth

2. quake, bound, boat, pass

3. book, word, less, yard

4. play, case, stick, mark

5. down, ground, bill, load

6. hog, fold, field, reach

7. wild, work, wash, back

8. life, cloth, cat, week

9. night, end, saver, long

10. fun, glad, club, peace

CROSS PATHS

Start at the arrow. There are four circles in that box, so move four boxes, either across or up. Each time you land in a box, move the number of dots in that box in only one direction, up, down, or across until you reach Finish (F). You may cross your own path, but do not retrace it.

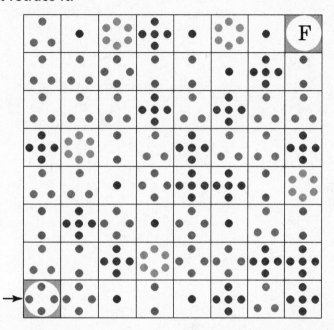

TRIANGULAR SQUARE

Place the nine numbered squares into the diagram so that the four numbers in each of the diagram's four large triangles equal the number outside of it. The patterns have to match and you may not rotate the squares.

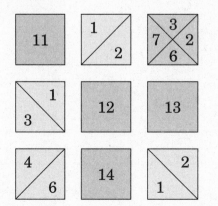

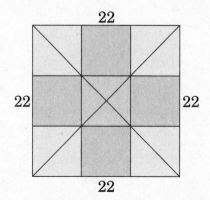

257

WEEK 40

POP!

The balloons in a dart game are arranged so their letters spell out the word "BLOWING." To win, you must pop six different balloons with six different darts, but after each pop the remaining letters must spell out a new word reading across from left to right. Do not rearrange the balloons. Can you determine the order of the balloons to pop and the words formed? Your words may differ from ours.

IN THE BALANCE

MATH ◆ LOGIC

Scales 1, 2, and 3 are perfectly balanced. Determine how many triangles it takes to balance scale 4.

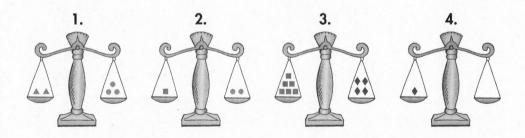

CROSS PATHS

WEEK 40

Directions for solving are on page 257.

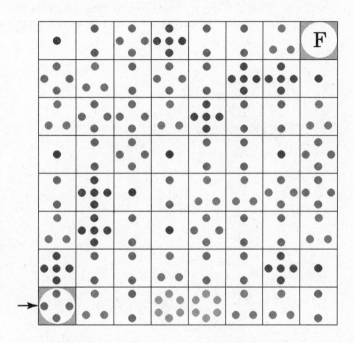

F

→

MATH

IN THE MONEY

How quickly can you convert each bag of money into dollars and cents and determine which one contains the greatest amount?

1. 921 nickels

2. 183 quarters

3. 4,559 pennies

4. 468 dimes

HOLE IN ONE

LOGIC

Twenty-four golfers entered a hole-in-one contest. Each golfer was given a ball with a different 4-digit number combination using the numbers 1, 2, 7, and 8 on it. Looking at the 23 balls still on the green, can you figure out what combination is on the ball that won the contest?

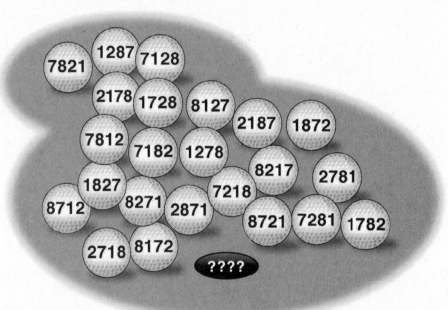

POP!

LANGUAGE

Directions for solving are on page 258. This time, you'll be using the letters in the word "CLATTER."

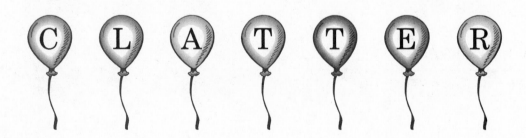

IN THE BALANCE

WEEK
40

Scales 1, 2, and 3 are perfectly balanced. Determine how many triangles it takes to balance scale 4.

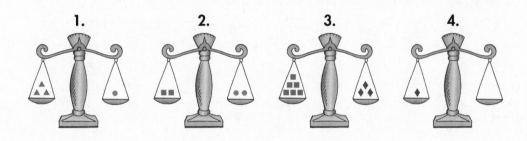

1. 2. 3. 4.

TRIANGULAR SQUARE

Directions for solving are on page 257.

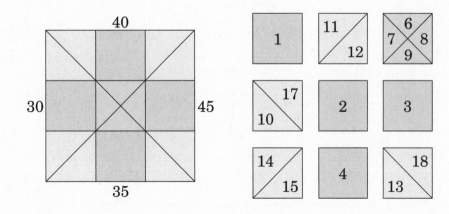

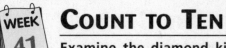

COUNT TO TEN

VISUAL ◆ MATH

Examine the diamond kites and box kites and then answer these questions: 1. Which row contains the most diamond kites? 2. Which row contains the most box kites? 3. Which row contains an equal number of diamond kites and box kites?

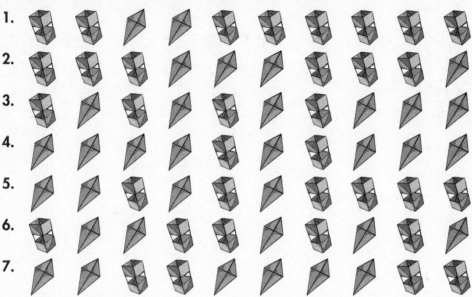

1.
2.
3.
4.
5.
6.
7.

STATE LIMITS

LANGUAGE

This list consists of the names of seven U.S. states, but we've removed all of the letters between the first and last ones. Can you complete the names?

O _____ O

N _____ E

M _____ S

I _____ O

T _____ S

V _____ A

M _____ E

HEXAGON HUNT

In this diagram of six-sided figures, there are 10 "special" hexagons. These 10 are special because the six numbers around each one are all different from each other and the center. We've circled one of the 10. Can you find the other 9?

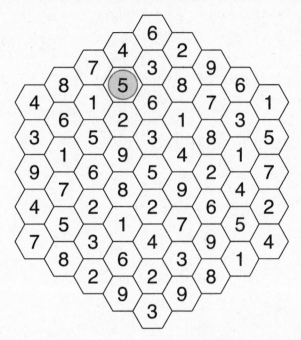

VISUAL ◆ LANGUAGE

NEXT TO NOTHING

In the first row, the D is next to the number zero and the C is next to the letter O. Circle all of the letters next to zeroes and then scramble these circled letters to spell out a woman's name.

D0	CO	QO	SO
HO	E0	A0	WO
LO	YO	MO	AO
R0	UO	B0	IO
FO	XO	KO	ZO
GO	VO	PO	N0

FILLING STATION

Place the given consonants on the dashes to form words. The vowels have already been placed for you, and as an additional help, each entry lists its category beside its given consonants.

1. C C G H (city)

   __ __ I __ A __ O

2. B C H K L N T T (household sight)

   __ I __ __ __ E __   __ A __ __ E

3. D G H R T T (movie)

   " __ __ E   __ __ A __ U A __ E "

4. C D L R S S (food)

   __ A E __ A __   __ A __ A __

5. G L L R (animal)

   __ O __ I __ __ A

MAGIC NUMBER SQUARES

Fill in the empty boxes so these groups add up to the number below each diagram: 1. each row; 2. each column; 3. each long diagonal; 4. the four center squares; 5. the four corner squares; and 6. each quarter of the diagram. A number will be used only once per diagram.

1.

14			
9		12	11
	10	8	

38

2.

	7		
9	13		16
8		5	

42

GOING IN CIRCLES

Directions for solving are on page 232.

1.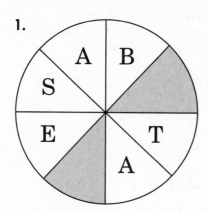

2.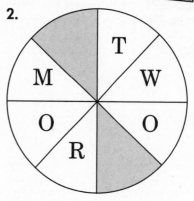

VISUAL ◆ LANGUAGE

WORD CHARADE

Directions for solving are on page 244.

My first letter is a vowel that appears directly next to an S.

My second letter is the last letter in a column of eight consecutive letters of the alphabet that are not in order.

My third letter appears to the immediate right of a J and directly above a V.

My fourth letter appears either directly above or directly below wherever my third letter appears.

My fifth letter is the seventh letter of a 9-letter name of a short-legged dog that starts reading down one column then continues reading up an adjacent column.

My sixth letter appears only once in the diagram.

____ ____ ____ ____ ____ ____

O	F	Z	U	Q	Y	B	U
H	L	I	K	O	L	E	C
X	Y	G	P	T	Z	X	W
E	D	N	V	R	K	L	P
Y	N	D	Q	M	J	Y	T
L	U	A	B	P	C	V	F
V	H	C	K	N	W	D	A
A	S	H	J	S	R	G	I

KEEP ON MOVING

WEEK 41

VISUAL

The goal is to move from the shaded square to the asterisk. Since the shaded square has the number 3 in it, you must move three squares up, down, left, or right, but not diagonally. In the new square will be another number; move that number of squares up, down, left, or right, continuing in this way until you reach the asterisk. It's okay to cross your own path.

4	3	4	1	2	5
2	3	1	3	4	1
3	2	2	1	4	3
1	3	**3**	3	3	2
2	1	2	4	2	4
2	✳	5	2	3	3

STAR WORDS

VISUAL ◆ LOGIC

Only five of the eight words given will fit together in the diagram. Place them in the directions indicated by the arrows.

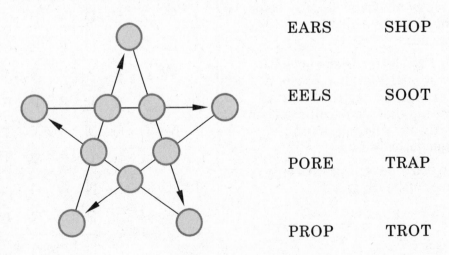

EARS   SHOP

EELS   SOOT

PORE   TRAP

PROP   TROT

266

WORD WHEEL

WEEK 41

Starting with the "B" at the arrow, see how many everyday words of three or more letters you can find going clockwise. Don't skip over any letters. For example, if you saw the letters C, A, R, E, D, you would form five words: CAR, CARE, CARED, ARE, RED. We found 30 words.

CHANGELINGS

Can you change the first word into the second word (in each set) by changing only one letter at a time? Do not rearrange the order of the letters with each change. Each change must result in an everyday word, and words beginning with a capital letter, slang, or obsolete words aren't allowed. The number in parentheses indicates the number of changes we used for that Changeling.

1. BUSY

_____

_____

_____

DESK
(4 changes)

2. WORK

_____

_____

_____

BANK
(4 changes)

3. GOOD

_____

_____

_____

BOSS
(4 changes)

CODE WORD

DECODING

Directions for solving are on page 231.

$\overline{1}\ \ \overline{2}\ \ \overline{3}\ \ \overline{4}\ \ \overline{5}\ \ \overline{6}\ \ \overline{7}\ \ \overline{8}\ \ \overline{9}\ \ \overline{10}\ \ \overline{11}$

W 2 4 H   2 4 3   11 9 15 6 2 9 G   3 4 6 11 9 G 4 H   8 9 1

5 9 6 2 V 8 L 11 1   P 11 6 3 11 V 11 6 8 9 10 11,   4 H 11

H O 6 3 11   1 11 M O 9 3 4 6 8 4 11 3   4 H 8 4   11 V 11 9

4 H 11   H 11 8 V 2 11 3 4   O F   7 5 6 11 19 3   10 8 9

7 11   10 8 6 6 2 11 1   W 2 4 H   G 6 8 10 11.

IN THE ABSTRACT

VISUAL ◆ SPATIAL

Directions for solving are on page 229.

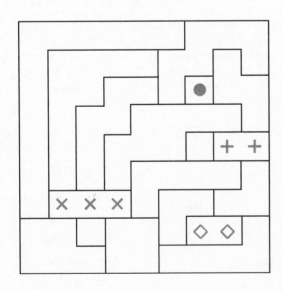

ONLINE NETWORK

Directions for solving are on page 239.

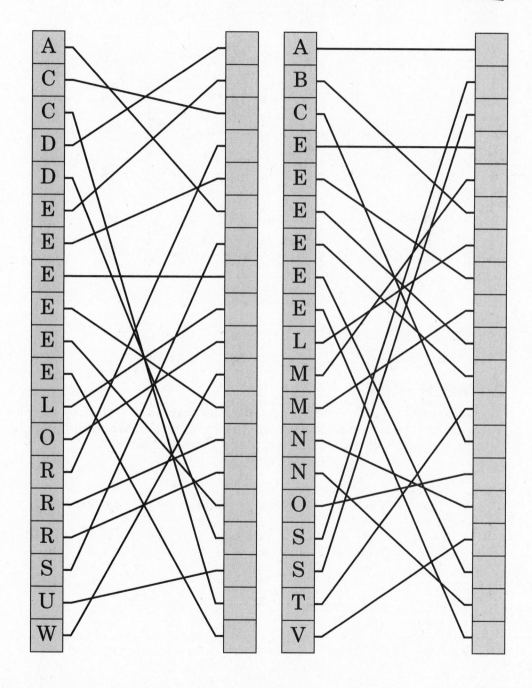

COUNTDOWN

VISUAL

Directions for solving are on page 231.

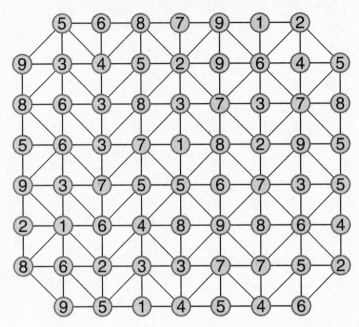

SYMBOL-ISM

DECODING

This is simply a Cryptogram that uses symbols instead of letters to spell out a truism. Each symbol stands for the same letter throughout. For this puzzle, we've already indicated that ☀ = F and 👁 = W.

LETTER, PLEASE

The numbers below stand for certain letters on the telephone dial. You will see that one number may stand for more than one letter — for example, 3 may be D, E, or F. By finding the correct letter for each number, you will have spelled out a thought.

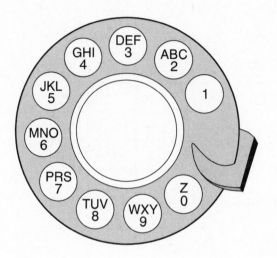

93 733 469

6824 2 626 427

263 93 3689 446;

43 93 26853 733

469 548853 43

365697, 93 96853

7489 446.

CROSS-UPS

Using only the letters given above each diagram, fill in the boxes in such a way that an everyday compound word is formed, one part reading across and the other part reading down. The letter already in the diagram is a letter shared by both parts of the word. Note: Each part of the compound word is an entire word on its own.

1. D N N O O T

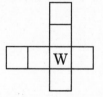

2. C K L P S T

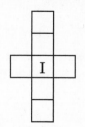

MARCHING ORDERS

MATH ◆ LOGIC

Using a different two-step sequence of addition and/or subtraction, can you make your way from Start to Finish in each puzzle by moving up, down, or diagonally? We've started the first one for you using the sequence +3 and -1; continue this sequence to reach Finish. You will not cross your own path or pass through any square twice.

1. FINISH ↑

10	9	12	11	12	14
7	8	10	13	16	15
4	6	7	9	10	11
3	5	6	8	9	8
1	2	4	6	10	12
0	3	9	7	8	11

↑ START

2. FINISH ↑

18	12	17	16	21	26
17	13	8	14	23	20
12	11	9	12	19	18
6	8	4	10	17	20
3	5	7	12	21	15
0	2	9	14	16	23

↑ START

QUICK FILL

LANGUAGE

Directions for solving are on page 230.

A C C E I L M N O O

1. Letter 9 is a vowel.

2. Letter 3 is from the second half of the alphabet.

3. Letters 4 and 5, in order, spell out a word of denial.

4. In the alphabet, letter 10 is immediately before letter 6.

5. Letter 2 appears elsewhere in the word.

6. Letters 7, 8, and 1, in order, spell out a word that means frozen water.

$$\overline{1}\ \overline{2}\ \overline{3}\ \overline{4}\ \overline{5}\ \overline{6}\ \overline{7}\ \overline{8}\ \overline{9}\ \overline{10}$$

STACKED UP

The box on the left can be formed by three of the numbered boxes superimposed on top of each other; do not turn them in any way. Can you figure out which three work?

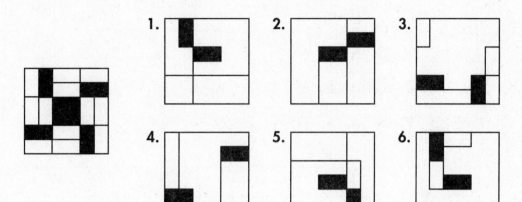

LOGIC

SUDOKU

Directions for solving are on page 232.

			2				3	7
8		2				9	4	
3	1		6		4			
9			5	1		7		4
		4		6		5		
1		5		7	2			9
			1		3		9	6
	2	3				1		5
5	9				6			

ALPHABET SOUP

VISUAL ◆ LANGUAGE

Cross off each letter from the alphabet list that appears in the larger group of letters. Then rearrange the letters not crossed out to form the name of an African capital city.

K	S	E	V	E	K	H	E	S	T	F	K	S	T	H	V
H	F	T	E	N	U	K	L	F	S	V	T	B	Z	U	N
B	N	J	L	H	S	P	T	D	K	B	Y	V	U	F	T
V	B	Y	S	W	X	G	V	U	N	K	Q	T	B	P	M

A	B	C	D	E	F	G	H	I	J	K	L	M	N	O	P	Q	R	S	T	U	V	W	X	Y	Z

Capital city: _____

DOVETAILED WORDS

LANGUAGE

Directions for solving are on page 240.

1. R P R A B I E B S I T   _____ _____

2. M S U C O F F I N N E   _____ _____

3. T B A H S Y M I E L   _____ _____

4. W M H A A R R I F N A   _____ _____

5. B P O L W U D S E H R   _____ _____

274

TRI, TRI AGAIN

Directions for solving are on page 233.

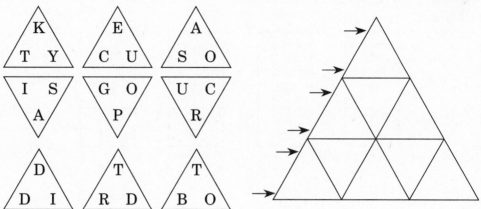

LANGUAGE

ANIMAL CHARADES

Directions for solving are on page 233.

My FIRST is in CATFISH and in BRASH; _____

My SECOND is in PANTHER and in STASH; _____

My THIRD is in MOLE but not in DRONE; _____

My FOURTH is in COUGAR but not in GROWN; _____

My FIFTH is in CORMORANT and in FRAME; _____

My SIXTH is in BAT and in BLAME; _____

My SEVENTH is in LEMMING but not in GLUM; _____

My EIGHTH is in DOVE but not in SOME; _____

My NINTH is in GROUSE and in BLUE; _____

My TENTH is in OSTRICH and in TRUE; _____

My WHOLE is a critter with nary a scale;
It's an amphibian with limbs and a tail.

_____

WHAT'S YOUR NUMBER?   MATH ◆ LOGIC

Can you figure out the sequence of the numbers in the boxes and what missing number goes into the space with the question mark?

35	102	86	?
9	30	4	15
8	12	74	10

RELATIONSHIPS QUIZ   LANGUAGE

KENNEL is to DOG as STY is to PIG because a DOG lives in a KENNEL and a PIG lives in a STY. Each of the statements below is a relationship of some kind. Can you select the right word from the four following each?

1. THERMOMETER is to TEMPERATURE as CLOCK is to _____.

   (a) watch   (b) time   (c) alarm   (d) minute

2. CIRCLE is to GLOBE as SQUARE is to _____.
   (a) cube   (b) house   (c) rectangle   (d) dance

3. TRUMAN is to MISSOURI as OBAMA is to _____.
   (a) Hawaii   (b) Maine   (c) California   (d) Michigan

4. SCARY is to FEARFUL as DARING is to _____.
   (a) villain   (b) bold   (c) timid   (d) battle

5. KEY is to TYPEWRITER as FLUTIST is to _____.
   (a) music   (b) reed   (c) orchestra   (d) piano

MISSING DOMINOES

Directions for solving are on page 245.

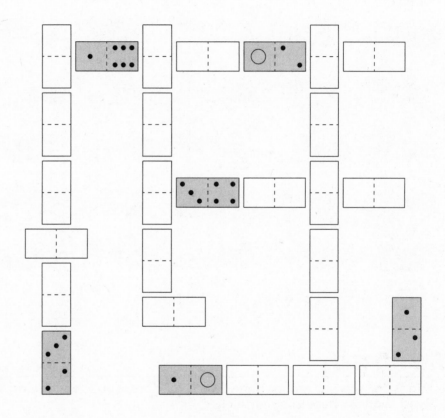

DOMINOES

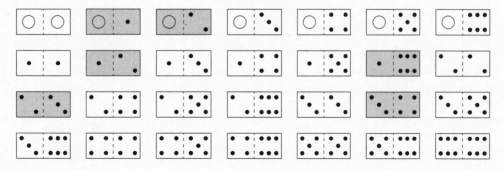

VISION QUEST

VISUAL

Find the row or column that contains
five DIFFERENT vegetables.

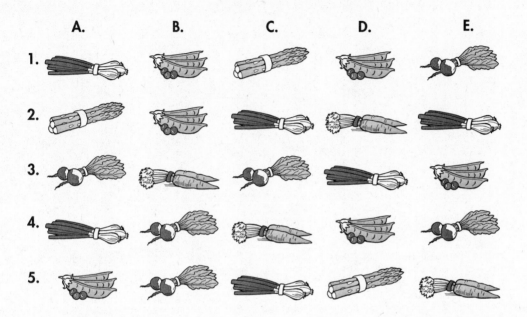

A. B. C. D. E.

1.
2.
3.
4.
5.

WAYWORDS

LANGUAGE

Directions for solving are on page 254. This time, you'll be looking for
a 9-word thought beginning with IT.

BLEND	DIFFICULT	HARD	TAKES
FREEDOM	WORK	IT	PLASTIC
TO	PURCHASE	EASY	LOOK
COINCIDENCE	MAKE	ANYTHING	CRUNCH

ELIMINATION

Directions for solving are on page 234. Once again, the remaining words will form a thought.

ESCORT ROME NEVER RAIDERS STARS CONSORT
MISS WASN'T SWELTER AN HAWKEYE OF STRIPES
OPPORTUNITY BUILT CORNHUSKER TO RED THE
PASSPORT DENTIST EXPRESS IN LOST WHITE
QUIT YOUR A COMFORT LOVE DAY BLUE ARK

Eliminate…

1. the five words that form the title of the first movie that featured Indiana Jones.

2. the four words that end with the same three letters.

3. the six words that form a saying that means "It required more than 24 hours for fabrication of The Eternal City."

4. the word that is the nickname of a resident of Iowa and the other word that is the nickname of a resident of Nebraska.

5. the two words that, when the first three letters of each word are put together, form the name of a country.

6. the word that forms the name of a South American capital when a vowel is added to the end of it.

7. the two words in the nickname of the American flag and the three names of its colors.

EASY PICKINGS

To solve, simply cross out one letter in each pair. When the puzzle is completed correctly, the remaining letters will spell out a quote by Virgil.

AO OS   TU HO BE   WT NW IN GT

IM OS   NB EK RN TD   MT OH EN

TF IR ER ES   EI NY KC UL IW NH TE VS.

BULL'S-EYE LETTER

LANGUAGE

Directions for solving are on page 236.

_ _ _ _

_ _ _ _

_ _ _ _

_ _ _ _

_ _ _ _

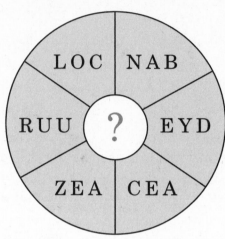

CARD SENSE

LOGIC

Directions for solving are on page 241.

1. Both black cards are somewhere below the six.

2. Neither diamond is on top.

3. One face card is second from the top, and the other is on the bottom.

ANAGRAM MAZE

Directions for solving are on page 249. This time, there are 19 words to anagram and the first word you'll be anagramming is PATS.

1 PATS	2 STUD	3 SACK	4 ZINC	5 PRAY	6 ZOOS
7 WHIP	8 CALL	9 MUSH	10 CUED	11 TWIN	12 WISE
13 TURN	14 BEAN	15 SPAS	16 SUNS	17 FANG	18 TOOK
19 CARE	20 LEND	21 COPY	22 HATE	23 APES	24 GRIN
25 EARL	26 POPS	27 HEWN	28 HARE	29 LILY	30 COLA
31 LAMP	32 AWRY	33 DADS	34 WOOL	35 LESS	36 MARE

S COUNT

Directions for solving are on page 251. This time, see how many S's you can count in the sentence.

"STOP STASHING SUCH SILLY

STUFF AS SUNGLASSES, SASHES,

SWIMSUITS, BUS PASSES, CLASS

RINGS, AND SWISS CHEESES,"

HISSED SISSY'S SPOUSE RUSS

SENSELESSLY LAST SUNDAY.

SUDOKU

Directions for solving are on page 232.

				2			7	1
3					8			
7					6	8		
1				8		4	2	
	9		7		1		6	
	6	8		5				9
		2	8					4
			5					3
8	3			9				

MAGNIFIND

Figure out which area of the drawing has been enlarged.

SLIDE RULE

WEEK 44

Directions for solving are on page 251. Here, you're to form 4-letter words. We found 26 words, including DUNK.

Your list of words:

THE LINEUP

While scrutinizing the lineup of letters below, can you answer the five given questions correctly in five minutes or less?

SULCOVBFJKISSGEXERCISEYZITEMDPRACTICALQTHAWFT

1. Which letter of the alphabet does not appear in the lineup? _____

2. What 8-letter word — with its letters in correct order and appearing together — can you find in the lineup? _____

3. Which letter of the alphabet appears exactly three times in the lineup? _____

4. What 9-letter word — with its letters in correct order and appearing together — can you find in the lineup? _____

5. Other than the answers to Questions 2 and 4, how many everyday words — with their letters in correct order and appearing together — of four or more letters can you find in the lineup? _____

OVERLAY

VISUAL ◆ **SPATIAL**

Directions for solving are on page 242.

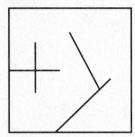

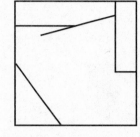

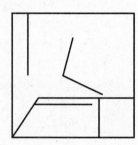

A.

B.

C.

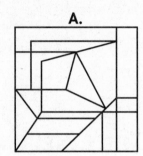

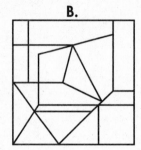

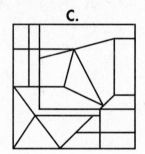

CIRCLE SEARCH

LANGUAGE

Directions for solving are on page 247. Here you're looking to form 14 words.

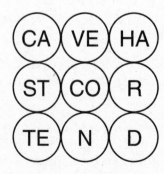

LOOSE TILE

The tray on the right seemed the ideal place to store the set of loose dominoes. Unfortunately, when the tray was full, one domino was left over. Determine the arrangement of the dominoes in the tray and which is the Loose Tile.

ASSOCIATIONS

Directions for solving are on page 236.

WHAT DO SNAKES DO AFTER HAVING AN ARGUMENT?

MOSQUITO TEAM SAVOR HEAVY LOOK EAGER ERIE

RELISH YEAR UTTER HAPPY OBSERVE BALLAD

INTIMATE HOUSEFLY SATISFY HURON SONG SLOPPY

PRONOUNCE ANCHOVY WRONG KNOWLEDGEABLE

NATURAL GNAT DANGLE SEE INCORRECT MUTUAL

SMART MELODY ACTIVITY SAY KETCHUP ENJOY

EARLY SUPERIOR URGENT WISE UNTRUE PETUNIA

ROUND TRIP

VISUAL ◆ LOGIC

Directions for solving are on page 240.

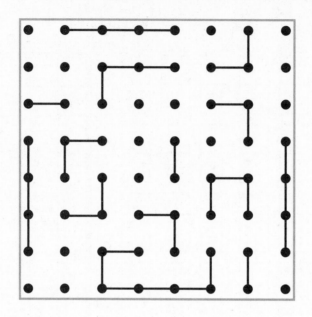

TARGET SHOOT

LANGUAGE

Directions for solving are on page 242.

1.

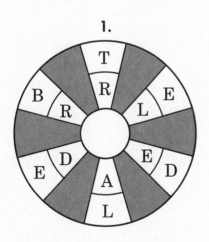

2.

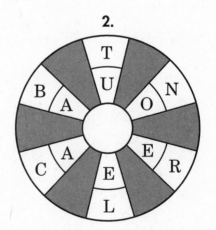

RING LOGIC

Directions for solving are on page 247.

1. The pattern is symmetrical from left to right.

2. Each ring is linked at least twice.

3. The right side of rings B, H, and Q are to the front.

4. The bottom of rings E and U are to the front.

ALL IN A ROW

Directions for solving are on page 228. This time, look for the most groups of consecutive numbers adding up to 12.

A. 5 8 1 2 1 6 4 9 7 3 5 1 1 6 2 4 5 8 3 2 4 3 6 3

B. 9 2 3 4 7 1 5 8 6 1 4 1 2 3 6 1 9 2 4 1 5 6 4 7

C. 1 5 2 3 1 9 4 7 2 8 6 1 3 7 1 8 3 1 2 1 3 9 1 4

FUN WITH FACTS AND FIGURES   MATH

Directions for solving are on page 250.

1. Take the number of vowels in the word IGLOO
   and subtract the number of consonants in the word.   _____

2. Next, multiply by the number of letters in the
   name of the continent that contains Brazil,
   Argentina, and Peru.   _____

3. Now add the number of pencils in a gross.   _____

4. Divide by the number sides on a hexagon.   _____

5. Add the number of hours in a day.   _____

The answer is the number of U.S. states. *Is yours?*

HEXAGON HUNT   VISUAL

Directions for solving are on page 263.

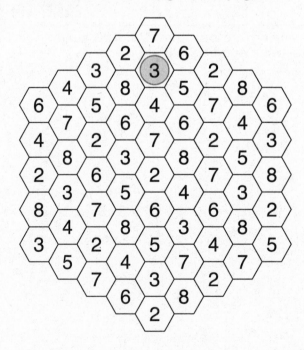

WHIRLIGIG

WEEK 45

In each numbered section are five letters. Rearrange each group of letters so that when you add "CHA" from the middle of the diagram to the front of each group, you will form 12 common 8-letter words.

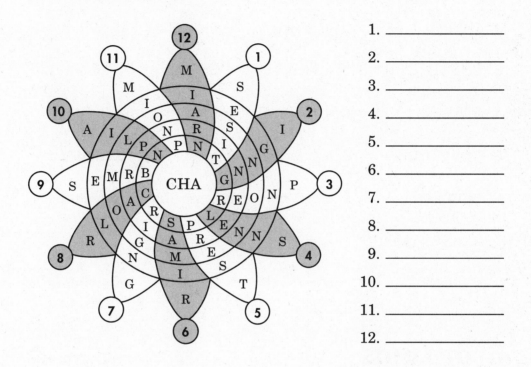

1. _____

2. _____

3. _____

4. _____

5. _____

6. _____

7. _____

8. _____

9. _____

10. _____

11. _____

12. _____

LANGUAGE

COMPOUND IT

Directions for solving are on page 256.

1. blue, child, ward, play

2. bird, room, proof, ground

3. read, call, house, breaking

4. plant, coat, hold, out

5. come, over, some, up

6. haul, spin, back, beat

7. stage, bean, dry, link

8. coach, wall, pleasant, hand

9. cuff, bag, maiden, writing

10. trick, fare, pipes, love

ANTONYMS QUIZ

LANGUAGE

Directions for solving are on page 254.

1. SURREPTITIOUS   a. bankrupt   b. direct   c. enthralling

2. JOVIAL   a. greedy   b. farfetched   c. sullen

3. CONTRACT   a. elongate   b. nominate   c. assent

4. STRIFE   a. concord   b. boon   c. bluster

5. COVETOUS   a. irascible   b. giving   c. nimble

6. BRAZEN   a. infernal   b. compelling   c. demure

7. BLASPHEMOUS   a. divine   b. buoyant   c. liable

8. FLAUNT   a. conceal   b. impart   c. standardize

STATE LIMITS

LANGUAGE

Directions for solving are on page 262.

A _____ S

W_____ G

P _____ A

I _____ S

K _____ S

O _____ N

R _____ D

CIRCLE MATH

Directions for solving are on page 252. We've started you off by telling you A = 6.

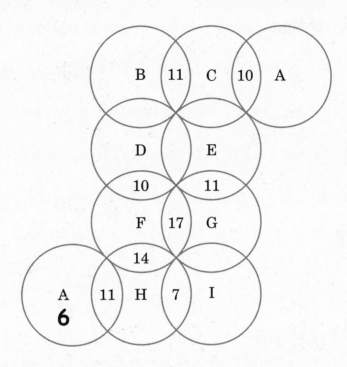

CROSS-UPS

Directions for solving are on page 271.

1. G H I O R U

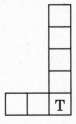

2. E H N R T T W Y

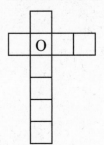

WORD EQUATIONS

Directions for solving are on page 253.

1. provide party food + support column = many-legged insect

2. except that + 2,000-pound weight = shirt fastener

3. overtake on the highway + ship harbor = travel-abroad document

4. bees' production + lunar body = newlyweds' vacation

5. birthday mailing + piece of lumber = carton material

SQUARE LINKS

Solving directions are on page 252.

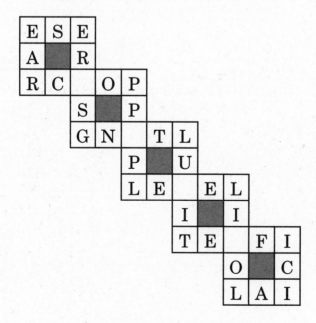

SUDOKU

Directions for solving are on page 232.

		1					8	
7				5	2			
			2	1			4	5
		7			6		9	4
3			8		1			2
2	6		4			1		
4	1			8	3			
		2	1					6
	9					4		

WORD HUNT

Directions for solving are on page 241. This time, you'll be searching for 6-letter last names of men who have won an Oscar award for Best Actor, such as (Ronald) COLMAN. We found 12 names, including COLMAN.

C	R	V	C	B	O
O	A	B	I	A	G
L	M	N	O	R	N
M	W	E	D	T	E
O	H	L	S	C	Y
N	O	N	I	P	A

Your list of words:

LICENSE PLATES

LANGUAGE

Each box contains five or six letters of a 2-word means of transport. The top letters are a part of the first word and the bottom letters are a part of the second word, in order.

1.
```
T I O
W A G
```

2.
```
O U N
I K E
```

3.
```
O T O
C O O
```

4.
```
R T S
 C A
```

5.
```
L L E
U S
```

6.
```
I C K
R U C
```

RINGERS

LANGUAGE ◆ SPATIAL

Directions for solving are on page 246.

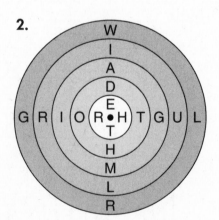

1.

2.

ARROW MAZE

Solving directions are on page 235.

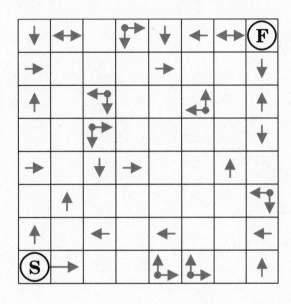

KEEP ON MOVING

Directions for solving are on page 266. Here, start in the shaded square with the number 1.

2	3	1	1	3	2
*	3	1	1	3	4
2	3	3	1	4	5
2	1	3	2	1	3
4	4	5	3	1	5
3	3	1	1	5	4

TRI, TRI AGAIN

Directions for solving are on page 233.

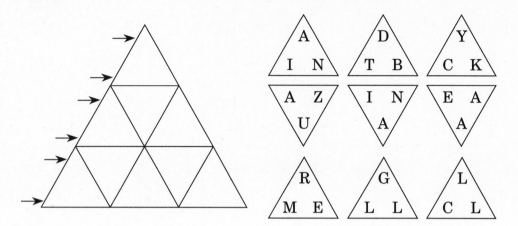

LETTER, PLEASE

Directions for solving are on page 271.

843   896   6678

232884385   96737

46   843   3645474

52648243   273

"24325   36256733."

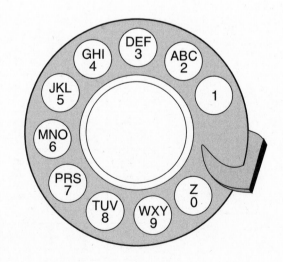

TIPS OF THE ICEBERG

We're back at the Iceberg Diner. After doing some careful addition, answer the following questions:

1. Who made the most in total tips?
2. Who made the least?
3. Which two waitpersons made exactly the same amount?

EMPLOYEE	TIP 1	TIP 2	TIP 3	TIP 4	TIP 5
Hank	$2.15	$1.25	$1.25	$1.30	$1.10
Inez	$1.10	$1.10	$1.00	$1.20	$0.60
Jack	$0.45	$2.20	$2.10	$2.05	$0.45
Ken	$1.50	$1.50	$1.35	$1.25	$2.05
Laura	$2.95	$2.80	$1.20	$1.00	$1.00
Marty	$2.20	$2.00	$2.35	$0.40	$0.85
Noel	$1.00	$2.10	$0.85	$2.00	$1.10

COUNT TO TEN

VISUAL ◆ MATH

Examine the angelfish and starfish and then answer these questions: 1. Which row contains the most angelfish? 2. Which row contains the most starfish? 3. Which row contains an equal number of angelfish and starfish?

BLOCK PARTY

VISUAL ◆ SPATIAL

Directions for solving are on page 235.

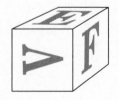 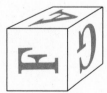  

STAR WORDS

Directions for solving are on page 266.

DAIS   LIED

DEAD   LIVE

DIAL   SAID

DOES   SELL

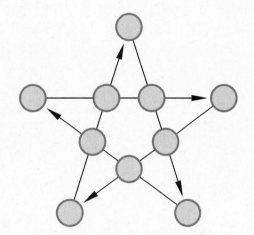

WORD VISIBILITY

See page 248 for solving directions.

1. W K U W A
   S A O N G

2. B L N O K
   Y E E A M

3. D A L M Y
   F E U A N

4. F G E S H
   L A I T V

5. N U V E P
   R I X A T

6. M H T O H
   W Y I C R

COUNT ON IT!

LANGUAGE

Directions for solving are on page 249.

1. S M A T B E   2. I V U H O   3. E C R E N
4. R K U R N   5. E T Y E   6. S E R

$$\frac{}{1}\ \frac{}{2}\ \frac{}{3}\ \frac{}{4}\ \frac{}{5}\ \frac{}{6}\ '\quad \frac{}{1}\quad \frac{}{1}\ \frac{}{2}\ \frac{}{3}\ \frac{}{4}\ \frac{}{5}\ \frac{}{6}$$

$$\frac{}{1}\ \frac{}{2}\ \frac{}{3}\ \frac{}{4}\quad \frac{}{1}\ \frac{}{2}\ \frac{}{3}\ \frac{}{4}\ \frac{}{5}\quad \frac{}{1}\ \frac{}{2}\ \frac{}{3}\ \frac{}{4}\ \frac{}{5}\ \frac{}{6}\ .$$

RELATIONSHIPS QUIZ

LANGUAGE

Directions for solving are on page 276.

1. NEBRASKA is to CORN as IDAHO is to _____.
   (a) potatoes (b) wheat (c) pears (d) onions

2. POTENTIAL is to ACTUAL as FUTURE is to _____.
   (a) space (b) past (c) present (d) tomorrow

3. RED is to PURPLE as YELLOW is to _____.
   (a) green (b) pink (c) banana (d) brown

4. NEW YORK is to YANKEES as CINCINNATI is
   to _____.
   (a) Indians (b) Reds (c) Brewers (d) Rangers

5. MATH is to GEOMETRY as SCIENCE is to _____.
   (a) geography (b) physics (c) history (d) philosophy

WORD WHEEL

WEEK
47

Directions for solving are on page 267. Beginning with the "W" at the top of the wheel, we formed 30 words of three or more letters.

SYMBOL-ISM

Directions for solving are on page 270. For this puzzle, we've already indicated that ✎ = S.

301

Directions for solving are on page 234. Once again, the remaining words will form a thought.

HEAD DOUBLE CORNUCOPIA MEN EXODUS
FRAGRANCE TIME ARE INDEMNITY WEIGH SWAYED
JUDGES HEALS EVACUATION MORE COUPON BY
OVER PROVERBS FEAR STRUTS JOB ALL
NUMBERS THAN HEELS WOUNDS GENESIS
REVERENCE SINGULARITY

Eliminate…

1. the six words that are names of books of the Bible.

2. the three words that form a phrase that means "completely or deeply in love."

3. each word that ends with three consecutive letters of the alphabet, in some order.

4. the two words that make up the title of a 1944 movie starring Barbara Stanwyck and Fred MacMurray.

5. the word that forms the name of a country when its first three letters and last three letters are put together.

6. the four words that form a phrase meaning "an indefinite interval remedies an aggregate of traumas."

7. each word that has five syllables.

SKILLS TEST

VISUAL ◆ LOGIC

Which figure does not belong in the group?

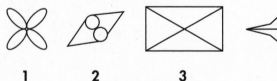

1   2   3   4   5   6

FILLING STATION

Directions for solving are on page 264.

1. H H R S S S (game)

__ O __ __ E __ __ O E __

2. C G G L N R (actor)

__ E O __ __ E   __ __ O O __ E Y

3. G M N R S T (TV show)

" __ __ E Y ' __   A __ A __ O __ Y "

4. C C R S T (country)

__ O __ __ A   __ I __ A

5. C H L R R S T T (fictional character)

__ __ A __ __ E __ __   O ' __ A __ A

MATH ◆ LOGIC

MARCHING ORDERS

Directions for solving are on page 272. We've started the first one for you using the sequence +6 and −2.

1.   FINISH ↑

14	19	22	20	22	28
11	15	17	16	26	30
9	13	10	18	21	24
7	4	8	14	12	20
5	6	9	10	13	16
0	3	2	7	11	14

↑ START

2.   FINISH ↑

13	16	19	18	20	25
9	17	15	16	22	21
8	14	10	11	12	13
2	6	3	8	9	12
4	5	7	5	10	11
0	3	4	6	8	9

↑ START

COUNT THE RECTANGLES VISUAL ◆ SPATIAL

To solve this puzzle, write down the four letters that describe each rectangle (a 4-sided figure) in this diagram. We found 38 rectangles; how many can you locate?

WEEK 47

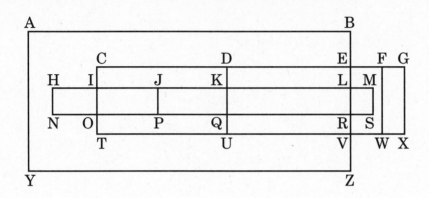

CARD SENSE

LOGIC

Directions for solving are on page 241.

1. The cards in one suit pair are adjacent; but the cards in the other are not.

2. The top three cards include two cards of matching suits and two cards of matching numbers.

3. The tens are both somewhere above the ace.

4. The seven of diamonds isn't adjacent to the ace.

GRAND TOUR

WEEK **48**

Directions for solving are on page 248. This time, you'll be looking for a chain of 5-letter words, starting with CA-CHE-ST (cache, chest).

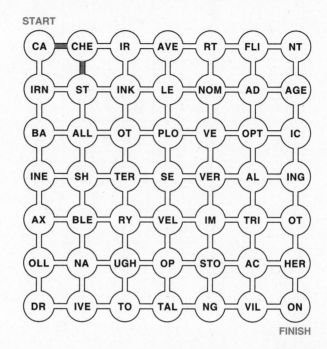

CROSS EXAMINATION

In each set, cross out three groups of letters so that the remaining groups, in order, spell out a word.

1. UN BR AIN PRE OKE DICT ABLE

2. FOR TEL TUN EV ISI ING ON

3. RE ULT VER SI AT ME BLE

4. AR EX CHI PE RI THAN MENT

5. CAT AC AL TI PHE VA TED

6. ST MEC ELO HA NI IRAN SM

7. OP SA PO VER SI ICE TION

8. GE DA TUM OG RA ARY PHY

SUDOKU

LOGIC

Directions for solving are on page 232.

4	1				2	5		
			1				6	8
7				4	2			
	8			9	7			
	4		7		3			
	7	1				4		
	2	9						4
6	7			3				
		3	6				9	7

SWITCHEROO

DECODING

In each group, for the first word and its number equivalent given, determine what the number equivalent is for the second word.

1. LIFE is to 3175 as FILE is to:
   (a) 7531 (b) 3157 (c) 7135 (d) 5173

2. RIOT is to 8462 as TRIO is to:
   (a) 2846 (b) 4862 (c) 6482 (d) 2468

3. RUBY is to 9573 as BURY is to:
   (a) 9537 (b) 3957 (c) 3795 (d) 7593

4. ROCK is to 1329 as CORK is to:
   (a) 2931 (b) 2139 (c) 2913 (d) 2319

5. FOAL is to 8024 as LOAF is to:
   (a) 4082 (b) 4028 (c) 2048 (d) 4208

6. WHAT is to 5786 as THAW is to:
   (a) 6785 (b) 6875 (c) 8657 (d) 6857

WHAT'S YOUR NUMBER?

Can you figure out the sequence of numbers in the left-hand, top, and right-hand spokes and what missing number goes into the circle with the question mark in the bottom spoke?

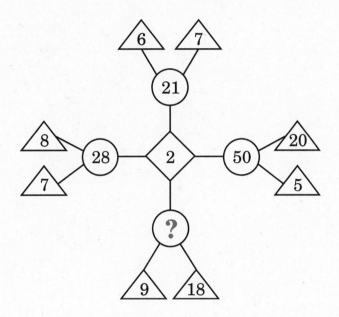

WAYWORDS

Directions for solving are on page 254. This time, you'll be looking for a 10-word thought beginning with A.

JUSTICE	WON	AS	NOBLE
ENEMY	LOST	IS	BAD
FRIEND	AN	AS	BRING
FLIMSY	A	PARTICIPANT	PILLOW

SEVEN WORD ZINGER

LANGUAGE

Directions for solving are on page 253.

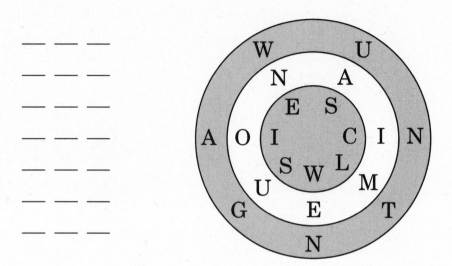

___ ___ ___

___ ___ ___

___ ___ ___

___ ___ ___

___ ___ ___

___ ___ ___

___ ___ ___

EASY PICKINGS

LANGUAGE

To solve, simply cross out one letter in each pair below. When the puzzle is completed correctly, the remaining letters will spell out a quote by Francis Bacon.

NE AC OT CU RS ME,   RT OT   EB EM

HC EO ML OM AO YN ED EN DR,

SM NU SF TO   NB EA   OW BR HE EY RE TD.

308

IN THE ABSTRACT

WEEK
48

Directions for solving are on page 229.

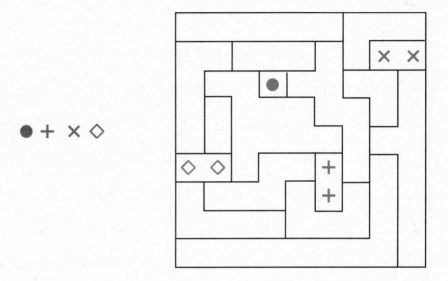

● + × ◇

ARROW MAZE

Solving directions are on page 235.

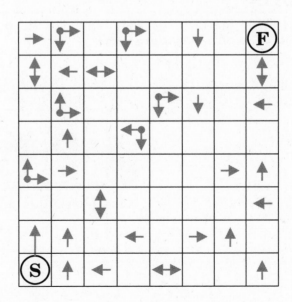

ASSOCIATIONS LANGUAGE

Directions for solving are on page 236.

WHAT WAS THE HEADLINE FOR THE REVIEW OF THE RESTAURANT ON THE MOON?

GRATEFUL HAWK ACHE REASON SPECTATOR EXACT

ROME PAIN ATTITUDE ECCENTRIC TASTEFUL

FALCON FANCY LEMONADE OPULENT OBSERVER

OMINOUS VENICE DUSTY JUICE NOBLE BIZARRE

OTTER INQUISITIVE ARTISTIC NEGLECT TICKLE

EAGLE MONEY CURIOUS OVEN EYEWITNESS SYRUP

ODD PLANET SORE HEROIC OVERLOOK EXPLAIN

CIDER RICE NAPLES DISREGARD ELEVATOR NOSY

SLIDE RULE LANGUAGE

Directions for solving are on page 251. Here, you're to form 4-letter words. We found 27 words, including CART.

Your list of words:

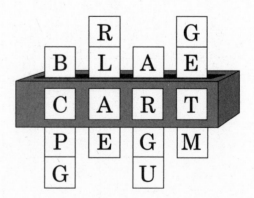

ANAGRAM MAZE

WEEK
48

Directions for solving are on page 249. This time, there are 21 words to anagram and the first word you'll be anagramming is SAIL.

1 LIEU	2 FLIT	3 WAKE	4 ROCK	5 PROD	6 SAIL
7 TINY	8 HOES	9 FOIL	10 QUIT	11 ZONE	12 LOCK
13 CLAP	14 NEON	15 STUB	16 TEAM	17 AFAR	18 GONE
19 FINE	20 ALOE	21 CUKE	22 CHIN	23 LIVE	24 LIPS
25 KNEE	26 DIET	27 RAPS	28 FAIL	29 POUT	30 PACE
31 SHIP	32 CLEF	33 LEAP	34 FURS	35 SHAM	36 STEP

ALL IN A ROW

Directions for solving are on page 228. This time, look for the most groups of consecutive numbers adding up to 16.

A. 8 2 6 3 1 7 5 2 4 3 2 6 9 8 2 4 6 1 3 2 8 3 6 9

B. 1 3 4 9 8 6 3 1 5 4 3 8 2 7 6 3 2 4 8 3 5 6 3 5

C. 5 6 8 3 2 4 6 1 8 7 3 3 5 6 1 8 3 2 3 7 4 5 4 9

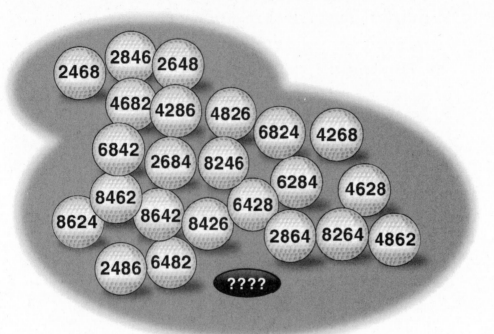

HOLE IN ONE

Twenty-four golfers entered a hole-in-one contest. Each golfer was given a ball with a different 4-digit number combination using the numbers 2, 4, 6, and 8 on it. Looking at the 23 balls still on the green, can you figure out what combination is on the ball that won the contest?

IN THE MONEY

MATH

How quickly can you convert each bag of money into dollars and cents and determine which one contains the greatest amount?

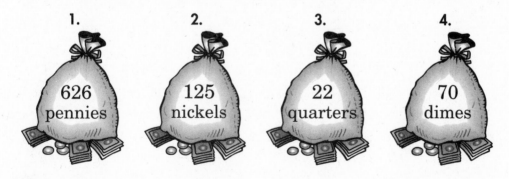

CARD SENSE

Five playing cards — the three of diamonds, the eight of clubs, the ace of spades, and the ace and queen of hearts — were shuffled and put in a pile, one on top of another. Using the information in the clues below, can you identify each card's position in the pile?

1. The aces are adjacent.

2. The diamond is below the club.

3. The eight is below a heart.

4. The three is above the spade.

5. Two red cards are adjacent.

WORD WHEEL

Starting with the "C" at the arrow, see how many everyday words of three or more letters you can find going clockwise. Don't skip over any letters. For example, if you saw the letters C, A, R, E, D, you would score five words: CAR, CARE, CARED, ARE, RED. We formed 33 words.

PRESIDENTIAL FINALES

LANGUAGE

The list below consists of the names of 10 U.S. Presidents, but we've removed all of their letters except for the last letters in their first and last names. Can you write one letter on each dash to complete the names of the Chief Executives?

1. _ _ _ _ _ E   _ _ _ H

2. _ _ _ L   _ _ _ _ _ _ _ N

3. _ _ _ _ Y   _ _ _ _ _ N

4. _ _ _ _ _ _ _ N   _ _ _ _ _ _ _ _ _ T

5. _ _ _ _ _ E   _ _ _ _ _ _ _ _ _ N

6. _ _ _ _ _ T   _ _ _ _ _ _ _ _ _ R

7. _ _ _ _ _ _ D   _ _ _ _ N

8. _ _ _ _ _ D   _ _ _ _ _ N

9. _ _ _ _ _ _ T   _ _ _ _ _ R

10. _ _ _ N   _ _ _ _ S

DEDUCTION PROBLEM

LOGIC

Andrew, Bill, Charlie, Dan, and Ernie were seated around a circular table. Ernie's brother, who was sitting to Charlie's right, noticed that no two people whose names start with consecutive letters of the alphabet were sitting next to each other. Where was each man sitting in relation to Charlie?

COUNT TO TEN

Examine the smiles and frowns below and then answer these questions: 1. Which row contains the most SMILES? 2. Which row contains the most FROWNS? 3. Which row contains an equal number of SMILES and FROWNS?

1.
2.
3.
4.
5.
6.
7.
8.
9.
10.

ON THE LINE

Can you trace this figure without lifting your pencil from the paper, crossing, or retracing your own path?

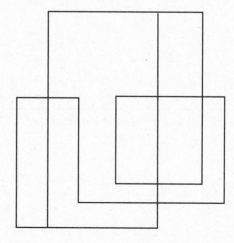

ALPHABET SOUP

LANGUAGE ◆ VISUAL

Not every letter of the alphabet appears in the diagram below. When you spot a letter that does, cross it off the alphabet provided. Next, anagram the letters that do not appear in the diagram to form the name of a rock star.

Q	L	K	U	A	M	R	D	E	X	P	F
V	U	B	H	R	K	Z	P	W	D	J	M
X	Y	U	K	W	E	P	A	F	H	M	O
D	M	O	R	E	C	X	U	Y	L	J	Q
M	B	Z	A	P	K	W	Q	X	H	L	Y
B	R	M	Q	W	D	X	L	K	Y	V	H
C	B	U	P	Q	W	J	F	V	R	E	K
Z	W	P	K	R	A	Q	Y	V	J	L	O
K	B	F	E	P	R	W	M	Z	D	X	Q
W	J	H	R	F	Y	O	C	V	A	Z	P

A	J	S
B	K	T
C	L	U
D	M	V
E	N	W
F	O	X
G	P	Y
H	Q	Z
I	R	

_____

SKILLS TEST

LANGUAGE ◆ LOGIC

Determine which tile of letters does not belong with the others below.

BE	WZ	MP	FI	QU	OR

TIPS OF THE ICEBERG

This chart shows the gratuities each waiter earned on a recent breakfast shift at the Iceberg Diner. All you have to do is some careful addition and then answer the following questions:

1. Who made the most in total tips?
2. Who made the least?
3. Which two waiters made exactly the same amount?

EMPLOYEE	TIP 1	TIP 2	TIP 3	TIP 4	TIP 5
Al	$2.10	$1.70	$1.75	$1.30	$2.95
Brenda	$1.25	$2.10	$0.65	$2.00	$1.65
Charlie	$0.75	$1.70	$1.70	$1.70	$1.70
Dena	$1.90	$1.70	$0.75	$2.00	$1.10
Ed	$1.45	$0.70	$1.15	$1.75	$1.00
Flora	$1.70	$2.25	$1.05	$0.95	$1.90
Greta	$1.70	$1.05	$1.15	$1.10	$4.00
Hank	$0.75	$1.45	$1.25	$4.50	$1.05
Inez	$1.10	$3.20	$2.10	$2.00	$1.90
Jack	$2.25	$1.30	$1.90	$1.35	$1.95

ALPHABET CIRCLE MAZE

VISUAL

Start at A at the bottom, continue through the alphabet only once, and finish at the Z in the center. You will pass through other letters when going from one letter to the next, but move in only one direction, either around a circle or along a spoke. Don't enter or cross through the Z until you are finished.

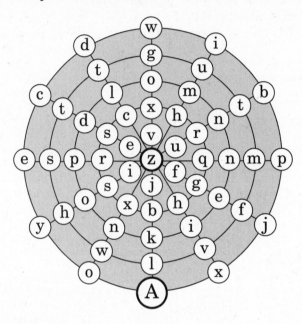

TARGET SHOOT

LANGUAGE

Find the two letters which, when entered into the center circle of each target, will form three 6-letter words reading across.

1.

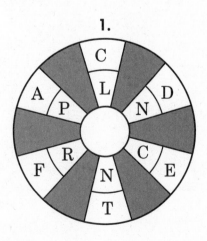

2.

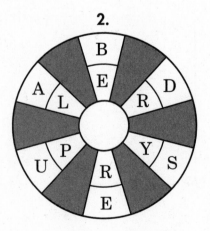

KEEP ON MOVING

The goal is to move from the shaded square to the asterisk. Since the shaded square has the number 3 in it, you must move three squares up, down, left, or right, but not diagonally. In the new square will be another number; move that number of squares up, down, left, or right, continuing in this way until you reach the asterisk. It's okay to cross your own path.

1	3	2	1	5	3
2	1	4	2	2	2
3	3	3	4	4	1
5	3	*	1	4	4
4	3	2	2	1	3
2	4	4	1	4	5

SUDOKU

Place a number into each box so each row across, column down, and small 9-box square within the larger square (there are 9 of these) contains 1 through 9.

	7			8	6			
	1	8	3				2	
3			2	9				8
		6			3	8	5	2
				6				
1	2	7	5			3		
5				7	9			6
	4				1	7	3	
			6	3			1	

319

FUN WITH FACTS AND FIGURES   MATH

This puzzle tests you on five little facts and figures. Solve the quiz in the order given since each answer is used in the next statement. There are no fractions used here.

1. Take the number of seasons in the year and multiply it by the number on the black ball in a game of pool.

2. Next, subtract the number of Great Lakes.

3. Now divide by the supposed number of a cat's lives.

4. Add the number of E's in the phrase CREEPIER EERINESS.

5. Add the number of steering wheels in a standard car.

Our answer is Bo Derek's rating in a famous 1970s movie.
Is yours?

RINGERS   VISUAL ◆ LANGUAGE

Each Ringer is composed of five rings. Use your imagination to rotate the rings so that you spell out four 5-letter words reading from the outside to the inside when all five rings are aligned correctly.

1.
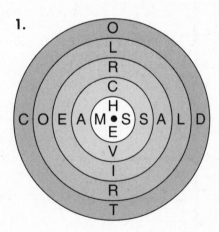

2.
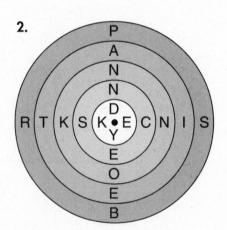

GRAND TOUR

WEEK
50

Form a continuous chain of 5-letter words moving through the maze from START to FINISH. The second part of one word becomes the first part of the next word. This puzzle starts with LUR-CH-AMP (lurch, champ).

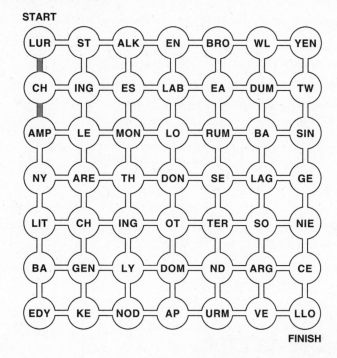

START

FINISH

ANIMAL CHARADES

In the Charade below, each line contains a clue to a letter of the alphabet. These letters, in the given order, will spell out the name of an animal. The animal's identity is also hinted at in the last sentence of the Charade.

My FIRST is in WOODCHUCK but not in CLOCK;

My SECOND is in FALCON but not in FLOCK;

My THIRD is in OPOSSUM and in MUST;

My FOURTH is in HORSE and in RUST;

My FIFTH is in BOBCAT but not in BASSOON;

My SIXTH is in HERRING but not in HARPOON;

My SEVENTH is in OSTRICH and in CLARINET.

My WHOLE is a rodent often kept as a pet.

321

ANTONYMS QUIZ

LANGUAGE

An antonym is a word that is opposite in meaning to another word; for example, "cold" is the antonym of "hot." One of the words following each capitalized word is the antonym of that word.

1. DISMAL   a. inferior   b. efficient   c. cheerful

2. VALOR   a. cowardice   b. duty   c. exhilaration

3. CAPTIVITY   a. enormity   b. freedom   c. flair

4. INDUSTRIOUS   a. lazy   b. sporty   c. boorish

5. MINUTE   a. enlightened   b. fluent   c. immense

6. DEARTH   a. wealth   b. enmity   c. spoof

7. PLIABLE   a. discrete   b. madcap   c. rigid

8. MISER   a. dunce   b. spendthrift   c. cleric

BULL'S-EYE LETTER

LANGUAGE

Add the SAME single letter to each group of three letters, then rearrange the letters to form six everyday 4-letter words.

— — — —

— — — —

— — — —

— — — —

— — — —

— — — —

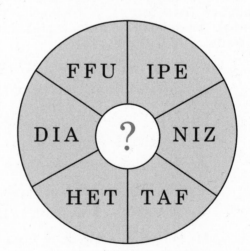

ARROW MAZE

Starting at the S and following the arrow leading out of it, see if you can find your way to F. When you reach an arrow, you MUST follow its direction and continue in that direction until you come to the next arrow. When you reach a two-headed arrow, you can choose either direction. It's okay to cross your own path.

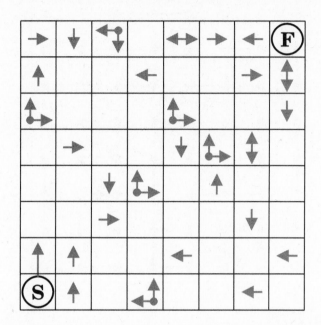

LANGUAGE

LICENSE PLATES

Each box contains six letters of the names of former cast members from "Saturday Night Live." The top three letters are part of the first name and the bottom three are part of the last name, in order.

1.
```
D A M
S A N
```

2.
```
 I K E
 M Y E
```

3.
```
E V Y
A S E
```

4.
```
D I E
P H Y
```

5.
```
A N E
U R T
```

6.
```
I L L
F E R
```

ROUND TRIP

When this puzzle has been completed correctly, you will have made a round trip through its set of dots. You must visit every dot exactly once, make no diagonal moves, and return to your starting point. Parts of the right paths are shown; can you find the rest?

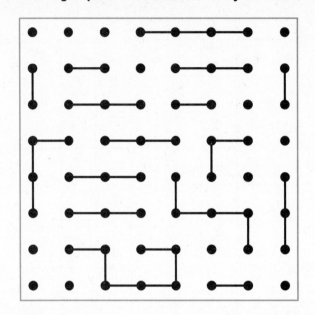

ELIMINATION

Cross off the capitalized words below according to the instructions given. The remaining words, in order, will form a truism.

PRINCES SOLEMN SIZING FIRST TRUDGE MELONS IMPRESSIONS CAROUSEL ARE ADORATION THE LEMONS MOST PLANKS LASTING THERE

Eliminate...

1. the word that is a title of a Broadway musical.
2. the word that can be split into two words, one meaning "fuss" and the other meaning "allowance."
3. the two words that can mean "lumber."
4. the three words that are anagrams of each other.
5. the word that is a plural, but becomes a singular word when "s" is added at the end.
6. the word that becomes a new word when "lender" is inserted somewhere inside.
7. the word that becomes its opposite when the first letter is deleted.

CARD SENSE

Directions for solving are on page 313.

1. Neither club is on the bottom.

2. The spade is below the ten.

3. The red cards are adjacent.

4. The diamond is below the queen.

5. The sevens are adjacent.

6. The ace is below the heart.

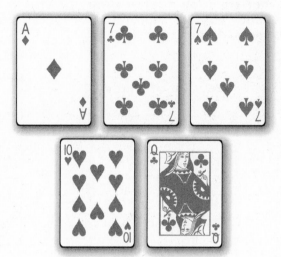

DOVETAILED WORDS

Two related words, with their letters in the correct order, are combined in each row of letters. Can you find both words? In a line like POBOOXDELER, or POboOxDeLEr, you can see the two words POODLE and BOXER.

1. P A R U P R I N C E O T   _____ _____

2. P E A A I S N E T E L R   _____ _____

3. M A N O G A V E Z I L N E   _____ _____

4. O Y E R A L L O N W G E   _____ _____

5. W I C L A L O C T U W S   _____ _____

WORD HUNT

LANGUAGE

Find words by moving from one letter to any adjoining letter. You may start a word with any letter in the diagram. In forming a word you may return to a letter as often as you wish, but do not stand on a letter using it twice in direct succession. In this Word Hunt, you are searching for 5-letter names of girls (like BETTY). We found 10 girls' names.

Your list of words:

T	E	B	U	S
T	K	H	I	A
Y	C	A	R	N
C	M	D	O	E
A	N	I	L	H

U.S. M's

LANGUAGE

The list below consists of the names of six U.S. states, but we've removed all of their letters except for the M's. Can you write one letter on each dash to complete the names of the states?

1. __ __ __ __ __ M __

2. M __ __ __ __

3. __ __ __   __ __ __ __ __ __

4. __ __ __   __ __ M __ __ __ __ __ __

5. M __ __ __ __ __ __ __ __

6. __ __ __ __ __ __ M __

RING LOGIC

Complete the diagram below by drawing in the links between the rings using the statements below. Assume that all the rings in the picture are locked rigidly into position and cannot be moved in any direction. Consider yourself a true ringmaster if you can find the solution in under six minutes!

1. Every ring except for rings E and M is linked at least twice.

2. Ring E is in front of both A and I.

3. Ring M is behind both I and Q.

4. The right sides of rings F, L, and P are to the front.

5. The bottom of ring J is to the front.

6. The pattern is symmetrical from left to right.

SLIDE RULE

Slide each column of letters up or down in the box and form as many everyday 4-letter words as you can in the windows where SENT is now. We formed 23 words.

Your list of words:

PROGRESSION

Which of the numbered figures, 1 through 5, replaces the question mark?

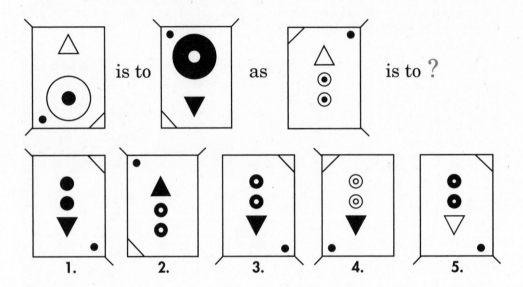

is to ... as ... is to ?

CIRCLE MATH

MATH

Each overlapping circle is identified by a letter having a different number value from 1 to 9. Where some circles overlap, there is a number: It is the SUM of the values of the letters in those overlapping circles. Can you figure out the correct values for the letters? We've started you off by telling you that B equals 8.

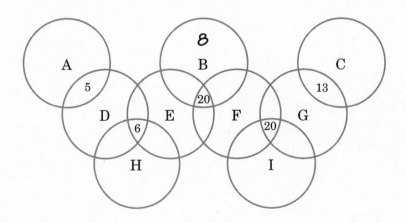

LOOSE TILE

WEEK
51

The tray on the right seemed the ideal place to store the set of loose dominoes. Unfortunately, when the tray was full, one domino was left over. Determine the arrangement of the dominoes in the tray and which is the Loose Tile.

WHAT'S YOUR NUMBER?

Can you figure out the sequence of numbers in the boxes below and what missing numbers go into the spaces with the question marks?

| 3 | 7 | | 8 | 17 | | 23 | 47 | | ? | ? |

329

WORD WHEEL

Directions for solving are on page 313. Beginning with the "C" at the top of the wheel, we formed 32 words of three or more letters.

KEEP ON MOVING

Directions for solving are on page 319.
It's okay to cross your own path.

3	1	3	4	3	3
1	3	2	2	3	3
4	3	2	✳	3	2
3	1	2	3	2	3
1	3	1	3	4	2
4	2	2	2	3	2

COUNT THE TRAPEZOIDS

Write down the four letters that describe each trapezoid (a four-sided figure with only two parallel sides). We found 24 trapezoids; how many can you find?

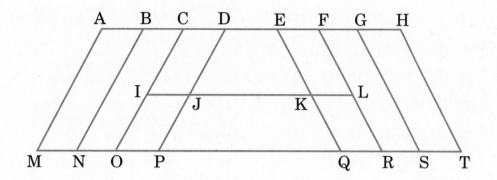

SENTENCE TEASER

LOGIC

Read the four statements A–D below, and assume that these statements are all true. Next, read statements 1–4 and, using the information received from statements A–D, try to determine if the final four statements are true or false.

A. All Martians have six feet.

B. Only Venusians have four hands.

C. Aliens with four hands always have six feet.

D. Only aliens with four hands have tails.

• • •

1. Venusians have tails.

2. Martians have tails.

3. Venusians have six feet.

4. A Venusian has four hands, a tail, and six feet.

WORD CHARADE

VISUAL ◆ SPATIAL

Find each letter in the diagram according to the instructions, and write each letter on its dash to spell out a 6-letter word.

My first letter is surrounded only by letters from the first half of the alphabet.

M	O	P	V	X	N	U	M
Z	L	E	M	I	O	S	A
N	F	T	D	K	B	F	N
Q	I	K	B	T	F	N	P
A	Q	S	G	C	L	P	S
N	G	B	Z	K	D	Z	I
Z	R	Z	E	B	N	J	R
U	O	I	M	E	L	B	C

My second letter has the same letter to its immediate left and its immediate right.

My third letter appears only in the first and eighth columns.

My fourth letter appears directly below a Q and to the immediate left of a B.

My fifth letter appears only in even rows.

My sixth letter is the first letter of a word reading upwards in one of the columns.

SUDOKU

LOGIC

Directions for solving are on page 319.

	2	3	8					1
	4			1	2	9		
9					4	2		
	5	8			6			
	9			5			8	
			4			5	2	
		4	2					7
		5	6	4			9	
	3				8	1	4	

OVERLAY

When you overlay the three diagrams in the top row, which of the three lettered diagrams, A, B, or C, will be formed?

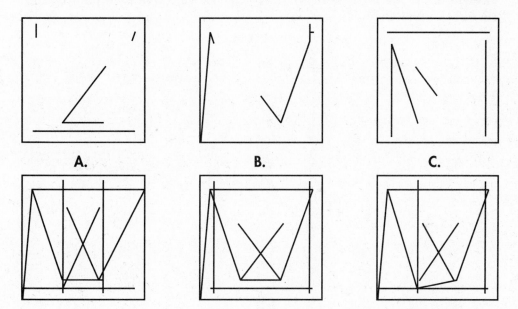

A.   B.   C.

DEDUCTION PROBLEM

The ages of Ms. Ullman and three other women are different whole numbers from 38 to 41. Some of the women are sensitive about the subject so that in any conversation in which ages are mentioned, while those under 40 always tell the truth, those 40 and over always lie. From the following statements made in one such conversation, can you determine each woman's full name and age?

Ella said, "Hannah is 40, and Grace is younger than Flo."

Flo said, "I am not Ms. Tripp."

Grace said, "Ms. Smith is older than Ella."

Hannah said, "Ms. Tripp is older than Ms. Ryan, and I am 40."

COUNT TO TEN

Examine the apples and pears below and then answer these questions: 1. Which row contains the most APPLES? 2. Which row contains the most PEARS? 3. Which row contains an equal number of APPLES and PEARS?

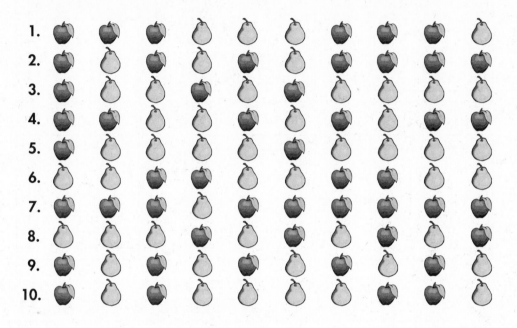

BLOCK PARTY

Study the different views of the block, and draw what should appear on the face that has a question mark.

MISSING DOMINOES

In this game you use all 28 dominoes that are in a standard set. Each one has a different combination from 0-0, 0-1, 0-2, to 6-6. Domino halves with the same number of dots lie next to each other. To avoid confusion we have used an open circle to indicate a zero. Can you fill in the missing white dominoes to complete the board?

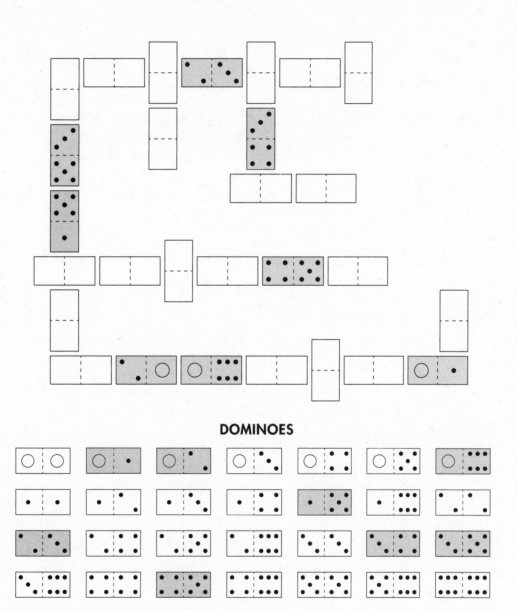

DOMINOES

335

ANSWERS

BULL'S-EYE LETTER (Week 1)
The Bull's-Eye Letter is I: bike, main, lied (or idle), wait, taxi, bill.

MAGIC NUMBER SQUARES
(Week 1)

1.

7	21	20	10
18	12	13	15
14	16	17	11
19	9	8	22

2.

33	23	31	9
13	27	19	37
11	29	21	35
39	17	25	15

ANAGRAM MAZE (Week 1)

1			4	5	6
7			10		12
13	14	15	16		18
				23	24
				29	
				35	36

The path through the maze, with only one anagram given for each is 1. lane; 7. dire; 13. neon; 14. rent; 15. stub; 16. lips; 10. acne; 4. chum; 5. ours; 6. calm; 12. heat; 18. done; 24. chin; 23. evil; 29. lacy; 35. step; 36. team.

ALL IN A ROW (Week 1)
Row C. Row A contains 4 groups: 32122, 1225, 1261, and 352. Row B contains 3 groups: 622, 42121, and 73. Row C contains 5 groups: 55, 3133, 82, 271, and 4123.

WAYWORDS (Week 1)
Every sorrow will pass and be forgotten.

SENTENCE TEASER (Week 1)
1. False. Clue D states that dogs with green eyes have black fur, but says nothing about cats. Therefore, it can't be stated that short-haired cats do not have black fur; 2. True. Long-haired dogs with long tails have green eyes (clue B). By clue D, dogs with green eyes have black fur; 3. True. Short-haired cats have long tails (clue A). By clue C, cats with long tails have blue eyes. 4. False. Cats with long tails have blue eyes (clue C), but cats with short tails may also have blue eyes.

ARROW MAZE (Week 1)

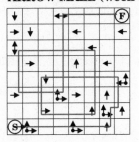

SYMBOL-ISM (Week 1)
People who look backward with worry are likely to bump into trouble ahead.

DEDUCTION PROBLEM (Week 1)
Both parrot #1 and parrot #2 say that parrot #2 is Polly. Since only one parrot is telling the truth, these two aren't both telling the truth. They both are lying and parrot #2 isn't Polly. Parrot #3, then, is telling the truth, and said that parrot #1 isn't Polly. By elimination, parrot #3 is Polly.

MIXED MENAGERIE (Week 1)
Row 2 contains five different birds.

SUDOKU (Week 1)

2	3	4	9	7	5	8	1	6
1	7	6	2	3	8	4	9	5
5	8	9	1	4	6	3	2	7
7	1	8	4	5	3	2	6	9
4	6	5	7	2	9	1	8	3
3	9	2	8	6	1	7	5	4
6	5	1	3	8	4	9	7	2
9	2	3	6	1	7	5	4	8
8	4	7	5	9	2	6	3	1

THE LINEUP (Week 1)
1. Q; 2. threatened; 3. D; 4. crying; 5. wilt, threat, threaten, eaten, defy, bite.

TARGET SHOOT (Week 2)
1. RE: stress, agreed, barely; 2. LK: folksy, silken, walked.

FUN WITH FACTS AND FIGURES (Week 2)
1. 4 x 4 = 16; 2. 16 + 13 = 29; 3. 29 x 3 = 87; 4. 87 − 29 = 58; 5. 58 + 2 = 60.

WHAT'S YOUR NUMBER? (Week 2)
25 — first and second numbers in each row and column add up to the third.

IN THE ABSTRACT (Week 2)
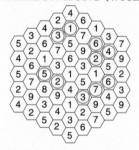

U.S. N's (Week 2)
1. North Carolina; 2. Pennsylvania; 3. Indiana; 4. Connecticut; 5. Rhode Island; 6. Montana; 7. Wisconsin; 8. Maine; 9. Nevada; 10. Oregon.

ANTONYMS QUIZ (Week 2)
1. c; 2. a; 3. b; 4. c; 5. b; 6. c; 7. a; 8. c.

CARD SENSE (Week 2)
Since no two black cards are adjacent (clue 1), the three of diamonds and the ace of hearts are second and fourth, in some order. By clue 2, then, the four of spades is on top, the three of diamonds is second, and the ace of hearts is fourth. The queen of clubs is third and the four of clubs is on the bottom (clue 3). In summary, from top to bottom: four of spades, three of diamonds, queen of clubs, ace of hearts, four of clubs.

W COUNT (Week 2)
There are 29 W's.

ELIMINATION (Week 2)
1. onion; 2. predict (cider); 3. bleach; 4. plume (plum); 5. fortune (four, ten); 6. carve (crave); 7. pinnacle (pelican). "Every day should offer something new."

WORD VISIBILITY (Week 2)
1. thigh; 2. grown; 3. easel; 4. scout; 5. truth; 6. grape.

LICENSE PLATES (Week 2)
1. Martha Stewart; 2. Oprah Winfrey; 3. Rosie O'Donnell; 4. Ellen DeGeneres; 5. Tyra Banks; 6. Kelly Ripa.

ASSOCIATIONS (Week 2)
rat, squirrel, mouse; bound, jump, leap; flannel, linen, burlap; bravery, courage, valor; marigold, lilac, daisy; screwdriver, hammer, pliers; diamond, emerald, ruby; pecan, cashew, almond. Answer to riddle: "Because he was a cheetah."

SKILLS TEST (Week 3)
Columbus, Ohio; Topeka, Kansas; Lansing, Michigan; Phoenix, Arizona; Hartford, Connecticut.

HEXAGON HUNT (Week 3)

PATCH PUZZLE (Week 3)

CODE WORD (Week 3)
Code Word: culminates. Small coins are not of much value nowadays, but a dime can be a terrific screwdriver.

MARCHING ORDERS (Week 3)

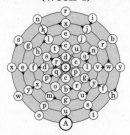

DOVETAILED WORDS (Week 3)

1. uncle, aunt; 2. pelican, duck; 3. squash, radish; 4. cherry, apple; 5. yellow, green.

SYMBOL-ISM (Week 3)

It is far better to have failed than not to have tried at all.

PRESIDENTIAL VOWELS (Week 3)

1. Abraham Lincoln; 2. Ronald Reagan; 3. George Washington; 4. Theodore Roosevelt; 5. Ulysses Grant; 6. Dwight Eisenhower; 7. Calvin Coolidge; 8. John Quincy Adams; 9. James Monroe; 10. Bill Clinton.

COUNT THE TRIANGLES (Week 3)

There are 13 triangles: ACB, ADB, ADC, ADF, AFB, AFE, AGE, AGF, BCF, BDF, BFE, CDF, and DGF.

EASY PICKINGS (Week 3)

If there's no alternative, there's no problem.

TRI, TRI AGAIN (Week 3)

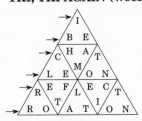

MAGNIFIND (Week 3)

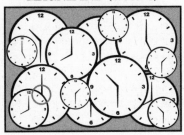

ALPHABET CIRCLE MAZE (Week 4)

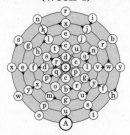

SALT & PEPPER (Week 4)

1. the seventh row; 2. the fourth row; 3. the second row.

ONLINE NETWORK (Week 4)

The man who reads has riches in himself.

WAYWORDS (Week 4)

Far from the eyes is far from the heart.

THE LINEUP (Week 4)

1. N; 2. hieroglyphics; 3. S; 4. giraffe; 5. jams, exit, zest.

BLOCK PARTY (Week 4)

WORD CHARADE (Week 4)

R	D	W	Ⓝ	H	A	X	B
K	C	U	J	B	G	Ⓛ	S
P	Ⓝ	P	H	T	Ⓟ	U	Q
I	Ⓛ	Q	O	W	R	Ⓣ	G
J	T	S	Ⓔ	R	C	Ⓝ	O
X	F	Ⓐ	W	Ⓛ	M	I	C
M	B	Ⓝ	F	O	U	A	K
S	R	T	U	H	E	F	P

planet

MAGIC NUMBER SQUARES (Week 4)

1.

55	13	16	46
22	40	37	31
34	28	25	43
19	49	52	10

2.

14	56	53	23
47	29	32	38
35	41	44	26
50	20	17	59

DEDUCTION PROBLEM (Week 4)

If Al gets his wish of playing center field, both Bob and Chuck could get their wishes also, so Al will play either right or left field. If he will play right field, Bob and Chuck could still get their wishes, with Bob playing left field and Chuck in center. Al, then, will play left field. By elimination, Chuck is the one boy that gets his wish by not playing left field. Chuck will play right field and Bob will play center field.

SUDOKU (Week 4)

5	4	6	8	1	9	7	2	3
7	8	2	6	3	5	9	1	4
1	3	9	4	2	7	8	5	6
2	9	5	3	8	1	6	4	7
4	7	3	9	5	6	2	8	1
6	1	8	7	4	2	5	3	9
3	2	7	5	6	4	1	9	8
8	6	1	2	9	3	4	7	5
9	5	4	1	7	8	3	6	2

BULL'S-EYE LETTER (Week 4)

The Bull's-Eye Letter is Y: myth, zany, hymn, very, year, yarn.

SENTENCE TEASER (Week 4)

1. Yes, people who eat carrots have good memories (A), and therefore work hard (D). 2. No, according to C, people with good memories are generous, but it does not follow that all people who are generous have good memories and hence work hard (D). 3. Yes, people who eat carrots have good memories (A), and therefore are generous (C). 4. No, people who eat broccoli are generous (B), but as in number 2, it does not follow that all people who are generous have good memories.

ARROW MAZE (Week 4)

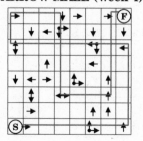

WORD HUNT (Week 5)

1. bean, corn, date, fig, kale, leek, lime, okra, pea, pear, plum, yam.

2. apple, berry, cress, grape, guava, lemon, mango, melon, onion, peach, prune.

ALL IN A ROW (Week 5)

Row C. Row A contains 5 groups: 4128, 3165, 16521, 9321, and 582. Row B contains 5 groups: 7143, 143331, 96, 112353, and 9222. Row C contains 7 groups: 78, 285, 546, 62232, 3291, 744, and 1644.

FUN WITH FACTS AND FIGURES (Week 5)

1. $12 \div 3 = 4$; 2. $4 + 4 = 8$; 3. 8×4 (Ohio) = 32; 4. $32 - 26 = 6$; 5. $6 + 3 = 9$.

ANAGRAM MAZE (Week 5)

1	2				
7			10	11	12
13	14		16		18
	20	21	22		24
				29	30
				35	

The path through the maze, with only one anagram given for each is 2. owns; 1. tone; 7. shot; 13. free; 14. peas; 20. cups; 21. oils; 22. blot; 16. dais; 10. what; 11. drop; 12. tape; 18. arms; 24. hubs; 30. went; 29. meat; 36. kiss.

MARCHING ORDERS (Week 5)

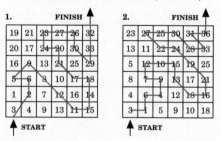

TIPS OF THE ICEBERG (Week 5)

1. Charlie ($17.05); 2. Dena ($9.55); 3. Al and Jack ($16.65).

CROSS PATHS (Week 5)

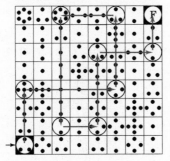

POP! (Week 5)

abridge, bridge, bride (or ridge), ride, rid, id, I.

CARD SENSE (Week 5)

Since the nine of hearts is between the diamonds (clue 2) and the diamonds are between the fours (clue 1), the order of the cards is four, diamond, nine of hearts, diamond, four. The top card is not the four of clubs (clue 3), so it is the four of spades and the bottom card is the four of clubs. Also by clue 3, the three of diamonds is second from the top, and by elimination, the ace of diamonds is fourth. In summary, from top to bottom: four of spades, three of diamonds, nine of hearts, ace of diamonds, and four of clubs.

IN THE MONEY (Week 5)

1. $13.75; 2. $16.00; 3. $12.02; 4. $13.50. Bag #2 contains the most money.

TRIANGULAR SQUARE (Week 5)

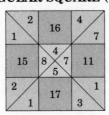

IN THE BALANCE (Week 5)

Four triangles. Scale 1 shows that one triangle equals three circles, so two triangles equal six circles. Since scale 2 shows that two circles equal one square, six circles equal three squares. Two triangles, then, equal three squares, and eight triangles equal 12 squares. Four squares equal two diamonds on scale 3, so 12 squares equal six diamonds. Since eight triangles equal six diamonds, four triangles equal three diamonds to balance scale 4.

CARD SENSE (Week 6)

The king of clubs isn't on the bottom (clue 2). By clue 4, then, the king of clubs is on top or directly between the four of clubs and the two of spades, in some order. If it were on top, the second card would be black (clue 4). By clue 2, the second card wouldn't be the two of spades, so it would be the four of clubs. This, however, contradicts clue 3. Therefore, the king of clubs isn't on top; it's directly between the four of clubs and the two of spades, in some order. The four of clubs, then, rests on the king of clubs, and the king of clubs rests on the two of spades (clue 2). The six of hearts is somewhere above the four of clubs (clue 3) but isn't on top (clue 1), so the jack of diamonds is on top and the six of hearts is second from the top. In summary from top to bottom: jack of diamonds, six of hearts, four of clubs, king of clubs, two of spades.

POP! (Week 6)

streams, steams, teams, team, tam, am, a.

CROSS PATHS (Week 6)

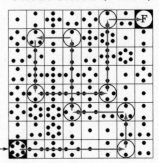

TRIANGULAR SQUARE (Week 6)

IN THE ABSTRACT (Week 6)

ASSOCIATIONS (Week 6)

deer, moose, elk; scare, frighten, startle; drop, dive, plunge; waterless, dry, arid; magenta, scarlet, crimson; fennel, rosemary, tarragon; ton, pound, ounce; grapefruit, lemon, lime. Answer to riddle: "He uses the paws button."

TARGET SHOOT (Week 6)

1. CH: orchid, itched, richer; 2. AZ: blazer, amazed, snazzy.

ELIMINATION (Week 6)

1. mouth (myth); 2. livid; 3. nectar (Nebraska, Connecticut, Arkansas); 4. hungry (Hungary); 5. eerie; 6. kayak; 7. sprout. "Opportunity lost cannot be recalled."

V COUNT (Week 6)

There are 34 V's.

WORD WHEEL (Week 6)

abs, absolve, absolvent, sol, solve, solvent, vent, entry, try, tryst, star, starch, tar, arc, arch, archway, way, wayward, war, ward, wardrobe, rob, robe, before, for, fore, ore.

SEVEN WORD ZINGER (Week 6)

bed, cry, nag, zoo, gum, soy, ale.

WORD VISIBILITY (Week 6)

1. tickle; 2. parent; 3. stripe; 4. silent; 5. carpet; 6. throne.

PATCH PUZZLE (Week 7)

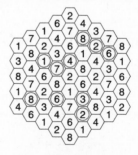

EASY PICKINGS (Week 7)

Children under twelve must be accompanied by money.

BLOCK PARTY (Week 7)

HEXAGON HUNT (Week 7)

WHAT'S YOUR NUMBER? (Week 7)

4 — sum of the first and second numbers in each row and column equals the sum of the third and fourth numbers.

CODE WORD (Week 7)

Code Word: dragonflies. The larger the island of knowledge, the longer the shoreline of wonder.

MAGNIFIND (Week 7)

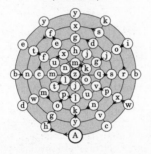

ALPHABET CIRCLE MAZE (Week 7)

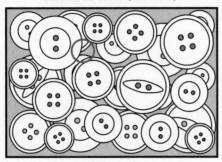

LICENSE PLATES (Week 7)

1. John Grisham; 2. Stephen King; 3. Nora Roberts; 4. Anne Rice; 5. James Patterson; 6. Danielle Steel.

DOVETAILED WORDS (Week 7)

1. penguin, owl; 2. blue, purple; 3. February, July; 4. grape, honeydew; 5. onion, eggplant.

ONLINE NETWORK (Week 7)

One can bear grief, but it takes two to be glad.

ANTONYMS QUIZ (Week 7)

1. a; 2. c; 3. a; 4. c; 5. a; 6. c; 7. b; 8. b.

COUNT THE SQUARES (Week 7)

There are 9 squares: ABFE, ACJH, ADNL, BCGF, CDKJ, EFIH, FGJI, HJML, and JKNM.

TRI, TRI AGAIN (Week 8)

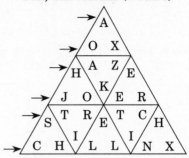

FRUIT-FOR-ALL (Week 8)

Row 4 contains five different fruits.

SHOES & SOCKS (Week 8)

1. the first row; 2. the third row; 3. the fifth row.

SLIDE RULE (Week 8)

aid, ail, all, and, ant, any, art, cod, cog, cot, coy, cry, hid, hit, hog, hot, pig, pit, ply, pod, pot, pry, sit, sly, sod, soy.

SKILLS TEST (Week 8)

Brenda has 20 marbles, Bobby 29, Buzz 35, and Billy 39, for a total of 123.

SUDOKU (Week 8)

4	5	8	1	7	2	9	3	6
6	2	1	8	9	3	7	4	5
9	7	3	4	6	5	1	2	8
5	6	4	7	8	1	2	9	3
3	1	7	5	2	9	6	8	4
2	8	9	6	3	4	5	7	1
7	9	6	3	5	8	4	1	2
8	4	2	9	1	6	3	5	7
1	3	5	2	4	7	8	6	9

SENTENCE TEASER (Week 8)

1. Yes, provided he has a mustache (A). 2. Yes, provided he is tall (B), but he need not be wealthy. Although people with mustaches are tall (C), one can be tall without being wealthy (D). 3. Yes, provided he has a mustache (A). 4. No, people with mustaches are tall (C).

WAYWORDS (Week 8)

Few things are as good as they seem in advance.

343

WORD CHARADE (Week 8)

O	U	H	F	J	Z	D	Q
K	G	P	O	Ⓡ	A	Ⓒ	V
B	D	Ⓡ	I	L	Ⓡ	T	N
S	N	Ⓔ	C	P	G	Ⓐ	Ⓡ
F	O	Ⓜ	H	B	I	J	G
E	V	Q	G	Ⓢ	L	N	K
V	I	T	Ⓒ	F	H	Z	B
D	P	A	U	T	O	Ⓒ	T

scream

SYMBOL-ISM (Week 8)

No moment is ever the same as another.

DEDUCTION PROBLEM (Week 8)

Each spotted puppy has as many spots as there are spotted puppies. If each gave away one spot, they would each have one fewer spot than there are spotted puppies. The unspotted puppy, then, would receive one spot from each spotted puppy and would have as many spots as there are originally spotted puppies, or one more spot than all the others.

IN THE ABSTRACT (Week 8)

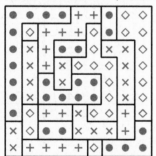

THE LINEUP (Week 8)

1. Z; 2. physicians; 3. E; 4. hogtie; 5. free, hull, back.

SKILLS TEST (Week 8)

neigh, ninth, north, notch, nymph.

ARROW MAZE (Week 9)

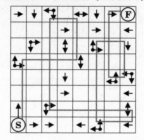

ALL IN A ROW (Week 9)

Row A. Row A contains 6 groups: 551, 7121, 218, 92, 326, and 12431. Row B contains 5 groups: 29, 533, 641, 74, and 4331. Row C contains 4 groups: 62111, 11432, 137, and 245.

WORD HUNT (Week 9)

cider, cocoa, coffee, eggnog, juice, punch, soda, water.

ASSOCIATIONS (Week 9)

gorilla, baboon, chimpanzee; pine, elm, spruce; indigo, azure, blue; lessen, diminish, reduce; firm, rigid, stiff; Edam, brie, Cheddar; downpour, thunderstorm, cloudburst; rotate, whirl, spin. Answer to riddle: "Chase parked cars."

FUN WITH FACTS AND FIGURES (Week 9)

1. $100 \div 5 = 20$; 2. $20 + 21 = 41$; 3. $41 - 9 = 32$; 4. $32 \div 16 = 2$; 5. $2 + 5$ (Spain) $= 7$.

MARCHING ORDERS (Week 9)

1. FINISH

10	16	13	18	17	14
11	9	8	10	15	13
12	14	7	14	18	16
8	9	12	11	16	12
12	11	14	10	15	19
16	7	13	16	13	16

START

2. FINISH

16	12	21	26	25	34
24	17	22	16	31	26
18	21	8	11	23	28
14	13	24	19	21	20
5	9	18	14	26	25
10	7	17	13	22	17

START

344

TARGET SHOOT (Week 9)

1. HI: achier, behind, ethics; 2. GL: piglet, bugler, eagles.

WORD VISIBILITY (Week 9)

1. cashew; 2. anchor; 3. tinsel; 4. encore; 5. casino; 6. basket.

ANIMAL CHARADES (Week 9)

donkey

WORD WHEEL (Week 9)

mar, march, marcher, arc, arch, archer, cherub, her, rub, ruby, bylaw, law, lawbook, boo, book, booked, educate, ducat, cat, ate, ten, tend, end, endow, dowager, wag, wage, wager, age, germ.

HEXAGON HUNT (Week 9)

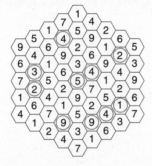

EASY PICKINGS (Week 9)

Nature always wins.

CARD SENSE (Week 10)

Since no two red cards are adjacent (clue 1), the six of spades and the nine of clubs are second and fourth from the top, in some order. By clue 2, then, the two of hearts is on top, the six of spades is second, and the nine of clubs is fourth. The ace of diamonds isn't on the bottom (clue 3), so it is third from the top. By elimination, the four of diamonds is on the bottom. In summary, from top to bottom: two of hearts, six of spades, ace of diamonds, nine of clubs, four of diamonds.

X COUNT (Week 10)

There are 18 X's.

ANAGRAM MAZE (Week 10)

	2	3	4	5	6
	8				
		14	15	16	
				22	23
25	26	27		29	
31			33	34	35

The path through the maze, with only one anagram given for each is 6. cola; 5. flee; 4. lacy; 3. fats; 2. bush; 8. vein; 14. bran; 15. ripe; 16. egos; 22. lamp; 23. mine; 29. life; 35. able; 34. beak; 33. last; 27. mile; 26. peat; 25. swap; 31. rife.

BLOCK PARTY (Week 10)

SLIDE RULE (Week 10)

bag, ban, bat, bee, beg, bet, bog, bow, sag, sat, saw, see, set, sew, son, sow, tag, tan, tat, tee, ten, toe, ton, tot, tow, urn, use, van, vat, vee, vet, vow.

LICENSE PLATES (Week 10)

1. Brad Pitt; 2. Matt Damon; 3. George Clooney; 4. Ellen Barkin; 5. Andy Garcia; 6. Elliott Gould.

DOVETAILED WORDS (Week 10)

1. banana, strawberry; 2. Italy, Spain; 3. robin, loon; 4. celery, carrot; 5. brown, gold.

COUNT THE TRAPEZOIDS (Week 10)

There are 24 trapezoids: ACGE, ACKI, ACOM, ADHE, ADLI, ADPM, BCGF, BCKJ, BCON, BDHF, BDLJ, BDPN, EGKI, EGOM, EHLI, EHPM, FGKJ, FGON, FHLJ, FHPN, IKOM, ILPM, JKON, and JLPN.

MAGNIFIND (Week 10)

CODE WORD (Week 10)

Code Word: downstream. Some men see things as they are and ask why. Others dream things that never were and ask why not. (George Bernard Shaw)

ONLINE NETWORK (Week 10)

It is easier to make war than to make peace.

ANTONYMS QUIZ (Week 11)

1. b; 2. a; 3. c; 4. a; 5. b; 6. a; 7. c; 8. c.

WHAT'S YOUR NUMBER? (Week 11)

14 — in each row and column, the third number equals one less than the sum of the first and second.

BULL'S-EYE LETTER (Week 11)

The Bull's-Eye Letter is H: bath, whom, hazy, then, math, hack.

TRI, TRI AGAIN (Week 11)

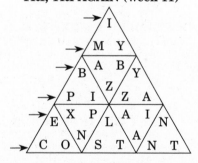

SKILLS TEST (Week 11)

Madison; Roosevelt; Garfield; Washington; Harrison; Van Buren.

ALPHABET SOUP (Week 11)

(Mark) Twain

SUDOKU (Week 11)

6	1	3	2	7	4	5	9	8
7	9	8	1	5	6	2	4	3
4	2	5	8	3	9	1	7	6
5	4	2	6	8	3	9	1	7
3	6	1	7	9	5	4	8	2
9	8	7	4	2	1	6	3	5
8	7	9	5	1	2	3	6	4
1	5	6	3	4	8	7	2	9
2	3	4	9	6	7	8	5	1

WAYWORDS (Week 11)

Forgiving another will set you free.

ALPHABET CIRCLE MAZE (Week 11)

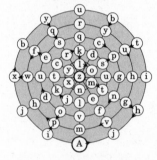

MAGIC NUMBER SQUARES (Week 11)

1.

63	7	11	51
19	43	39	31
35	27	23	47
15	55	59	3

2.

72	16	20	60
28	52	49	40
44	36	32	56
24	64	68	12

FRUIT CHARADES (Week 11)

grape.

LOOK TO THE SKIES (Week 11)

Column B contains five different sky sights.

DEDUCTION PROBLEM (Week 12)

The regular red tape was originally 12 inches long, and the extra-sticky piece was 24 inches long.

ARROW MAZE (Week 12)

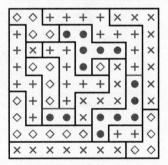

THE LINEUP (Week 12)

1. F; 2. phosphorus; 3. X; 4. streaky; 5. streak, game, wild, jive.

IN THE ABSTRACT (Week 12)

WORD CHARADE (Week 12)

catnip

ALL IN A ROW (Week 12)

Row B. Row A contains four groups: 544, 4612, 823, and 373. Row B contains six groups: 715, 5224, 1912, 274, 823, and 2128. Row C contains four groups: 535, 232213, 922, and 2641.

SKILLS TEST (Week 12)

1. coffee; 2. hello; 3. withhold; 4. toboggan.

WORD HUNT (Week 12)

aster, daisy, lilac, lotus, pansy, peony, poppy, tulip.

Y COUNT (Week 12)

There are 26 Y's.

SLIDE RULE (Week 12)

fare, file, fire, flip, floe, flop, fold, folk, food, ford, fore, fork, hale, hard, hare, hark, harp, hire, hold, hole, hood, hook, hoop, maid, male, mare, mark, mild, mile, milk, mire, mold, mole, mood, more, said, sale, silk, sire, slid, slip, slop, sold, sole, sore.

SUDOKU (Week 12)

2	9	8	7	6	4	3	5	1
7	1	5	2	9	3	6	4	8
4	6	3	1	8	5	9	7	2
5	8	4	3	7	1	2	6	9
1	2	7	9	5	6	4	8	3
6	3	9	8	4	2	5	1	7
8	7	6	5	3	9	1	2	4
3	5	2	4	1	8	7	9	6
9	4	1	6	2	7	8	3	5

SYMBOL-ISM (Week 12)

Why are there always hurdles to clear on the way to success?

COUNT THE RECTANGLES (Week 13)

There are 30 rectangles: ABEF, ABHG, ABKL, ABNM, ACDF, ACIG, ACJL, ACOM, BCDE, BCIH, BCJK, BCON, EDIH, EDJK, EDON, FDIG, FDJL, FDOM, FEHG, FEKL, FENM, GHKL, GHNM, GIJL, GIOM, HIJK, HION, KJON, LKNM, and LJOM.

ASSOCIATIONS (Week 13)

catsup, mayonnaise, mustard; falcon, hawk, eagle; helium, methane, oxygen; sycamore, cedar, maple; faint, dim, pale; dog, canine, pooch; witty, humorous, funny; shake, vibrate, quake. Answer to riddle: "Fish and ships."

347

ANIMAL CHARADES (Week 13)
rabbit.

HEXAGON HUNT (Week 13)

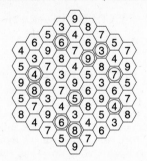

TARGET SHOOT (Week 13)
1. RP: purple, warped, carpet; 2. OI: oboist, choice, booing.

LICENSE PLATES (Week 13)
1. Atlanta Braves; 2. Chicago Cubs; 3. Detroit Tigers; 4. Cincinnati Reds; 5. Baltimore Orioles; 6. Houston Astros.

WORD VISIBILITY (Week 13)
1. dollar; 2. cradle; 3. stream; 4. prompt; 5. orange; 6. candle.

SEVEN WORD ZINGER (Week 13)
few, shy, ask, elf, opt, wed, ebb.
(*Other answers may be possible.*)

BLOCK PARTY (Week 13)

DOVETAILED WORDS (Week 13)
1. white, red; 2. tomato, yam; 3. flamingo, stork; 4. Mercury, Venus; 5. pear, orange.

BULL'S-EYE LETTER (Week 13)
The Bull's-Eye Letter is V: cave, void, oven, ever (or veer), vent, wavy.

CODE WORD (Week 13)
Code word: switchable. "The best way to convince a fool that he is wrong is to let him have his own way." (humorist Josh Billings)

SUDOKU (Week 13)

6	3	2	7	8	9	4	5	1
8	9	5	3	4	1	2	7	6
1	4	7	5	6	2	3	9	8
5	2	4	9	7	6	1	8	3
9	1	3	8	5	4	6	2	7
7	8	6	2	1	3	9	4	5
4	5	1	6	2	7	8	3	9
2	7	9	1	3	8	5	6	4
3	6	8	4	9	5	7	1	2

MAGNIFIND (Week 13)

ANAGRAM MAZE (Week 14)

		3	4	5	6
					12
13	14	15	16		18
19			22	23	24
25	26				
	32	33	34		

The path through the maze, with only one anagram given for each is 3. toga; 4. form; 5. deaf; 6. peas; 12. fare; 18. cool; 24. surf; 23. pans; 22. sewn; 16. evil; 15. each; 14. buys; 13. aunt; 19. sale; 25. bear; 26. palm; 32. fits; 33. coin; 34. skid.

WHAT'S YOUR NUMBER?
(Week 14)
46 — on each spoke, the number in the circle minus two times the number in the square equals 8, the number in the diamond.

HOLE IN ONE (Week 14)
The golf ball in the hole is 4295.

IN THE MONEY (Week 14)
1. $8.40; 2. $8.25; 3. $8.48; 4. $8.50. Bag #4 has the most money.

CROSS PATHS (Week 14)

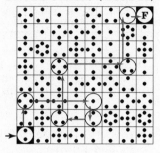

POP! (Week 14)
clicked, licked, liked, lied, lid, id, I.

IN THE BALANCE (Day 23)
Three triangles. Scale 1 shows that three triangles equal two circles, so nine triangles equal six circles. Since scale 2 shows that one circle equals two squares, six circles equal twelve squares. Nine triangles, then, equal twelve squares. Scale 3 shows that six squares equal three diamonds, so twelve squares equal six diamonds and nine triangles equal six diamonds. Three triangles, then, equal two diamonds, and would balance scale 4.

TRIANGULAR SQUARE (Week 14)

POP! (Week 14)
oranges, orange, range, rang, ran, an, a.

HOLE IN ONE (Week 14)
The golf ball in the hole is 8637.

KEEP ON MOVING (Week 14)
Move two squares down, two squares right, one square down, two squares right, and four square up to the asterisk.

OVERLAY (Week 14)
Diagram B.

SWITCHEROO (Week 14)
1. d; 2. a; 3. b; 4. a; 5. c; 6. c.

GOING IN CIRCLES (Week 14)
1. magazine; 2. campaign.

ANIMAL CHARADES (Week 15)
turkey

WORD HUNT (Week 15)
calf, chin, face, foot, hand, heel, lash, nose, palm, shin, sole.

RELATIONSHIPS QUIZ (Week 15)
1. a; 2. a; 3. c; 4. d; 5. b.

ANTONYMS QUIZ (Week 15)
1. b; 2. a; 3. c; 4. c; 5. a; 6. b; 7. a; 8. c.

ROUND TRIP (Week 15)

349

COMPOUND IT (Week 15)

1. hot; 2. house; 3. boat; 4. yard; 5. work; 6. shop; 7. lift; 8. off; 9. stage; 10. coach (hothouse, houseboat, boatyard, yardwork, workshop, shoplift, liftoff, offstage, stagecoach).

WORD CHARADE (Week 15)

E	Z	R	V	P	K	G	Q
B	S	Q	F	W	O	C	G
Q	T	I	(D)	E	R	C	X
(O)	Z	F	H	L	(P)	N	J
X	J	(Y)	M	D	V	U	Q
W	L	B	D	U	I	E	B
G	I	K	N	P	(R)	T	W
J	U	M	I	E	X	C	E

parody

SLIDE RULE (Week 15)

bale, balm, blew, blot, blow, bolt, boom, boot, brew, brow, face, fact, flee, flew, floe, flow, foot, free, fret, from, pace, pact, pale, palm, plot, plow, poem, poet, pole, prom, prow, race, role, room, root.

SENTENCE TEASER (Week 15)

1. true, westerns are in color and last over 100 minutes (A and C), thrillers were made before 2000, and these also last over 100 minutes (B and D); 2. false, it does not follow from A that only westerns are in color; 3. false, it does not follow from B that only thrillers were made before 2000; 4. false, as can be seen from answer #3, some westerns could be made before 2000, and all westerns are in color (A).

SUDOKU (Week 15)

8	5	6	3	1	2	9	7	4
2	1	7	9	6	4	5	8	3
3	4	9	7	5	8	2	6	1
6	9	1	4	8	5	7	3	2
4	3	5	2	7	9	8	1	6
7	2	8	1	3	6	4	5	9
1	7	4	8	2	3	6	9	5
9	6	3	5	4	7	1	2	8
5	8	2	6	9	1	3	4	7

CODED PRESIDENTS (Week 15)

1. Abraham Lincoln; 2. Barack Obama; 3. John Quincy Adams; 4. Ronald Reagan; 5. Ulysses Grant; 6. Martin Van Buren; 7. Theodore Roosevelt; 8. Bill Clinton; 9. Richard Nixon; 10. Lyndon Johnson.

WORD WHEEL (Week 15)

she, shear, hear, heart, hearth, ear, earth, earthen, earthenware, art, the, then, hen, war, ware, are, area, react, reactor, act, actor, tor, torrid, rid, ridge, gel, gelid, elide, lid, idea, ideal, deal, alas, las, lash, ash.

CIRCLE SEARCH (Week 16)

dale, dance, dancer, let, ounce, out, outer, par, parcel, pare, parer, pat, pate, relet, tout.

STACKED UP (Week 16)

Boxes 1, 5, and 6.

WHIRLIGIG (Week 16)

1. barbecue; 2. barnyard; 3. barracks; 4. baritone; 5. barefoot; 6. bargains; 7. bartered; 8. baroness; 9. barbells; 10. barbaric; 11. barnacle; 12. barrette.

RHYMING REPLACEMENTS (Week 16)

1. stars & stripes; 2. soup & salad; 3. over & out; 4. black & blue; 5. buttons & bows; 6. soap & water 7. king & queen; 8. sweet & sour; 9. moan & groan; 10. rank & file.

COUNT ON IT! (Week 16)

It's an offer you can't refuse.

FILLING STATION (Week 16)

1. Little Orphan Annie; 2. Kate Winslet; 3. shamrock; 4. "The Wizard of Oz"; 5. Baton Rouge.

CARD SENSE (Week 16)

By clue 2, one of the spades is on top. It's not the five of spades (clue 4), so it's the four of spades. Since one red card is on top of the other (clue 3) and the heart is on top of the ace of clubs (clue 1), the two of diamonds is above the king of hearts, which is above the ace of clubs. By clue 4, the ace of clubs is above the five of spades. In order, then, from top to bottom: four of spades, two of diamonds, king of hearts, ace of clubs, five of spades.

ALL IN A ROW (Week 16)

Row A. Row A contains six groups: 354, 6141, 4125, 57, 741, and 813. Row B contains five groups: 516, 1632, 282, 84, and 651. Row C contains four groups: 52131, 831, 1128, and 426.

GRAND TOUR (Week 16)

burro, robot, botch, champ, ample, lever, verve, venom, nomad, adobe, obese, sepia, piano, noble, blear, armor, moral, allot, lotto, totem, tempo, poser, serge, genie, niece, cease.

BLOCK PARTY (Week 16)

VISION QUEST (Week 16)

Column C.

LETTER, PLEASE (Week 16)

A promise is a cloud; fulfillment is rain.

HEXAGON HUNT (Week 17)

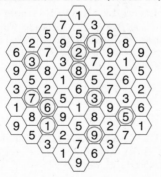

DEDUCTION PROBLEM (Week 17)

By clue 2, dance is on Friday. Fencing is on the day before karate (clue 1). By clue 4, then, aerobics, karate, and fencing are on, in some order, Monday, Tuesday, and Wednesday, so bowling is on Thursday. Since aerobics isn't on Wednesday (clue 3), it is on Monday; fencing, then, is on Tuesday and karate is on Wednesday. In summary, Jenny's schedule from Monday through Friday is aerobics, fencing, karate, bowling, and dance.

MAGNIFIND (Week 17)

CROSS-UPS (Week 17)

1. folklore; 2. woodwork.

ASSOCIATIONS (Week 17)

meeting, assembly, congregation; cheat, bilk, swindle; simple, plain, straightforward; stream, current, flow; wise, judicious, prudent; shape, figure, form; Kansas, Oklahoma, Iowa; chimpanzee, lemur, monkey.

Answer to riddle: He was stuffed.

ALPHABET CIRCLE MAZE (Week 17)

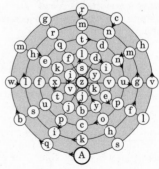

ONLINE NETWORK (Week 17)

leave, separate, part; pepper, nutmeg, thyme.

COUNTDOWN (Week 17)

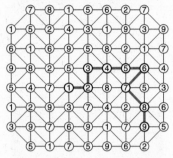

EASY PICKINGS (Week 17)

You won't sink if at first you think.

LOOSE TILE (Week 17)

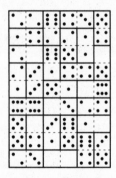

The 3-6 is the Loose Tile.

U.S. S'S (Week 17)

1. Massachusetts; 2. West Virginia; 3. Louisiana; 4. Texas; 5. Wisconsin; 6. Alaska.

ELIMINATION (Week 18)

1. shipshape, featherweight, honeybunch; 2. neutral; 3. sale and sail, worn and warn, meet and meat; 4. magical, edifice, chalice; 5. powerful; 6. kiss, and, tell (kiss-and-tell); 7. truth, is, stranger, than, fiction (truth is stranger than fiction). Cool words will not burn the tongue or ear.

WHAT'S YOUR NUMBER?
(Week 18)

7. The difference between the numbers in the top two boxes equals the difference between the numbers in the bottom two boxes.

ALPHABET SOUP (Week 18)

Chile.

SLIDE RULE (Week 18)

lake, lane, lank, leak, liar, like, line, link, loll, lone, sake, sale, sane, sank, seal, sear, sell, silk, sill, sine, sink, soak, soar, sole, vale, vane, veal, vial, vile, vine, vole, yank, year, yell, yoke, yolk.

IN THE ABSTRACT (Week 18)

LICENSE PLATES (Week 18)

1. Tucson, Arizona; 2. Orlando, Florida; 3. Detroit, Michigan; 4. Pittsburgh, Pennsylvania; 5. Austin, Texas; 6. Seattle, Washington.

BULL'S-EYE LETTER (Week 18)

The Bull's-Eye Letter is T: trip, stay, math, cart, jilt, tell.

SUDOKU (Week 18)

1	9	6	4	8	2	3	5	7
2	5	3	1	7	9	6	8	4
4	7	8	3	5	6	1	2	9
9	8	5	6	4	7	2	3	1
6	2	4	5	3	1	9	7	8
3	1	7	9	2	8	4	6	5
8	4	9	7	6	3	5	1	2
7	6	1	2	9	5	8	4	3
5	3	2	8	1	4	7	9	6

ANAGRAM MAZE (Week 18)

		4	5	6
		10		
		16	17	
19	20	21		23	24
25		27	28		30
31			34	35	36

The path through the maze, with just one anagram given for each, is 6. reed; 5. dote; 4. swap; 10. scar; 16. fate; 17. live; 23. none; 24. clam; 30. mare; 36. nail; 35. from; 34. deal; 28. dust; 27. bore; 21. prod; 20. peat; 19. loaf; 25. face; 31. sink.

SYMBOL-ISM (Week 18)
We must remember that it takes both rain and sunshine to make a rainbow.

THE LINEUP (Week 18)
1. X; 2. coconut; 3. O; 4. promenade; 5. three words (sulk, mitt, what).

SKILLS TEST (Week 18)
Box #2. Box #1 has 18 O's and Box #2 has 19 O's.

WORD EQUATIONS (Week 19)
1. for + bid = forbid; 2. dam + age = damage; 3. scar + let = scarlet; 4. thin + king = thinking; 5. kit + ten = kitten.

STAR WORDS (Week 19)

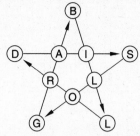

Your sequence of words may begin in any circle.

WAYWORDS (Week 19)
It takes a brave man to love a brave woman.

FUN WITH FACTS AND FIGURES (Week 19)
1. 8 x 5 = 40; 2. 40 − 4 = 36; 3. 36 ÷ 6 (Africa) = 6; 4. 6 + 6 = 12; 5. 12 − 3 = 9.

TRI, TRI AGAIN (Week 19)

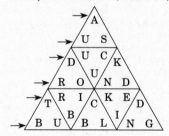

OVERLAY (Week 19)
Diagram A.

ANTONYMS QUIZ (Week 19)
1. a; 2. c; 3. b; 4. a 5. c; 6. a; 7. b; 8. b.

LETTER, PLEASE (Week 19)
Always remember to be happy because you never know who's falling in love with your smile.

ARROW MAZE (Week 19)

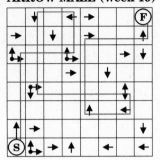

P COUNT (Week 19)

There are 32 P's in the sentence.

COUNT TO TEN (Week 19)

1. row 5; 2. row 10; 3. row 8.

BLOCK PARTY (Week 19)

CARD SENSE (Week 20)

Since there are five cards, three red and two black, the colors alternate from top to bottom (clue 1) and the stack is red, black, red, black, red. The eight of hearts is the top card of the stack (clue 3). By clue 2, the bottom card is the two of diamonds, the next-to-bottom card is the king of spades, and the seven of diamonds is the middle card. By elimination, the ace of clubs is second from the top. In summary, from top to bottom: eight of hearts, ace of clubs, seven of diamonds, king of spades, two of diamonds.

QUICK FILL (Week 20)

dictionary.

CIRCLE MATH (Week 20)

A = 5, B = 7, C = 1, D = 2, E = 9, F = 6, G = 8, H = 4, and I = 3.

RINGERS (Week 20)

1. urban, ghost, delta, rumor; 2. bayou, slump, hinge, optic.

COUNT ON IT! (Week 20)

Too many cooks spoil the broth.

IN THE ABSTRACT (Week 20)

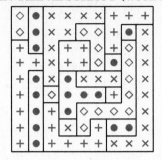

MARCHING ORDERS (Week 20)

RELATIONSHIPS QUIZ (Week 20)

1. d; 2. a; 3. d; 4. c; 5. b.

RING LOGIC (Week 20)

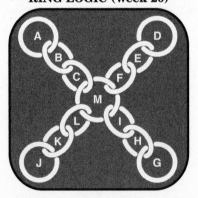

CIRCLE SEARCH (Week 20)

base, bat, cop, copy, cot, ease, eat, leap, lease, pea, peal, peat, release, rely, tea, teal, tease.

354

ANIMAL CHARADES (Week 20)
wolverine.

SKILLS TEST (Week 20)
John.

MISSING DOMINOES (Week 20)

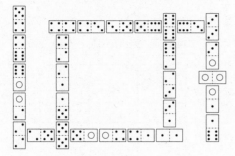

SEVEN WORD ZINGER (Week 21)
ale, dab, ego, fur, inn, law, row.

ON THE LINE (Week 21)

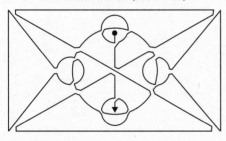

TARGET SHOOT (Week 21)
1. IN: clinic, dainty, fringe; 2. LV: pelvis, silver, velvet.

NEXT TO NOTHING (Week 21)
Quincy.

WORD HUNT (Week 21)
wade, wake, wand, want, ward, warm, warn, warp, wart, wary, weak, wean, wear, weed, weld, went, wept, whim, whip, wide, wife, wolf, wont.

SUDOKU (Week 21)

8	2	9	7	3	6	1	5	4
3	4	6	8	1	5	7	2	9
7	1	5	2	9	4	8	6	3
6	7	8	3	4	2	5	9	1
9	3	2	6	5	1	4	7	8
1	5	4	9	7	8	6	3	2
5	9	7	4	8	3	2	1	6
4	6	3	1	2	7	9	8	5
2	8	1	5	6	9	3	4	7

STACKED UP (Week 21)
Boxes 1, 2, and 4.

DOVETAILED WORDS (Week 21)
1. raise, boost; 2. frost, snow; 3. jungle, forest; 4. petite, slight; 5. panda, bamboo.

ROUND TRIP (Week 21)

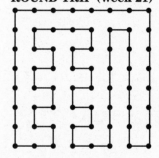

SQUARE LINKS (Week 21)
flaunted, academic, mechanic, kangaroo, marathon.

ARROW MAZE (Week 21)

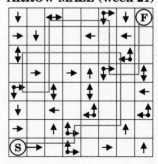

CODE WORD (Week 21)

Code Word: unseaworthy. Many of life's failures are men who did not realize how close they were to succeeding when they gave up.

KEEP ON MOVING (Week 21)

Move four squares down, four squares left, three squares up, one square right, and two squares up to the asterisk.

WORD CHARADE (Week 21)

C	W	Z	N	U	Ⓣ	G	Y
W	Ⓗ	A	Ⓡ	Ⓖ	V	Ⓣ	
Q	Ⓣ	D	F	B	E	M	S
N	Ⓡ	L	D	F	Q	Ⓣ	Z
F	Ⓑ	U	Ⓗ	I	Ⓖ	Y	E
D	Q	V	M	O	S	B	L
Ⓘ	Y	B	Ⓘ	Ⓗ	Ⓘ	Ⓡ	G
Z	S	Ⓡ	C	W	Ⓖ	A	N

bright

HEXAGON HUNT (Week 22)

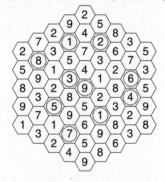

GOING IN CIRCLES (Week 22)

1. aardvark; 2. nonsense.

WHAT'S YOUR NUMBER?
(Week 22)

2. The bottom number is one more than the product of the numbers in the top three boxes.

ELIMINATION (Week 22)

1. "Psycho," "Vertigo," "Notorious"; 2. a, chip, off, the, old, block (a chip off the old block); 3. verbalize, express, articulate; 4. cabdriver; 5. green, bay, grand, rapids, little, rock (Green Bay, Grand Rapids, Little Rock); 6. ambulatory, communicable, representation; 7. stun, coconut, surmount. Pressure is what turns coal into diamonds.

ANAGRAM MAZE (Week 22)

1	2	3			
		9			
	14	15			
19	20				
25		27	28	29	
31	32	33		35	36

The path through the maze, with just one anagram given for each, is 1. huts; 2. peek; 3. dose; 9. arid; 15. toga; 14. beak; 20. rare; 19. dome; 25. ever; 31. near; 32. tans; 33. blow; 27. knee; 28. owns; 29. tide; 35. wand; 36. odor.

EASY PICKINGS (Week 22)

Your smile helps you and others around you.

ASSOCIATIONS (Week 22)

Oslo, Copenhagen, Helsinki; ant, termite, beetle; red, green, blue; energy, pep, vigor; remarkable, fantastic, extraordinary; manage, direct, supervise; quick, speedy, fast; delicate, fine, dainty. A garbage truck.

ALL IN A ROW (Week 22)

Row C. Row A contains five groups: 1264, 1822, 8221, 22171, and 94. Row B contains five groups: 652, 5215, 49, 26131, and 319. Row C contains six groups: 85, 5143, 14323, 238, 4531, and 166.

TARGET SHOOT (Week 22)

1. IT: critic, switch, edited; 2. ED: pledge, credit, needle.

IN THE ABSTRACT (Week 22)

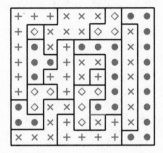

COUNTDOWN (Week 22)

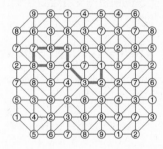

EASY PICKINGS (Week 22)

To teach is to learn.

SEVEN WORD ZINGER (Week 23)

mat, nun, odd, awe, pry, vow, arm.

WORD VISIBILITY (Week 23)

1. birch; 2. green; 3. scent; 4. plane; 5. fault; 6. write.

ANAGRAM MAZE (Week 23)

1	2	3	4	5	
7					
13		15	16	17	18
19	20	21			24
			28	29	30
	32	33	34		

The path through the maze, with only one anagram given for each, is 5. noel; 4. vote; 3. robs; 2. goes; 1. laid; 7. lure; 13. avid; 19. lack; 20. page; 21. bury; 15. rock; 16. mane; 17. teem; 18. grin; 24. weak; 30. peas; 29. risk; 28. tabs; 34. neat; 33. coal; 32. rats.

CIRCLE SEARCH (Week 23)

dome, done, ease, easel, eat, false, fame, nee, net, seldom, tea, tease.

ONLINE NETWORK (Week 23)

The more you say, the less people remember.

SUDOKU (Week 23)

6	4	9	1	5	8	7	3	2
2	8	7	6	3	9	1	4	5
1	3	5	7	4	2	9	8	6
3	6	4	5	9	1	2	7	8
9	5	8	3	2	7	4	6	1
7	2	1	4	8	6	5	9	3
8	9	3	2	1	4	6	5	7
4	1	6	8	7	5	3	2	9
5	7	2	9	6	3	8	1	4

CODE WORD (Week 23)

Code Word: personality. The problem with this country is that too many people go around saying, "The problem with this country..."

MAGIC NUMBER SQUARES
(Week 23)

1.

2	16	15	5
13	7	8	10
9	11	12	6
14	4	3	17

2.

8	30	22	32
36	18	26	12
34	20	28	10
14	24	16	38

MAGNIFIND (Week 23)

STAR WORDS (Week 23)

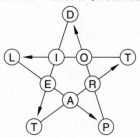

Your sequence of words may begin in any outer circle.

FUN WITH FACTS AND FIGURES
(Week 23)

1. 4 x 12 = 48; 2. 48 + 6 = 54; 3. 54 ÷ 27 = 2; 4. 2 + 10 = 12; 5. 12 - 4 = 8.

DEDUCTION PROBLEM
(Week 24)

If Lee were telling the truth, both he and Leroy would have broken even. Since just one man broke even, Lee is lying, and Leo is the one who told the truth and broke even. Lee, then, made $10,000 and Leroy lost that amount.

RELATIONSHIPS QUIZ (Week 24)

1. b; 2. d; 3. c; 4. a; 5. c.

TRI, TRI AGAIN (Week 24)

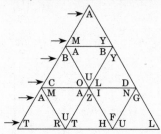

ALL IN A ROW (Week 24)

Row B. Row A contains 4 groups: 4332, 255, 5511, and 264. Row B contains 6 groups: 93, 32214, 525, 8112, 112413, and 48. Row C contains 5 groups: 336, 141114, 921, 543, and 4611.

THE LINEUP (Week 24)

1. X; 2. fragment; 3. E, I, and S; 4. drying; 5. kilt, deny, cite.

WHAT'S YOUR NUMBER?
(Week 24)

Top number 16 (-1 +2 -3 +4), bottom number 26 (+1 -2 +3 -4).

STACKED UP (Week 24)

Boxes 1, 3, and 4.

GOING IN CIRCLES (Week 24)

1. solDieRs (clockwise); 2. hesItaTe (counterclockwise).

ROUND TRIP (Week 24)

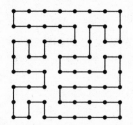

ANTONYMS QUIZ (Week 24)

1. b; 2. a; 3. b; 4. c; 5. a; 6. c; 7. a; 8. b.

RING LOGIC (Week 24)

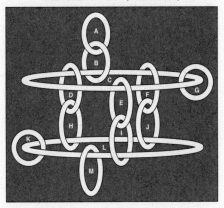

SYMBOL-ISM (Week 24)

No brain is stronger than its weakest think.

SKILLS TEST (Week 25)

The missing consonant is L: magnolia, lily, azalea, oleander, gladiolus, camellia, dahlia, violet.

MARCHING ORDERS (Week 25)

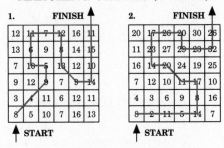

PATCH PUZZLE (Week 25)

B	I	D		C	O	G		S	M	O	G
O	N	E	S		E	W	E		E	A	R	N
S	C	A	T		A	L	L		A	R	E	A
S	H	R	U	B	S		A	R	R	E	S	T
			F	E	E		T	I	C			
C	R	A	F	T		N	I	G	H	T	L	Y
A	A	H		C	O	N		A	Y	E		
T	H	A	N	K	E	D		R	I	P	E	N
		A	I	R		G	U	M				
S	P	R	I	T	E		U	N	A	B	L	E
T	A	I	L		A	S	S		G	R	A	Y
O	G	L	E		L	E	T		E	A	V	E
W	E	E	D		S	A	Y		G	A	S	

PROGRESSION (Week 25)

1. Y (first row moves forward in the alphabet three letters, second row moves forward four letters, third row moves forward five letters); 2. V (each letter in the series is the consonant following one of the five vowels, in order).

R COUNT (Week 25)

There are 27 R's.

HEXAGON HUNT (Week 25)

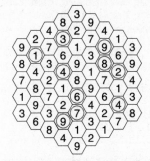

GRAND TOUR (Week 25)

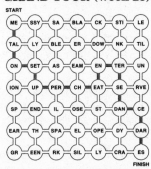

metal, talon, onset, setup, upper, perch, cheat, eaten, enter, terse, sedan, dance, cedar, dares.

ANIMAL CHARADES (Week 25)

bobcat

U.S. Y's (Week 25)

1. New York; 2. Kentucky; 3. Wyoming; 4. Pennsylvania; 5. New Jersey; 6. Maryland.

WORD HUNT (Week 25)

(Los Angeles) Angels, (Houston) Astros, (St. Louis) Cardinals, (San Francisco) Giants, (New York) Mets, (San Diego) Padres, (Texas) Rangers, (Cincinnati) Reds, (Detroit) Tigers, (Minnesota) Twins.

RINGERS (Week 25)

1. spout, layer, porch, grate; 2. boast, opera, haven, peril.

ELIMINATION (Week 25)

1. intestines; 2. lived (devil); 3. craftwork (two); 4. civic; 5. settle (Seattle); 6. begins; 7. banish. "He who wrestles with me strengthens me."

LICENSE PLATES (Week 26)

1. Montgomery, Alabama; 2. Honolulu, Hawaii; 3. Hartford, Connecticut; 4. Topeka, Kansas; 5. Richmond, Virginia; 6. Nashville, Tennessee.

WAYWORDS (Week 26)

Friends raise your standard of living.

COUNT THE SQUARES (Week 26)

The 17 squares are: ABGF, BCHG, BDMK, CDIH, CENL, DEJI, GHLK, HIML, HJRO, IJNM, LMPO, MNRP, PQTS, PRXV, QRUT, STWV, and TUXW.

CIRCLE MATH (Week 26)

A = 2, B = 5, C = 3, D = 7, E = 6, F = 4, G = 8, H = 1, and I = 9.

BULL'S-EYE LETTER (Week 26)

The Bull's-Eye Letter is Z: lazy, zinc, size, quiz, whiz, zany.

DOVETAILED WORDS (Week 26)

1. spinach, kale; 2. sparrow, finch; 3. lemon, peach; 4. circle, square; 5. black, gray.

SKILLS TEST (Week 26)

There are seven combinations: one quarter, one dime, and one nickel; one quarter and three nickels; four dimes; three dimes and two nickels; two dimes and four nickels; one dime and six nickels; and eight nickels.

LOOSE TILE (Week 26)

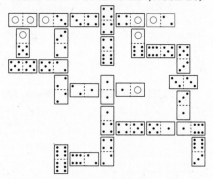

The 1-2 domino is the Loose Tile.

ARROW MAZE (Week 26)

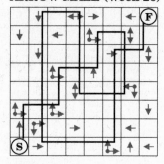

ASSOCIATIONS (Week 26)

Dalmatian, basset, bloodhound; walk, stroll, amble; shy, meek, bashful; circle, triangle, square; lager, beer, ale; stale, trite, timeworn; dime, nickel, quarter; pinkie, thumb, finger. Answer: baking soda.

MISSING DOMINOES (Week 26)

WORD WHEEL (Week 26)

mop, mope, open, pen, pend, end, endive, dive, diver, verb, verbal, ball, all, lunch, chop, hop, hope, pep, prim, primp, primper, rim, imp, per, pert, the, then, hen.

ALPHABET SOUP (Week 26)
"Jaws"

OVERLAY (Week 27)
Box B will be formed.

SLIDE RULE (Week 27)

aft, air, apt, ebb, elf, fib, fir, fit, fly, off, opt, sir, sit, sly, spy.

HOLE IN ONE (Week 27)
The golf ball in the hole is 4231.

IN THE MONEY (Week 27)
1. $7.20; 2. $10; 3. $10.25; 4. $11.50. Bag #4 has the most money.

CROSS PATHS (Week 27)

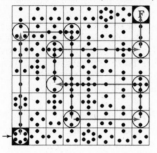

POP! (Week 27)
partied, parted, pared, pare, par, pa, a.

HOLE IN ONE (Week 27)
The golf ball in the hole is 7865.

IN THE BALANCE (Week 27)
Three triangles. Scale 1 shows that two triangles equal four circles, so one triangle equals two circles. Since scale 2 shows that two circles equal three squares, one triangle equals three squares. Six squares equal two diamonds on scale 3, so three squares equal one diamond. One triangle, then, equals one diamond; three triangles equal three diamonds and would balance scale 4.

TRIANGULAR SQUARE (Week 27)

CROSS PATHS (Week 27)

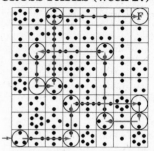

CREEPY CRAWLIES (Week 27)
Row 5.

SENTENCE TEASER (Week 27)
1. true (A, B, and C); 2. true (B and D); 3. false (it does not follow from B that all strongly scented flowers come out in summer, so A does not apply); 4. false (it does not follow from D that all flowers which do not last have a strong scent).

PRESIDENTIAL MONOGRAMS (Week 27)
1. Ronald Reagan; 2. Bill Clinton; 3. Abraham Lincoln; 4. Franklin Roosevelt; 5. Jimmy Carter; 6. Gerald Ford; 7. Barack Obama; 8. George Washington; 9. Herbert Hoover; 10. Harry Truman.

BATS & BALLS (Week 27)
1. the second row; 2. the ninth row; 3. the eighth row.

ON THE LINE (Week 27)

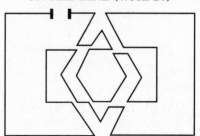

DEDUCTION PROBLEM (Week 28)

Since the boy who got the C was the only one telling the truth, Arthur's statement that his mark was a B was a lie, as was his comment that Cecil didn't get the A. Therefore, Cecil was the A student. Since Bert said that Cecil got an A, Bert told the truth; Bert's grade was a C. Cecil's statement that Arthur didn't get the D, then, was a lie, as was David's comment that he, himself, didn't get an F. Arthur got the D and David got the F. By elimination, Frank's statement was a lie, so he got a B. In summary:

    Arthur, D, liar
    Bert, C, truthful
    Cecil, A, liar
    David, F, liar
    Frank, B, liar

SKILLS TEST (Week 28)

gloat, globe, gloom, glory, glove.

WORD CHARADE (Week 28)

```
S D B J Ⓣ F C V
G F Ⓣ N L S B J
H G M Ⓘ M K H R
Z B J D A B G Ⓔ
P K Ⓢ H Ⓛ V Ⓣ M
V Ⓘ A Ⓘ Ⓝ P D A
L C G V A S F R
H N J G L Ⓣ M K
```

listen

ALPHABET CIRCLE MAZE (Week 28)

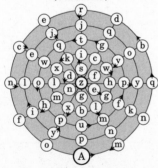

WHAT'S YOUR NUMBER? (Week 28)

1. 18 (twice the number diagonally across from it); 2. 21 (+2 +4 +6 +8).

TIPS OF THE ICEBERG (Week 28)

1. Al ($8.45); 2. Ed ($4.35); 3. Hank and Inez ($5.45).

ANAGRAM MAZE (Week 28)

1	2		4	5	6
	8		10		12
13	14		16		18
19		21	22		24
25	26	27			30
					36

The path through the maze, with only one anagram given for each, is 1. cork; 2. nail; 8. seam; 14. fuel; 13. slap; 19. barn; 25. drop; 26. bowl; 27. deli; 21. knee; 22. lift; 16. beat; 10. vats; 4. pile; 5. ages; 6. shoe; 12. char; 18. goat; 24. shut; 30. hear; 36. last.

TARGET SHOOT (Week 28)

1. CK: tackle, cuckoo, jacket; 2. UA: truant, square, iguana.

SUDOKU (Week 29)

3	7	8	2	1	6	9	4	5
1	6	4	9	5	8	2	7	3
2	5	9	4	3	7	8	1	6
7	8	5	6	9	3	1	2	4
6	1	3	7	2	4	5	9	8
4	9	2	5	8	1	6	3	7
9	4	7	8	6	2	3	5	1
8	2	1	3	4	5	7	6	9
5	3	6	1	7	9	4	8	2

CODE WORD (Week 29)

Code Word: chlorinates. Folks take credit for patience when they are simply putting off doing something that is unpleasant.

KEEP ON MOVING (Week 29)

Move one space down, three spaces left, two spaces up, two spaces right, and three spaces down to the asterisk.

MAGIC NUMBER SQUARES (Week 29)

1.

16	26	27	13
21	19	18	24
17	23	22	20
28	14	15	25

2.

26	46	30	74
66	38	54	18
70	34	50	22
14	58	42	62

CARD SENSE (Week 29)

Since no two face cards are adjacent (clue 1), the face cards are the top, bottom, and middle cards. By clue 2, then, the bottom card is the queen of diamonds. By clue 3, the king of spades is not on top; the king of spades is in the middle and the jack of clubs is on top. Also by clue 3, the six of diamonds is second from the top and the six of hearts is second from the bottom. In summary from top to bottom: jack of clubs, six of diamonds, king of spades, six of hearts, queen of diamonds.

EASY PICKINGS (Week 29)

Success is a journey, not a destination.

COUNTDOWN (Week 29)

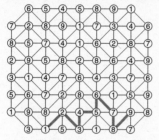

BLOCK PARTY (Week 29)

SEVEN WORD ZINGER (Week 29)

due, kid, why, egg, new, apt, cab.

SYMBOL-ISM (Week 29)

Surely, it must be better to know some of the questions than all of the answers.

ONLINE NETWORK (Week 29)

A fool can ask what the wise cannot answer.

IN THE ABSTRACT (Week 30)

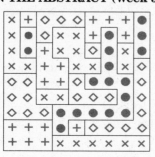

WORD VISIBILITY (Week 30)

1. guilt; 2. candy; 3. block; 4. strip; 5. joust; 6. crate.

MAGNIFIND (Week 30)

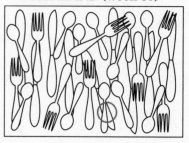

CIRCLE SEARCH (Week 30)

all, alp, ink, link, lip, opal, pal, pall, pink, pip, pop, port, portal, posh, prank, rank, rap, rash, shop, short, shrank.

STAR WORDS (Week 30)

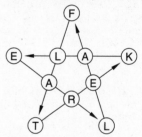

Your sequence of words may begin in any outer circle.

TRI, TRI AGAIN (Week 30)

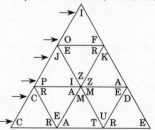

GOING IN CIRCLES (Week 30)

1. paVeMent (counterclockwise); 2. rHythMic (clockwise).

THE LINEUP (Week 30)

1. U; 2. cylinder; 3. J; 4. raffle; 5. jack, edit, jest.

STACKED UP (Week 30)

Boxes 3, 4, and 5.

FUN WITH FACTS AND FIGURES (Week 30)

1. 8 x 5 = 40; 2. 40 - 31 = 9; 3. 9 + 10 (California) = 19; 4. 19 + 1 = 20; 5. 20 ÷ 2 = 10.

ROUND TRIP (Week 30)

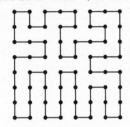

ALL IN A ROW (Week 30)

Row C. Row A has 4 groups: 554, 4613, 392, and 68. Row B has 3 groups: 4622, 77, and 14612. Row C has five groups: 1472, 842, 2129, 12731, and 266.

RINGERS (Week 30)

1. twirl, agree, right, knead; 2. infer, drift, rival, wrote.

RELATIONSHIPS QUIZ (Week 30)

1. b; 2. d; 3. a; 4. d; 5. a.

S COUNT (Week 31)

There are 44 S's.

MARCHING ORDERS (Week 31)

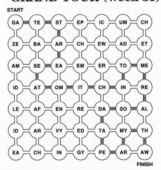

RING LOGIC (Week 31)

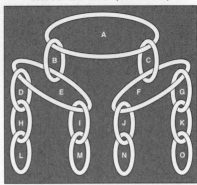

ANTONYMS QUIZ (Week 31)

1. a; 2. c; 3. a; 4. c; 5. b; 6. b; 7. a; 8. c.

HEXAGON HUNT (Week 31)

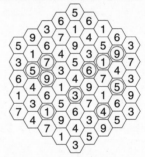

ANIMAL CHARADES (Week 31)

leopard

GRAND TOUR (Week 31)

gate, test, star, area, ease, seat, atom, omit, itch, chin, into, tome, mere, real, also, soda, data, tape, pear, army, myth, thaw.

LICENSE PLATES (Week 31)

1. Janet Jackson; 2. Celine Dion; 3. Tina Turner; 4. Mariah Carey; 5. Christina Aguilera; 6. Beyoncé Knowles.

BULL'S-EYE LETTER (Week 31)
The Bull's-Eye Letter is G: huge, aged, lung, glee, ugly, flag.

WAYWORDS (Week 31)
Experience is learning what not to do.

CARD SENSE (Week 31)
The top card is red (clue 1) but not the queen of hearts (clue 2), so it is the nine of diamonds. By clue 3, then, the second card from the top is the ace of clubs. Since the queen of hearts is below the jack of spades (clue 2) and the six of clubs is above the jack of spades (clue 4), the six of clubs is third from the top, the jack of spades is fourth, and the queen of hearts is the bottom card. In summary from top to bottom: nine of diamonds, ace of clubs, six of clubs, jack of spades, queen of hearts.

WHAT'S YOUR NUMBER?
(Week 31)
1. 64 (each number on the right is the square root of the number opposite it); 2. 18 (double each given number and subtract 10 from that total to get the next number in the sequence).

ELIMINATION (Week 31)
1. light; 2. magnum (gnu); 3. ado, torn (tornado); 4. grange (orange); 5. talk; 6. minimizing; 7. heart (earth). "Youth will never return once it is gone."

CIRCLE MATH (Week 31)
A = 3, B = 2, C = 7, D = 9, E = 4, F = 1, G = 5, H = 8, and I = 6.

PATCH PUZZLE (Week 32)

L	O	S	E		S	H	E		S	N	A	G
A	R	I	A		W	A	Y		H	O	L	E
P	E	N	S		A	D	E		R	O	O	M
			I	C	Y				N	I	N	E	S
O	T	H	E	R	S		D	E	N			
W	E	A	R	Y		C	O	C	K	P	I	T
E	E	L		S	H	A	N	K		A	R	E
S	N	O	R	T	E	D		T	A	C	K	S
		O	A	R		N	I	C	E	S	T
P	E	D	A	L			Y	E	T		
A	P	E	S		P	A	L		I	R	I	S
W	E	N	T		O	H	O		N	O	N	E
S	E	T	S		W	A	N		G	E	N	E

PROGRESSION (Week 32)
Figure 3 (items that are round and triangular in the first figure become square and inverted, respectively, in the second).

WORD HUNT (Week 32)
area, blab, bomb, bulb, chic, dead, died, kick, noun, pomp, prop, pulp, pump, rear, roar, tact, taut, tilt, tout.

OVERLAY (Week 32)
Box A will be formed.

SUDOKU (Week 32)

7	3	6	4	5	1	9	2	8
2	1	4	9	8	3	6	5	7
5	8	9	6	2	7	3	1	4
1	4	2	8	3	6	5	7	9
6	7	5	1	4	9	2	8	3
8	9	3	5	7	2	1	4	6
9	2	8	3	1	4	7	6	5
3	5	1	7	6	8	4	9	2
4	6	7	2	9	5	8	3	1

WORD WHEEL (Week 32)
was, wash, washed, ash, she, shed, hedge, edge, gear, ear, earl, early, lye, yea, yeas, yeast, east, star, start, tar, tart, art, task, ask, askew, skew, skewer, ewe, ewer, were, rent, entire, tire, ire.

WORD CHARADE (Week 32)

B	F	Q	T	W	(T)	J	G
Q	(A)	P	(E)	L	C	(E)	J
D	I	(L)	(A)	I	B	F	M
(A)	J	W	B	Q	(L)	(A)	D
M	(E)	(R)	M	J	(P)	F	Q
G	(C)	L	(A)	(C)	I	(E)	(C)
D	T	(E)	D	G	M	(R)	B
I	(A)	G	F	(R)	(T)	(E)	(A)

carpet

365

DOVETAILED WORDS (Week 32)

1. fork, spoon; 2. paper, eraser; 3. clarinet, oboe; 4. cushion, pillow; 5. wheat, corn.

MISSING DOMINOES (Week 32)

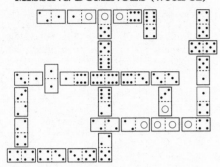

SLIDE RULE (Week 32)

can, cat, con, cot, coy, cry, cut, day, den, don, dot, dry, dun, gay, gel, get, got, gun, gut, guy, hat, hay, hen, hex, hey, hot, hut, wan, wax, way, wet, won, wry.

ALPHABET SOUP (Week 32)
Paris

BACON & EGGS (Week 33)

1. the tenth row; 2. the fifth row; 3. the first row.

ASSOCIATIONS (Week 33)

robin, cardinal, lark; cold, nippy, brisk; chemistry, biology, physics; land, earth, soil; calm, soothe, ease; lake, pond, stream; breathe, respire, inhale; foot, inch, yard. Answer: Spy-focals.

SENTENCE TEASER (Week 33)

1. false (D and C); 2. false (C and A); 3. true (even though all the animals with pedigrees won prizes, C, it does not necessarily follow that all the prize-winning animals had pedigrees); 4. true (even though all ten prizes were awarded to cats, A, it does not necessarily follow that all the cats won prizes).

366

TOOL BOX (Week 33)
Column D.

ALPHABET CIRCLE MAZE (Week 33)

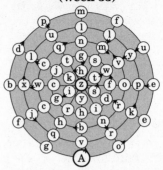

WHAT'S YOUR NUMBER? (Week 33)

11 (the numbers in each set of squares add up to 20).

KEEP ON MOVING (Week 33)

Move three spaces left, five spaces right, three spaces up, two spaces down, and three spaces left to the asterisk.

ON THE LINE (Week 33)

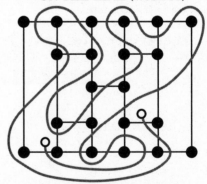

ARROW MAZE (Week 33)

COUNT THE RECTANGLES
(Week 33)
The 32 rectangles are: ABHG, ACIG, ACML, ACQP, ACSR, ADKG, ADOL, ADTR, BCIH, BDKH, CDFE, CDKI, CDOM, CDTS, EFKI, EFOM, EFTS, GIML, GIQP, GISR, GJNL, GKOL, GKTR, IJNM, IKOM, IKTS, JKON, LMQP, LMSR, LOTR, MOTS, and PQSR.

T COUNT (Week 33)
There are 36 T's.

DEDUCTION PROBLEM (Week 33)
Herbert won more than both Richard and Leo. Since Carl won less than Richard and more than Paul, Herbert won the most. Leo won more than Richard and less than Herbert. Leo, then, won the second highest amount and Richard the third highest. Since Carl received more than Paul, Paul received the least amount and Carl the second least. In summary, from least to most: Paul, Carl, Richard, Leo, and Herbert.

SKILLS TEST (Week 34)
1. $44 \div 4 = 11$. 2. $6 \times 6 + 66/66 = 37$.

SUDOKU (Week 34)

4	3	8	2	5	1	9	6	7
5	1	6	7	3	9	4	8	2
2	7	9	4	8	6	3	1	5
7	5	4	1	6	2	8	3	9
9	6	3	8	4	7	2	5	1
8	2	1	3	9	5	7	4	6
1	8	2	5	7	3	6	9	4
6	4	7	9	1	8	5	2	3
3	9	5	6	2	4	1	7	8

LOOSE TILE (Week 34)

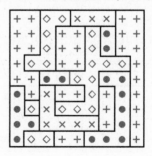

The 5-5 domino is the Loose Tile.

BLOCK PARTY (Week 34)

CARD SENSE (Week 34)
The top card is not the five of spades (clue 1), jack of clubs (clue 2), or two of hearts or six of diamonds (clue 4); it is the two of diamonds. The second card from the top is not the jack of clubs (clue 2), six of diamonds (clue 3), or two of hearts (clue 4), so it is the five of spades. By clue 2, then, the jack of clubs is third from the top. The six of diamonds is fourth from the top and the two of hearts is fifth (clue 4). In summary, from top to bottom: two of diamonds, five of spades, jack of clubs, six of diamonds, two of hearts.

TRI, TRI AGAIN (Week 34)

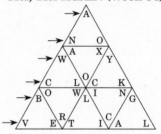

IN THE ABSTRACT (Week 34)

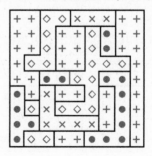

ANIMAL CHARADES (Week 34)
giraffe

TIPS OF THE ICEBERG (Week 34)
1. Inez ($10.30); 2. Brenda ($5.65); 3. Charlie and Dena ($7.65).

HEXAGON HUNT (Week 34)

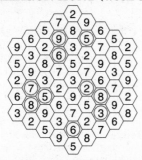

TARGET SHOOT (Week 34)
1. GH: eighth, highly, sighed; 2. OO: gloomy, choose, brooch.

ANAGRAM MAZE (Week 35)

1	2	3			6
7		9	10		12
13	14		16	17	18
	20	21			
		27			
31	32	33			

The path through the maze with only one anagram given for each is 6. thaw; 12. bolt; 18. link; 17. sobs; 16. tuna; 10. pace; 9. sore; 3. felt; 2. face; 1. oils; 7. made; 13. cats; 14. heat; 20. dome; 21. tide; 27. sway; 33. from; 32. tape; 31. mean.

MAGIC NUMBER SQUARES (Week 35)

1.

63	7	11	51
19	43	39	31
35	27	23	47
15	55	59	3

2.

72	16	20	60
28	52	48	40
44	36	32	56
24	64	68	12

FUN WITH FACTS AND FIGURES (Week 35)
1. 5 x 50 = 250; 2. 250 ÷ 25 = 10; 3. 10 + 60 = 70; 4. 70 ÷ 35 = 2; 5. 2 + 4 (Peru) = 6.

WORD HUNT (Week 35)
Dover, Idaho, Iowa, Maine, Miami, Nome, Ohio, Omaha, Reno, Tampa, Tulsa, Utah.

SEVEN WORD ZINGER (Week 35)
cab, rye, ash, dig, inn, now, awe.

MAGNIFIND (Week 35)

SHOE MANIA (Week 35)
Row 5.

DOVETAILED WORDS (Week 35)
1. watermelon, plum; 2. juice, soda; 3. pink, beige; 4. hawk, swan; 5. salt, pepper.

SUDOKU (Week 35)

2	1	5	7	6	4	8	3	9
7	9	4	8	2	3	6	1	5
6	3	8	1	5	9	4	7	2
9	8	7	3	4	6	5	2	1
3	2	1	5	8	7	9	4	6
4	5	6	2	9	1	7	8	3
8	4	9	6	3	2	1	5	7
1	6	2	4	7	5	3	9	8
5	7	3	9	1	8	2	6	4

BULL'S-EYE LETTER (Week 35)
The Bull's-Eye Letter is X: taxi, exit, jinx, apex, waxy, oxen.

MAGNIFIND (Week 35)

COUNTDOWN (Week 36)

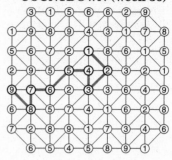

ALL IN A ROW (Week 35)

Row C. Row A contains four groups: 82, 2116, 721, and 21511. Row B contains six groups: 7111, 145, 5212, 91, 73, and 1234. Row C contains seven groups: 253, 532, 2152, 523, 23131, 262, and 6211.

CODE WORD (Week 36)

Code Word: personality. The guy who constantly loses at poker and still keeps on playing will never lack for friends.

SUDOKU (Week 36)

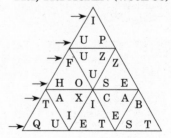

IN THE ABSTRACT (Week 35)

GOING IN CIRCLES (Week 36)

1. terrific; 2. discover.

EASY PICKINGS (Week 35)

The biggest city in Michigan is Detroit.

TRI, TRI AGAIN (Week 36)

THE LINEUP (Week 36)

1. D; 2. abbreviate; 3. B; 4. liberty; 5. jinx, mile, jolt.

QUICK FILL (Week 36)

reflection

ANIMAL CHARADES (Week 36)

muskrat

ELIMINATION (Week 36)

1. cousin, mother, uncle; 2. counter (counterpart, counterpoint, counterproductive); 3. grand, canyon (Grand Canyon); 4. sleeping, dogs (Let sleeping dogs lie); 5. nominate, strange, cabinet, federal; 6. animal, farm ("Animal Farm"); 7. turn, lad, pie. Joyfully live each moment of every day.

LICENSE PLATES (Week 36)

1. Claude Monet; 2. Marc Chagall; 3. Salvador Dalí; 4. Norman Rockwell; 5. Pablo Picasso; 6. Georgia O'Keeffe.

ARROW MAZE (Week 36)

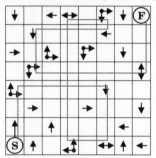

BLOCK PARTY (Week 36)

ASSOCIATIONS (Week 36)

terrier, beagle, poodle; odor, smell, scent; India, Pakistan, Nepal; shrewd, cunning, foxy; inquire, ask, question; Plato, Aristotle, Socrates; gamble, risk, hazard; maxim, adage, proverb. An acrocat.

BULL'S-EYE LETTER (Week 36)

The Bull's-Eye Letter is H: help, chap, achy, lash, echo, whip.

TIPS OF THE ICEBERG (Week 37)

1. Al ($10.85); 2. Dena ($5.80); 3. Ed and Flora ($9.70).

VISION QUEST (Week 37)
Column D

SKILLS TEST (Week 37)

Figure 4. The shaded, black, and white corners rotate positions counterclockwise; in figure 4, the shaded and white corners are not in the correct positions.

ONLINE NETWORK (Week 37)

quantity, amount, sum; catfish, bass, salmon.

ROUND TRIP (Week 37)

DOVETAILED WORDS (Week 37)

1. slide, chute; 2. baby, infant; 3. candle, incense; 4. walrus, otter; 5. garnet, ruby.

CARD SENSE (Week 37)

The bottom card is not the eight of spades (clue 1), ten of hearts (clue 2), seven of diamonds (clue 3), or five of diamonds (clue 4); it is the eight of clubs. By clue 3, the seven of diamonds is the fourth card. Since the ten of hearts is above the eight of spades (clue 2) and the eight of spades is above the five of diamonds (clue 1), the ten of hearts is the top card, the eight of spades is second, and the five of diamonds is third. In summary from top to bottom: ten of hearts, eight of spades, five of diamonds, seven of diamonds, eight of clubs.

WORD HUNT (Week 37)

daze, doze, faze, gaze, haze, hazy, laze, lazy, maze, ooze, quiz, size, whiz, zeal, zero, zest, zone, zoom.

TARGET SHOOT (Week 37)

1. RK: turkey, jerked, market; 2. UC: faucet, stucco, touchy.

OVERLAY (Week 37)
Diagram C

WAYWORDS (Week 38)

"The secret of happiness is to like what you do."

P COUNT (Week 38)
There are 31 P's.

WORD CHARADE (Week 38)

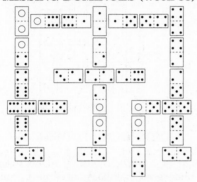

mosaic

WHAT'S YOUR NUMBER? (Week 38)

31. $3 \times 2 + 1 = 7$; $7 \times 2 + 1 = 15$; $15 \times 2 + 1 = 31$; $31 \times 2 + 1 = 63$.

MISSING DOMINOES (Week 38)

COUNT THE TRIANGLES (Week 38)

The 24 triangles are ABC, ABD, ACD, AEM, AEO, AIM, AIO, AMN, AMO, ANO, EFG, EFH, EGH, EIM, EIO, EMN, EMO, ENO, IJK, IJL, IKL, IMN, IMO, and INO.

RINGERS (Week 38)

1. snout, humor, trawl, laugh; 2. wordy, pitch, orbit, build.

RING LOGIC (Week 38)

CIRCLE SEARCH (Week 38)

able, arch, change, changeable, char, gent, gentle, lent, stab, stable, star, starch, tale, talent.

GRAND TOUR (Week 38)

renew, newel, elope, opera, raced, cedar, arbor, borne, never, verse, serum, rumba, baste, steel, elide, ideal, altar, tardy.

WORD VISIBLITY (Week 38)

1. tulip; 2. rugby; 3. aisle; 4. evict; 5. canoe; 6. plant.

ANAGRAM MAZE (Week 39)

	2	3	4		
7	8				
13			16	17	18
19	20	21	22		24
					30
		33	34	35	36

The path through the maze, with just one anagram given for each, is: 4. mope; 3. bowl; 2. over; 8. once; 7. slat; 13. node; 19. leak; 20. clay; 21. dent; 22. char; 16. veer; 17. legs; 18. dire; 24. coat; 30. isle; 36. dose; 35. till; 34. tuba; 33. drab.

COUNT ON IT! (Week 39)
Wake up and smell the coffee.

ALPHABET SOUP (Week 39)
opal

FUN WITH FACTS AND FIGURES (Week 39)
1. 4 x 25 = 100; 2. 100 +103 = 203; 3. 203 − 101 = 102; 4. 102 ÷ 3 = 34; 5. 34 + 2 = 36.

W COUNT (Week 39)
There are 23 W's.

SLIDE RULE (Week 39)
can, cap, cat, cee, con, cop, cot, coy, cry, cue, cup, cut, hat, hay, hen, hey, hoe, hop, hot, hue, hut, man, map, mat, may, men, met, mop, ran, rap, rat, ray, rep, roe, rot, rue, run, rut, tan, tap, tat, tee, ten, toe, ton, top, tot, toy, try, tut.

SQUARE LINKS (Week 39)
campfire, transfer, original, nonsense, humorous.

CIRCLE MATH (Week 39)
A = 2, B = 8, C = 3, D = 5, E = 1, F = 4, G = 6, H = 9, and I = 7.

SEVEN WORD ZINGER (Week 39)
any, bee, goo, kit, nun, shy, tip.

WORD EQUATIONS (Week 39)
1. idealist; 2. important; 3. medallion; 4. office; 5. settee.

WAYWORDS (Week 39)
You entertain a bore just by listening.

ANTONYMS QUIZ (Week 39)
1. b; 2. a; 3. a; 4. c; 5. b; 6. c; 7. b; 8. a.

STACKED UP (Week 40)
Boxes 1, 2, and 5.

SUDOKU (Week 40)

3	8	6	7	4	5	2	1	9
9	1	7	2	6	8	5	3	4
5	2	4	9	1	3	8	6	7
1	7	8	6	5	9	3	4	2
2	5	9	1	3	4	6	7	8
6	4	3	8	2	7	9	5	1
8	3	2	5	7	1	4	9	6
4	6	1	3	9	2	7	8	5
7	9	5	4	8	6	1	2	3

LOOSE TILE (Week 40)

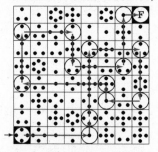

The 2-5 is the Loose Tile.

COMPOUND IT (Week 40)
1. under; 2. pass; 3. book; 4. mark; 5. down; 6. field; 7. work; 8. week; 9. night; 10. club (underpass, passbook, bookmark, markdown, downfield, fieldwork, workweek, weeknight, nightclub).

CROSS PATHS Week 40)

TRIANGULAR SQUARE (Week 40)

	1		4	
3	14			6
11	7	3 / 2 / 6	12	
1		13		2
	2		1	

POP! (Week 40)
blowing, bowing, owing, wing, win, in, I.

IN THE BALANCE (Week 40)
Two triangles. Scale 1 shows that two triangles equal three circles, so four triangles equal six circles. Since scale 2 shows that two circles equal one square, six circles equal three squares. Four triangles, then, equal three squares, and eight triangles equal six squares. Scale 3 shows that six squares equal four diamonds, so eight triangles equal four diamonds. Two triangles, then, equal one diamond, and would balance scale 4.

CROSS PATHS (Week 40)

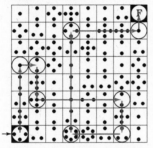

IN THE MONEY (Week 40)
1. $46.05; 2. $45.75; 3. $45.59; 4. $46.80. Bag #4 has the most money.

HOLE IN ONE (Week 40)
The golf ball in the hole is 2817.

POP! (Week 40)
clatter, latter, later, late, ate, at, a.

IN THE BALANCE (Week 40)
Six triangles. Scale 1 shows that three triangles equal one circle, so six triangles equal two circles. Since scale 2 shows that two circles equal two squares, so six triangles equal two squares. Scale 3 shows that six squares equal three diamonds, so two squares equal one diamond. Six triangles, then, equal one diamond, and would balance scale 4.

TRIANGULAR SQUARE (Week 40)

COUNT TO TEN (Week 41)
1. the fourth row; 2. the first row; 3. the sixth row.

STATE LIMITS (Week 41)
Ohio; New Hampshire; Massachusetts; Idaho; Texas; Virginia; Maine.

HEXAGON HUNT (Week 41)

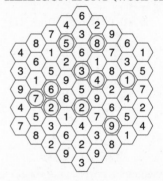

NEXT TO NOTHING (Week 41)
Brenda.

FILLING STATION (Week 41)
1. Chicago; 2. kitchen table; 3. "The Graduate"; 4. Caesar salad; 5. gorilla.

MAGIC NUMBER SQUARES (Week 41)

1.

2	5	15	16
14	17	3	4
9	6	12	11
13	10	8	7

2.

14	10	15	3
11	7	18	6
9	13	4	16
8	12	5	17

GOING IN CIRCLES (Week 41)
1. sabotage; 2. tomorrow.

WORD CHARADE (Week 41)

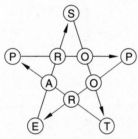

asylum

KEEP ON MOVING (Week 41)

Move three squares right, two squares up, one square left, four squares down, and three squares left to the asterisk.

STAR WORDS (Week 41)

Your sequence of words may begin in any circle.

WORD WHEEL (Week 41)

boa, boar, oar, arc, arch, archer, cherub, her, rub, breath, breathe, eat, the, their, heir, irate, rat, rate, ate, tea, tear, tearful, tearfully, ear, earful, full, fully, lye, yen, envy.

CHANGELINGS (Week 41)

1. BUSY, bust, dust, dusk, DESK; 2. WORK, pork, park, bark, BANK; 3. GOOD, mood, moos, moss, BOSS.

CODE WORD (Week 41)

Code Word: disturbance. With its enduring strength and unrivaled perseverance, the horse demonstrates that even the heaviest of burdens can be carried with grace.

IN THE ABSTRACT (Week 41)

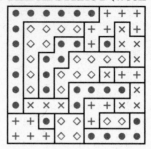

ONLINE NETWORK (Week 42)

decrease, lower, reduce; assemble, meet, convene.

COUNTDOWN (Week 42)

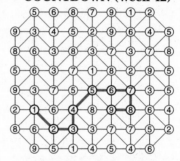

SYMBOL-ISM (Week 42)

The foolish look for happiness in the future, while the wise plant it and grow it under their feet.

LETTER, PLEASE (Week 42)

We see how much a man has and we envy him; if we could see how little he enjoys, we would pity him.

CROSS-UPS (Week 42)

1. downtown; 2. lipstick.

MARCHING ORDERS (Week 42)

374

QUICK FILL (Week 42)
economical.

STACKED UP (Week 42)
Boxes 2, 3, and 6.

SUDOKU (Week 42)

4	5	9	2	8	1	6	3	7
8	6	2	7	3	5	9	4	1
3	1	7	6	9	4	8	5	2
9	3	6	5	1	8	7	2	4
2	7	4	3	6	9	5	1	8
1	8	5	4	7	2	3	6	9
7	4	8	1	5	3	2	9	6
6	2	3	9	4	7	1	8	5
5	9	1	8	2	6	4	7	3

ALPHABET SOUP (Week 42)
Cairo.

DOVETAILED WORDS (Week 42)
1. rabbi, priest; 2. muffin, scone; 3. thyme, basil; 4. wharf, marina; 5. blush, powder.

TRI, TRI AGAIN (Week 43)

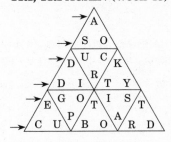

ANIMAL CHARADES (Week 43)
salamander.

WHAT'S YOUR NUMBER?
(Week 43)
55. In each rectangle, the top number minus three times the middle number equals the bottom number.

RELATIONSHIPS QUIZ (Week 43)
1. b; 2. a; 3. a; 4. b; 5. c.

MISSING DOMINOES (Week 43)

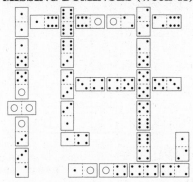

VISION QUEST (Week 43)
Row 5

WAYWORDS (Week 43)
It takes hard work to make anything look easy.

ELIMINATION (Week 43)
1. raiders, of, the, lost, ark ("Raiders of the Lost Ark"); 2. escort, consort, passport, comfort; 3. Rome, wasn't, built, in, a, day (Rome wasn't built in a day); 4. Hawkeye, Cornhusker; 5. swelter, dentist (Sweden); 6. quit (Quito); 7. stars, stripes, red, white, blue. Never miss an opportunity to express your love.

EASY PICKINGS (Week 43)
As the twig is bent the tree inclines.

BULL'S-EYE LETTER (Week 43)
The Bull's-Eye Letter is G: guru, clog, bang, edgy, cage, gaze.

CARD SENSE (Week 43)
The top card isn't the club or spade (clue 1) or either diamond (clue 2), so it is the nine of hearts. By clue 1, the king of clubs isn't second from the top. The jack of diamonds, then, is second from the top and the king of clubs is on the bottom (clue 3). By clue 1, the six of diamonds is third from the top and the seven of spades is fourth. In order, from top to bottom: nine of hearts, jack of diamonds, six of diamonds, seven of spades, and king of clubs.

ANAGRAM MAZE (Week 44)

1	2	3			
		9			
13	14	15			
19			22	23	24
25		27	28		30
31	32	33			36

The path through the maze, with just one anagram given for each, is: 1. spat; 2. dust; 3. cask; 9. hums; 15. pass; 14. bane; 13. runt; 19. race; 25. real; 31. palm; 32. wary; 33. adds; 27. when; 28. hear; 22. heat; 23. peas; 24. ring; 30. coal; 36. ream.

S COUNT (Week 44)
There are 45 S's.

SUDOKU (Week 44)

6	8	4	3	2	5	9	7	1
3	2	1	9	7	8	5	4	6
7	5	9	4	1	6	8	3	2
1	7	3	6	8	9	4	2	5
2	9	5	7	4	1	3	6	8
4	6	8	2	5	3	7	1	9
5	1	2	8	3	7	6	9	4
9	4	7	5	6	2	1	8	3
8	3	6	1	9	4	2	5	7

MAGNIFIND (Week 44)

SLIDE RULE (Week 44)
deal, dean, dent, desk, dial, dint, disk, dual, dunk, dusk, dust, heal, heat, hint, hunk, hunt, husk, neat, nest, weak, wean, went, west, what, whit, wink.

THE LINEUP (Week 44)
1. N; 2. exercise; 3. A; 4. practical; 5. kiss, item, thaw.

OVERLAY (Week 44)
Diagram B

CIRCLE SEARCH (Week 44)
cast, cave, con, concord, contend, contest, cord, cost, cove, hard, have, ten, tend, test.

LOOSE TILE (Week 44)

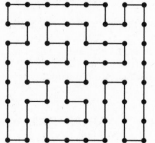

The 0-3 is the Loose Tile.

ASSOCIATIONS (Week 44)
mosquito, housefly, gnat; savor, relish, enjoy; look, observe, see; Erie, Huron, Superior; utter, pronounce, say; ballad, song, melody; wrong, incorrect, untrue; knowledgeable, smart, wise. They hiss and make up.

ROUND TRIP (Week 44)

TARGET SHOOT (Week 45)

1. IB: edible, bribed, tribal; 2. NN: cannon, banner, tunnel.

RING LOGIC (Week 45)

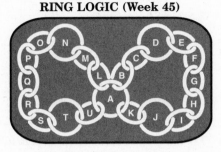

ALL IN A ROW (Week 45)

Row B. Row A contains four groups: 8121, 624, 3243, and 363. Row B contains seven groups: 471, 6141, 1236, 2361, 192, 2415, and 156. Row C contains five groups: 15231, 1371, 183, 831, and 39.

FUN WITH FACTS AND FIGURES (Week 45)

1. $3 - 2 = 1$; 2. 1×12 (South America) $= 12$; 3. $12 + 144 = 156$; 4. $156 \div 6 = 26$; 5. $26 + 24 = 50$.

HEXAGON HUNT (Week 45)

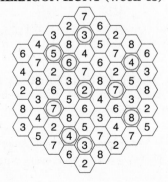

WHIRLIGIG (Week 45)

1 chastise; 2. changing; 3. chaperon; 4. channels; 5. chapters; 6. charisma; 7. charging; 8. charcoal; 9. chambers; 10. chaplain; 11. champion; 12. chairman.

COMPOUND IT (Week 45)

1. child; 2. proof; 3. read; 4. out; 5. come; 6. back; 7. stage; 8. hand; 9. bag; 10. pipes (childproof, proofread, readout, outcome, comeback, backstage, stagehand, handbag, bagpipes).

ANTONYMS QUIZ (Week 45)

1. b; 2. c; 3. a; 4. a; 5. b; 6. c; 7. a; 8. a.

STATE LIMITS (Week 45)

1. Arkansas; 2. Wyoming; 3. Pennsylvania; 4. Illinois; 5. Kansas; 6. Oregon; 7. Rhode Island.

CIRCLE MATH (Week 45)

A = 6, B = 7, C = 4, D = 1, E = 3, F = 9, G = 8, H = 5, and I = 2.

CROSS-UPS (Week 45)

1. outright; 2. noteworthy.

WORD EQUATIONS (Week 45)

1. caterpillar; 2. button; 3. passport; 4. honeymoon; 5. cardboard.

SQUARE LINKS (Week 45)

research, shopping, multiple, lifetime, official.

SUDOKU (Week 46)

5	2	1	7	6	4	3	8	9
7	8	4	9	3	5	2	6	1
9	3	6	2	1	8	7	4	5
1	5	7	3	2	6	8	9	4
3	4	9	8	5	1	6	7	2
2	6	8	4	9	7	1	5	3
4	1	5	6	8	3	9	2	7
8	7	2	1	4	9	5	3	6
6	9	3	5	7	2	4	1	8

WORD HUNT (Week 46)

(Humphrey) Bogart, (Marlon) Brando, (James) Cagney, (Art) Carney, (Ronald) Colman, (Robert) De Niro, (Charlton) Heston, (William) Holden, (Jack) Lemmon, (Lee) Marvin, (Paul) Newman, (Al) Pacino.

LICENSE PLATES (Week 46)

1. station wagon; 2. mountain bike; 3. motor scooter; 4. sports car; 5. trolley bus; 6. pickup truck.

RINGERS (Week 46)

1. royal, clump, shaft, murky; 2. wrath, light, rumor, glide.

ARROW MAZE (Week 46)

KEEP ON MOVING (Week 46)

Move one square right, five squares up, three squares left, three squares down, one square left, and two squares up to the asterisk.

TRI, TRI AGAIN (Week 46)

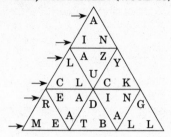

LETTER, PLEASE (Week 46)

The two most beautiful words in the English language are "check enclosed."

TIPS OF THE ICEBERG (Week 46)

1. Laura ($8.95); 2. Inez ($5.00); 3. Hank and Noel ($7.05).

COUNT TO TEN (Week 46)

1. the seventh row; 2. the fifth row; 3. the third row.

BLOCK PARTY (Week 46)

STAR WORDS (Week 47)

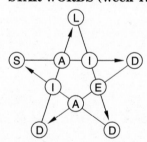

Your sequence of words may begin in any circle.

WORD VISIBLITY (Week 47)

1. sauna; 2. bleak; 3. delay; 4. faith; 5. rivet; 6. which.

COUNT ON IT! (Week 47)

There's a sucker born every minute.

RELATIONSHIPS QUIZ (Week 47)

1. a; 2. c; 3. a; 4. b; 5. b.

WORD WHEEL (Week 47)

wit, with, wither, the, her, hero, heroic, icon, con, conform, for, form, formal, formally, mall, all, ally, lye, yea, year, ear, earth, art, that, hat, hatband, ban, band, bandit, and.

SYMBOL-ISM (Week 47)

Friendship is somewhat like a bank account, since you cannot draw on it unless you make your deposits.

ELIMINATION (Week 47)

1. Exodus, Judges, Proverbs, Job, Numbers, Genesis; 2. head, over, heels (head over heels); 3. weigh, coupon, struts; 4. double, indemnity ("Double Indemnity"); 5. fragrance (France); 6. time, heals, all, wounds (Time heals all wounds); 7. cornucopia, evacuation, singularity. Men are swayed more by fear than reverence.

SKILLS TEST (Week 47)

Figure 5. All the other figures have four enclosed areas.

FILLING STATION (Week 47)

1. horseshoes; 2. George Clooney; 3. "Grey's Anatomy"; 4. Costa Rica; 5. Scarlett O'Hara.

MARCHING ORDERS (Week 47)

1.   FINISH ↑

14	19	22	20	22	28
11	15	17	16	26	30
9	13	10	18	21	24
7	4	8	14	12	20
5	6	9	10	13	16
0	3	2	7	11	14

↑ START

2.   FINISH ↑

13	16	19	18	20	25
9	17	15	16	22	21
8	14	10	11	12	13
2	6	3	8	9	12
4	5	7	5	10	11
0	3	4	8	8	9

↑ START

COUNT THE RECTANGLES (Week 47)

The 38 rectangles are ABZY, CDKI, CDQO, CDUT, CELI, CERO, CEVT, CFWT, CGXT, DELK, DERQ, DEVU, DFWU, DGXU, EFWV, EGXV, FGXW, HION, HJPN, HKQN, HLRN, HMSN, IJPO, IKQO, IKUT, ILRO, ILVT, IMSO, JKQP, JLRP, JMSP, KLRQ, KLVU, KMSQ, LMSR, OQUT, ORVT, and QRVU.

CARD SENSE (Week 47)

By clue 2, the top three cards are the ten of hearts, ten of clubs, and ace of clubs, in some order. Since the tens are both somewhere above the ace (clue 3), the ace is third from the top. The fourth and fifth cards, then, are the five and seven of diamonds, in some order. By clue 1, the ten of clubs is the top card and the ten of hearts is second. Since the seven of diamonds isn't adjacent to the ace (clue 4), it's the bottom card. By elimination, the five of diamonds is fourth from the top. In summary, from top to bottom: ten of clubs, ten of hearts, ace of clubs, five of diamonds, and seven of diamonds.

GRAND TOUR (Week 48)

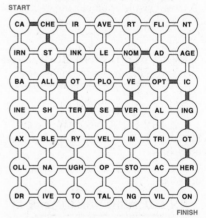

cache, chest, stall, allot, otter, terse, sever, verve, venom, nomad, adopt, optic, icing, ingot, other, heron.

CROSS EXAMINATION (Week 48)

1. unpredictable; 2. television; 3. reversible; 4. experiment; 5. activated; 6. mechanism; 7. opposition; 8. geography.

379

SUDOKU (Week 48)

4	1	6	8	9	2	5	7	3
9	2	5	7	1	3	4	6	8
7	3	8	5	6	4	2	1	9
2	8	1	3	4	9	7	5	6
5	9	4	2	7	6	3	8	1
3	6	7	1	5	8	9	4	2
1	5	2	9	8	7	6	3	4
6	7	9	4	3	1	8	2	5
8	4	3	6	2	5	1	9	7

SWITCHEROO (Week 48)

1. c; 2. a; 3. d; 4. d; 5. b; 6. a.

WHAT'S YOUR NUMBER? (Week 48)

81. On each spoke, the 2 in the diamond equals the two numbers in the triangles multiplied together and divided by the number in the circle.

WAYWORDS (Week 48)

A friend lost is as bad as an enemy won.

SEVEN WORD ZINGER (Week 48)

cat, emu, inn, low, sea, sun, wig.

EASY PICKINGS (Week 48)

Nature, to be commanded, must be obeyed.

IN THE ABSTRACT (Week 48)

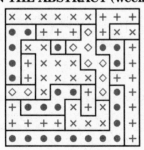

ARROW MAZE (Week 48)

ASSOCIATIONS (Week 48)

hawk, falcon, eagle; ache, pain, sore; spectator, observer, eyewitness; Rome, Venice, Naples; eccentric, bizarre, odd; lemonade, juice, cider; inquisitive, curious, nosy; neglect, overlook, disregard. Great food, no atmosphere.

SLIDE RULE (Week 48)

bare, beam, beat, blue, brag, brat, cage, care, cart, clam, clue, crag, cram, germ, glue, glum, glut, gram, page, pare, part, peat, perm, pert, plug, plum, pram.

ANAGRAM MAZE (Week 48)

	2	3	4	5	6
	8				
	14	15	16		
			22	23	24
25	26	27			30
31		33	34	35	36

The path through the maze, with just one anagram given for each, is: 6. ails; 5. drop; 4. cork; 3. weak; 2. lift; 8. shoe; 14. none; 15. tubs; 16. meat; 22. inch; 23. veil; 24. lisp; 30. cape; 36. pets; 35. mash; 34. surf; 33. peal; 27. spar; 26. tied; 25. keen; 31. hips.

ALL IN A ROW (Week 48)

Row A. Row A contains six groups: 826, 3175, 52432, 24613, 46132, and 3283. Row B contains four groups: 349, 31543, 763, and 835. Row C contains five groups: 32461, 187, 8323, 2374, and 745.

HOLE IN ONE (Week 49)

The golf ball in the hole is 6248.

IN THE MONEY (Week 49)

1. $6.26; 2. $6.25; 3. $5.50; 4. $7.00. Bag #4 has the most money.

CARD SENSE (Week 49)

The aces are adjacent (clue 1), so the three of diamonds is above both of them (clue 4). The three of diamonds is below the eight of clubs (clue 2), which is below a heart (clue 3). The three of diamonds, then, is third from the top, the eight of clubs is second, and the queen of hearts is on top. By clue 5, the ace of hearts is fourth and the ace of spades is fifth. In summary, from top to bottom: queen of hearts, eight of clubs, three of diamonds, ace of hearts, ace of spades.

WORD WHEEL (Week 49)

con, cons, constable, stab, stable, stabled, tab, table, tabled, able, bled, led, edgy, gym, mar, march, marcher, arc, arch, archer, archery, her, rye, yet, etch, chop, hop, opt, optic, optical, tic, call, all.

PRESIDENTIAL FINALES (Week 49)

1. George Bush; 2. Bill Clinton; 3. Harry Truman; 4. Franklin Roosevelt; 5. George Washington; 6. Dwight Eisenhower; 7. Richard Nixon: 8. Ronald Reagan; 9. Herbert Hoover; 10. John Adams.

DEDUCTION PROBLEM (Week 49)

Bill, Dan, and Ernie were not to Charlie's right, so Andrew was. Neither Bill nor Dan was to Charlie's left; Ernie was. By elimination, Bill was to Ernie's left and Dan was to Andrew's right, putting Bill and Dan next to one another. The order of men, beginning with Charlie and moving right, were Charlie, Andrew, Dan Bill, Ernie.

COUNT TO TEN (Week 49)

1. row 4; 2. row 10; 3. row 8.

ON THE LINE (Week 49)

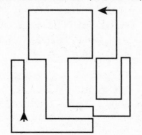

ALPHABET SOUP (Week 49)

Sting.

SKILLS TEST (Week 49)

QU. The other tiles have letters that are two letters apart from each other in the alphabet, but Q is three letters away from U.

TIPS OF THE ICEBERG (Week 49)

1. Inez ($10.30); 2. Ed ($6.05); 3. Greta and Hank ($9.00).

ALPHABET CIRCLE MAZE (Week 50)

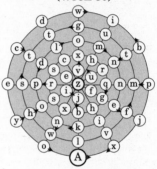

TARGET SHOOT (Week 50)

1. IE: friend, apiece, client; 2. WA: upward, always, beware.

KEEP ON MOVING (Week 50)

Move 3 squares down, 4 squares right, 5 squares up, 3 squares left, 2 squares down, 3 squares right, 1 square up, 2 squares left, 2 squares down, and 1 square left to the asterisk.

SUDOKU (Week 50)

2	7	4	1	8	6	5	9	3
9	1	8	3	5	4	6	2	7
3	6	5	2	9	7	1	4	8
4	9	6	7	1	3	8	5	2
8	5	3	9	6	2	4	7	1
1	2	7	5	4	8	3	6	9
5	3	1	4	7	9	2	8	6
6	4	9	8	2	1	7	3	5
7	8	2	6	3	5	9	1	4

FUN WITH FACTS AND FIGURES
(Week 50)
1. 4 x 8 = 32; 2. 32 - 5 = 27; 3. 27 ÷ 9 = 3; 4. 3 + 6 = 9; 5. 9 + 1 = 10.

RINGERS (Week 50)
1. olive, dream, torch, class; 2. penny, stock, baked, rinse.

GRAND TOUR (Week 50)

lurch, champ, ample, lemon, month, thing, ingot, otter, terse, serum, rumba, basin, singe, genie, niece, cello.

ANIMAL CHARADES (Week 50)
hamster.

ANTONYMS QUIZ (Week 50)
1. c; 2. a; 3. b; 4. a; 5. c; 6. a; 7. c; 8. b.

BULL'S-EYE LETTER (Week 50)
The Bull's-Eye Letter is C: cuff, epic, zinc, fact, etch, acid.

ARROW MAZE (Week 50)

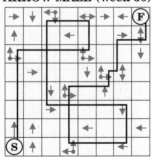

LICENSE PLATES (Week 50)
1. Adam Sandler; 2. Mike Myers; 3. Chevy Chase; 4. Eddie Murphy; 5. Jane Curtin; 6. Will Ferrell.

ROUND TRIP (Week 51)

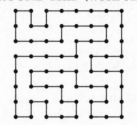

ELIMINATION (Week 51)
1. "Carousel"; 2. adoration (ado, ration); 3. trudge, planks; 4. solemn, melons, lemons; 5. princes (princess); 6. sizing (slenderizing); 7. there (here). "First impressions are the most lasting."

CARD SENSE (Week 51)
The ace of diamonds is adjacent to the ten of hearts (clue 3) and below it (clue 6). It is also below the queen of clubs (clue 4), and above the seven of spades (clue 2) and seven of clubs (clue 5). The ace of diamonds, then, is third from the top, the ten of hearts is second, and the queen of clubs is on top. Since the seven of clubs isn't the bottom card (clue 1), the seven of clubs is fourth from the top and the seven of spades is on the bottom. In summary from top to bottom: queen of clubs, ten of hearts, ace of diamonds, seven of clubs, seven of spades.

DOVETAILED WORDS (Week 51)
1. prune, apricot; 2. painter, easel; 3. magazine, novel; 4. yellow, orange; 5. cactus, willow.

WORD HUNT (Week 51)
Betty, Carol, Doris, Helen, Karen, Linda, Maria, Nancy, Sarah, Susan.

U.S. M's (Week 51)
1. Alabama; 2. Maine; 3. New Mexico; 4. New Hampshire; 5. Minnesota; 6. Oklahoma.

RING LOGIC (Week 51)

SLIDE RULE (Week 51)

bead, bear, beat, bend, bent, bump, bunt, lead, leap, lend, lent, lump, near, neap, neat, sear, seat, sect, send, sent, snap, star, stat.

PROGRESSION (Week 51)
Figure 3.

CIRCLE MATH (Week 51)

A = 4, B = 8, C = 7, D = 1, E = 3, F = 9, G = 6, H = 2, and I = 5.

LOOSE TILE (Week 51)

The 3-6 domino is the Loose Tile.

WHAT'S YOUR NUMBER? (Week 51)

left side: 68 (each left number is three times the previous left number minus one); right side: 137 (each right number is twice the left number plus one).

WORD WHEEL (Week 52)

chair, hair, air, airplane, plan, plane, planet, planetary, lane, net, eta, tar, rye, yea, yeas, yeast, east, stall, stallion, tall, all, lion, ion, one, new, newel, ewe, welfare, elf, far, fare, are.

KEEP ON MOVING (Week 52)

Move 2 squares down, 1 square right, 3 squares up, 2 squares right, 3 squares down, 2 squares up, and 2 squares left to the asterisk.

COUNT THE TRAPEZOIDS (Week 52)

The 24 trapezoids are: AEQM, AFRM, AGSM, AHTM, BEQN, BFRN, BGSN, BHTN, CEKI, CEQO, CFLI, CFRO, CGSO, CHTO, DEKJ, DEQP, DFLJ, DFRP, DGSP, DHTP, IKQO, ILRO, JKQP, and JLRP.

SENTENCE TEASER (Week 52)

1. true, Venusians have four hands (B) and four-handed aliens have tails (D); 2. false, only four-handed aliens have tails (D), and only Venusians have four hands (B); 3. true, Venusians have four hands (B), and aliens with four hands have six feet (C); 4. true, only Venusians have four hands (B), while four-handed aliens have six feet (C) and tails (D).

WORD CHARADE (Week 52)

M	O	P	V	X	N	U	M
Z	L	E	M	(I)	O	S	(A)
N	F	(T)	D	K	B	F	N
Q	(I)	K	B	(T)	F	N	P
(A)	Q	S	G	C	L	P	S
N	(G)	B	Z	K	D	Z	(I)
Z	(R)	Z	E	B	N	J	R
U	O	(I)	M	E	L	B	(C)

tragic

SUDOKU (Week 52)

6	2	3	8	9	5	4	7	1
5	4	7	3	1	2	9	6	8
9	8	1	7	6	4	2	3	5
7	5	8	9	2	6	3	1	4
4	9	2	1	5	3	7	8	6
1	3	6	4	8	7	5	2	9
8	1	4	2	3	9	6	5	7
2	7	5	6	4	1	8	9	3
3	6	9	5	7	8	1	4	2

OVERLAY (Week 52)
Diagram B.

DEDUCTION PROBLEM (Week 52)
The four ages are 38, 39, 40, and 41. Since the women who are 38 and 39 tell the truth, and the two who are 40 and 41 lie, Hannah, who said she is 40, lied, and is actually 41. Ella, then, also lied when she said Hannah is 40; Ella is 40. Since Ella also said that Grace is younger than Flo and lied, Flo is 38 and Grace is 39. Grace, then, told the truth when she said that Ms. Smith is older than Ella, so Ms. Smith is Hannah. Flo also told the truth so she isn't Ms. Tripp. Hannah lied when she said that Ms. Tripp is older than Ms. Ryan, so Ella is Ms. Ryan, Grace is Ms. Tripp, and Flo is Ms. Ullman. In summary:

    Ella Ryan, 40
    Flo Ullman, 38
    Grace Tripp, 39
    Hannah Smith, 41

COUNT TO TEN (Week 52)
1. row 7; 2. row 5; 3. row 9.

BLOCK PARTY (Week 52)

MISSING DOMINOES (Week 52)

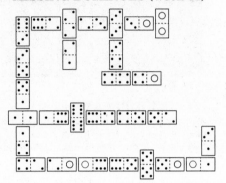

384